CRUISING GUIDE TO
SAN FRANCISCO BAY

Third Edition

Carolyn and Bob Mehaffy

Disclaimer: In devising the sailing directions and sketches of anchorages and harbors, we have relied on NOAA charts and personal observation and have made every effort to insure that the directions and sketches are accurate. However, they should not supplant your use of official charts and your own careful observation of conditions that may have changed since the publication of this book. Neither the publisher nor the authors assume any responsibility for property loss or risk to persons that might occur from the use or interpretation of any information in this book.

The text of this book is composed in Strayhorn Pro font.

ISBN 9781937196448

Published by Paradise Cay Publications
P.O. Box 29
Arcata, CA 95518-0029

Cover design by Robert Tripp

Charts by Raul Colocho

Book design by Linda Morehouse

Title page: Sailing in Raccoon Strait

Back cover: Author's photo by Frank Nugent

TABLE OF CONTENTS

This completely revised edition of the *Cruising Guide to San Francisco Bay*, still the only complete guide to the many destinations for cruising sailors in San Francisco and nearby coastal harbors, will continue to fill a much-needed niche for both local and visiting sailors. In this guide are general tips for safe, comfortable, and pleasurable Bay cruising as well as a description of each destination, including directions for the approach, the anchoring and berthing possibilities, the facilities available at each site, and some highlighted attractions nearby.

San Francisco Bay is not, strictly speaking, a bay at all but a part of an immense estuary. From Alviso at the southern end this estuary extends 75 miles to Suisun City at the northern end, and almost 100 miles from the Golden Gate to Stockton and Sacramento at the eastern ends.

The specific destinations have been grouped in this guide according to location. Local sailors generally designate as the Central, or Main, Bay that portion bounded by the Golden Gate, the Richmond-San Rafael Bridge, and Central Basin, immediately south of the Oakland-San Francisco Bay Bridge. The South Bay, according to sailors who live there, begins below the Dumbarton Bridge; however, other sailors on the Bay frequently use the term "South Bay" for anchorages and marinas below Central Basin on the west shore of the Bay and below the Bay Bridge on the east shore. For the purposes of this book, we have adopted this latter use. The North Bay commonly includes San Pablo Bay, the Carquinez Strait, Suisun Bay, and the most proximate of the river destinations, Petaluma and Napa.

The coastal and offshore destinations suitable for day or weekend cruises from San Francisco Bay have also been included. These are Bodega Bay, Tomales Bay, Drakes Bay, the Farallon Islands, and Pillar Point Harbor (Half Moon Bay).

For each destination the *Cruising Guide to San Francisco Bay* includes all public and private marinas as well as yacht clubs that accommodate visiting boaters. It includes as well all safe and legal anchorages we have been able to discover. We did not include some marginal anchorages used by local boaters because, after research, we judged these anchorages to be either illegal or unsafe without local knowledge and experience.

We have taken *Carricklee*, our Hardin 45 ketch, into virtually every marina and anchorage to determine the safety and comfort of the destination. In addition, we have explored marinas and anchorages by sportboat and by car to find out more about the facilities and attractions in and around each destination. We have talked with harbormasters, yacht club members, chandlery managers, shopkeepers, park rangers, and anyone else with local knowledge and a few minutes to spare for us.

In giving sailing directions for the approach to each marina and anchorage, we have given the bearing in degrees magnetic because we believe most small craft are fitted with magnetic compasses. We've given distances in nautical miles and depths in feet. Points of the compass are abbreviated, for example, N for north and SE for southeast.

Because we have calculated waypoints used in this book from the most current NOAA charts rather than on site with a GPS receiver, you will almost certainly find slight discrepancies between the waypoints you see in this book and those you see on your GPS receiver at the site. The prudent sailor will always be cautious when using waypoints, whether taken off a chart or a book or from another boater.

ACKNOWLEDGMENTS

We are deeply indebted to the scores of people who took the time to talk with us as we visited the many destinations covered in this book and to send us additional information when available. Our gratitude goes to our friends Frank Nugent and David Dawson for allowing us to use some of their photographs and Jack Wigmore for flying us over San Francisco Bay and environs for aerial photographs. Finally, we appreciate the advice and assistance of the staff of Paradise Cay Publications, including Jim Morehouse, CEO; mapmaker Raul Colocho; and independent editorial contractor Linda Morehouse.

SAILING SAN FRANCISCO BAY

Beautiful San Francisco

San Francisco Bay For sailors throughout the United States and around the world this wondrous estuary, including two smaller bays—San Pablo and Suisun, fed by the San Joaquin and Sacramento rivers and numerous small streams—has long been a destination to dream about. From the earliest written account of San Francisco Bay, set down in his log by Manuel de Ayala in August and September of 1775, this nearly perfect harbor for commercial and military ships has been lauded. While the number of these ships in San Francisco Bay diminished greatly in the second half of the 20th century, their absence has been more than compensated for by the numbers of pleasure boats—both sail and motor—afloat on these still voluminous and sparkling waters.

Richard Henry Dana, having sailed into this bay on a trade ship in 1835, alerted the world to the multitudinous beauties to which sailors might attend here:

"We sailed down this magnificent bay with a light wind, the tide, which was running out, carrying us at the rate of four or five knots. It was a fine day; the first of entire sunshine we had had for more than a month. We passed directly under the high cliff on which the Presidio is built, and stood into the middle of the bay, from whence we could see small bays making up into the interior, large and beautifully wooded Islands, and the mouths of several small rivers. If California ever becomes a prosperous country, this bay will be the centre of its prosperity. The abundance of wood and water; the extreme fertility of its shores; the excellence of its climate, which is as near to being perfect as any in the world; and its facilities for navigation affording the best anchoring-grounds in the whole western coast of America—all fit it for a place of great importance."

—*Two Years Before the Mast*

The *great importance* San Francisco Bay has for pleasure boaters results largely from the harmonious conjunction of water, weather, landscape, and "the City." The water, a deep, pure blue under the California sunshine, can be placid in one part of the Bay, accommodating the sailor seeking a relaxing sail, and roiled up in another part with current and wind, guaranteeing a rollicking ride for the thrill-seekers. A day without winds somewhere on the Bay is a rare day, especially during the spring, summer, and fall months. These winds are often in the 10-to-12-knot range early in the day, climbing in the afternoon, particularly in certain areas of the Bay, to 20, 25, or 30 knots. Those looking for the pleasures of some boisterous sailing need only to look around: somewhere in this bay they'll commonly find the right conditions. On the other hand, a motorboater can usually find a place somewhere on the Bay to escape unwelcome winds.

An extraordinary thing about cruising in the San Francisco Bay is the plethora of destinations. If you have but a week to spend here, your first emotion will almost surely be frustration at your inability to do any more than dabble in the possibilities. Do you want a cool day with little sunshine in a secluded anchorage? It's here. Do you want, the very next day, a slip in a sunny, warm marina near a large selection of facilities? It, too, is here, as are just about any other combinations you can desire. You can choose anchorages near nature preserves, mountain trails, sandy beaches, marshlands, and historic sites or marinas near biking and walking paths, museums, and libraries.

South Bay Yacht Club

Golden Gate Bridge

The one option you don't have in the Bay itself is tropical weather among palm trees. However, San Francisco Bay proper contains only a portion, though surely the major portion, of the destinations available to boaters. To the north, this Bay joins San Pablo Bay, which in turn connects through the Carquinez Strait to Suisun Bay to the east. The Petaluma and Napa rivers connect to the north end of San Pablo Bay. You can readily find the palm trees and hot, if not tropical, summers in the valleys accessible along these rivers. From San Francisco Bay, boaters can easily navigate these other bays and rivers to add to the enormous natural variety of this splendid destination.

The City of San Francisco is not the least of the many attractions this destination offers to boaters. Dylan Thomas, the Welsh poet, said of the *city* of San Francisco, "It is and has everything." Had he been a sailor, he could have said the same for the Bay. But he got it just right for the City as well as for the Bay he failed to include. And part of the *everything* of cruising by sailboat or motorboat in San Francisco Bay *is* the City, even if the only piece of the City the sailor takes in is its beauty seen from the water.

Thomas, writing to his wife, Caitlin, went on to describe San Francisco:

> The wonderful sunlight there, the hills, the great bridges, the Pacific at your shoes. . . . And the city is built on hills; it dances in the sun for nine months of the year; & the Pacific Ocean never runs dry.

John Steinbeck, a native Californian, was no less enthralled:

> When I was a child growing up in Salinas we called San Francisco "the City." . . . A strange and exclusive word is "city." Besides San Francisco, only small sections of London and Rome stay in the mind as the City. . . . San Francisco put on a show for me. I saw her across the bay, from the great road that bypasses Sausalito and enters the Golden Gate Bridge. The afternoon sun painted her white and gold—rising on her hills like a noble city in a happy dream. A city on hills has it over flat-land places. Over the green higher hills to the south, the evening fog rolled like herds of sheep coming to cote in the golden city. I've never seen her more lovely.
>
> —*Travels with Charley*

Because the City rises, sometimes precipitously, from the Bay to Nob Hill, to Telegraph Hill, to Russian Hill, her beauty is displayed as tableaux of many levels—white houses stepping up the steep streets, deeply tinted green trees interspersed; Presidio Park showing little but a swatch of dark green,

its eucalyptus and cedar trees concealing the many buildings squatting beneath them; Golden Gate Park extending an invitation into its emerald gardens; and, at dusk, the lights of Coit Tower and the Transamerica pyramid illuminating two eras in the City's history. If you never go ashore to discover all that makes this *the City*, you will nonetheless have savored much of its beauty from gliding along the waterfront.

Cruise Ship Visiting the Bay

Both Thomas and Steinbeck remark on San Francisco's glorious sunshine. A part of this city equally tantalizing, though not as much to those wanting to sail as to those sitting in marinas or anchorages enjoying the view, is the thick marine layer that frequently lies offshore, a backdrop for San Francisco, the Golden Gate Bridge, the Marin Headlands, and Sausalito during mid-day, waiting to come in like "sheep coming to cote," as Steinbeck says. When it does move in, in effusive white, woolly clouds, the fog horns of Point Bonita, Mile Rocks, Point Diablo, the Golden Gate Bridge, and Lime Point sound their deliciously mournful tunes, the sound most resonant of the sea.

The City, however, is not the only site of civilization drawing you to this Bay. Among the sites we invite you to explore in this book are the many anchorages that are relatively secluded, given the population around the Bay, and the many marinas and yacht clubs where you can moor your boat while you get acquainted with cities from the size and complexity of Oakland to the modesty and simplicity of Petaluma. Spend some time in the Berkeley

Fog Rolls Over the Hills of Sausalito

CG Cutter Under Way Near Alcatraz

Marina, from which you can get acquainted with one of the country's most prestigious universities. Or explore a former shrimp-processing operation from the anchorage at China Camp in San Pablo Bay.

San Francisco Bay has everything for your cruising pleasure: an extraordinary and intricate system of estuaries and rivers; varied winds and weather patterns; hills, mountains, and flat valleys; and cities and towns of every size.

Fishing Boats Rest in Harbor on Foggy Day

ABOUT THE BAY AND BOATING

A BRIEF HISTORY OF SAN FRANCISCO BAY

Sailing Toward the City and the Bay Bridge

If history is, as the historian Carl Becker claims, the record of the events of the past, then the history of San Francisco Bay is scant indeed before the Gaspar de Portolá expedition of 1769. Mistakenly believing the body of water he saw from atop Montara Mountain on November 4, 1769, to be a portion of the bay we now know as *Drakes Bay* (which Sebastian Cermeño had named *Bahía de San Francisco* in 1595), Portolá had no notion of the importance of his discovery. Only after Juan Manuel de Ayala, the first European to sail into the Bay, mapped it extensively in 1775 was this recognized as a separate and immensely significant bay.

THE PEOPLE

> "When the water went down and the land was dry O'-ye planted the buckeye and elderberry and oak trees, and all the other kinds of trees, and also bushes and grasses, all at the same time. But there were no people and he and Wek'-

wek wanted people. Then O'-ye took a quantity of feathers of different kinds and packed them up to the top of Oon'-nah-pi's [now called Sonora Mountain] and threw them up into the air and the wind carried them off and scattered them over all the country and they turned into people, and the next day there were people all over the land."

> —Coast Miwok tale

NATIVE AMERICANS

Despite its dearth of *history* in Becker's definition, the San Francisco Bay has nonetheless been the site of continuous human occupation for many centuries, probably for at least the past 5,000 years. Among the attractions for boaters are exhibits around the Bay that explain and illustrate how life along these shores might have been, based on the artifacts, or "records," left behind on the shores of the Bay before the arrival of the first Europeans in the late eighteenth century. The indigenous peoples who were hunting and fishing on the shores of San Francisco Bay when the first Europeans arrived in the late 18th century formed four tribes, each based on a common language: the Coast Miwoks, the Ohlones, the Wintuns, and the Yokuts. These groups seemingly lived a simple, relatively stress-free life, with abundant supplies of fish, game, and vegetation to provide food, clothing, shelter, and rudimentary tools.

That life has now disappeared entirely, with but a few descendants remaining from these four Bay Area groups. These early inhabitants were replaced, successively, by Spanish and then Mexican missionaries and ranchers, American merchant sailors and traders, gold miners and soldiers, and, today, urban dwellers of every occupation.

SPANISH AND MEXICAN EXPLORERS

Throughout the Bay Area are fascinating relics of the Spanish era that began in San Francisco some 200 years after it had begun along the Pacific Coast to the south. The pervasive fog that lies off the coast of San Francisco for many days of the year apparently shrouded the Bay from the view of mariners who had, under the command of Sir Francis Drake, discovered Drakes Bay in 1579. Once Ayala mapped San Francisco Bay in 1775, the Spanish began to change the civilization that had existed relatively unchanged for 5,000 years or more. In 1776 the Spaniards set up, first, a fort—the Presidio—and a church dedicated to San Francisco de Asís but today called *Mission Dolores*. In the 19th century the surrounding land on the north, east, and south sides of the Bay was divided into a few huge Spanish and, after 1821, Mexican land grants, the Vallejo and Peralta ranches among the largest with Vallejo's ranch estimated to have covered as much as 170,000 acres. The Hispanic era effectively ended with the Gold Rush.

Camp Reynolds, Angel Island

U. S. SETTLERS

Even before the Gold Rush, Americans had begun to arrive by both ship and the Oregon Trail. William Richardson's house, built in 1835 near Mission Dolores, was the first establishment of an American enclave here, called *Yerba Buena* ("Good Herb"). After U. S. soldiers captured the Presidio on July 9, 1846, they erected the Union flag over Yerba Buena, and the city was renamed *San Francisco* on January 30, 1847. The Treaty of Guadalupe Hidalgo made California a U.S. territory in 1848. The discovery of gold in the American River at Coloma, northeast of Sutter's Fort (Sacramento), hastened the granting of statehood to California in 1850, when it became the thirty-first state.

GROWTH OF THE CITY

The Gold Rush brought to San Francisco—and consequently to the Bay itself—dramatic changes, beginning with a jump in population from 300 to 25,000 in but a few months. Many men who did not make their fortunes in the gold fields returned to the Bay Area and stayed as squatters. Despite the provisions of the Treaty of Hidalgo of 1848 guaranteeing that the property rights of the *Californios* (as the residents from Mexico and Spain were called) would be respected, the *Californios* could not defend their ranches against these squatters because of the sheer sizes of the ranches and the enormous expense of guarding their boundaries. The financial drain of protracted legal battles led, in most cases, to the *Californios'* having to sell their holdings. Missions, forts, adobe houses, and their usual accoutrements from this Hispanic period survive around the Bay Area to give one a sense of life here before the Gold Rush changed it all.

Mission San Rafael

Of particular interest to sailors are the many modifications to the Bay itself that began with the gold miners and gold mining and have, to some degree, continued to this day. More than one-third of what was the San Francisco Bay before 1850 has been either filled in or diked off, beginning with the unusual filling in of the cove of Yerba Buena by the many ships abandoned by sailors with gold fever. Some of these ships became hotels or other commercial establishments. As the ships deteriorated from neglect and sank, they served as the foundation for new buildings along the waterfront. The gold mining itself also facilitated the filling of the

bay: hydraulic mining sent millions of tons of sediment down the Sacramento and San Joaquin rivers and into the Bay, altering not only its shoreline but its depth and composition as well. The damming of the rivers, and the diminished run-off, continues to affect the size and composition.

If the Gold Rush brought long-lasting and sometimes undesirable changes to the geography of San Francisco Bay, its effects on the City were no less enduring and, to some, no less unwelcome. Prosperity for the Bay Area was certainly not among those unwelcome changes. With the phenomenal growth of population in the 1850s and 1860s, the economy responded vigorously. Demands for beef, food crops, and lumber and the ever increasing need for freight, steamship, and stagecoach lines to transport both these products and the population resulted in many new jobs. In 1852 Wells Fargo began as an express and banking agency. The elite of the City built expansive and expensive homes on Rincon Hill and in South Park in the 1850s and on Nob Hill in the 1870s.

The hills of San Francisco gave these homeowners magnificent panoramic views of the Bay, but these same hills presented quite a challenge to transportation. The first cable car, demonstrated in 1873, promised a solution. For the next twenty years, the cable cars on as many as eight different lines not only climbed the hills in the center of the city but linked outlying areas to San Francisco. Electric street cars and trolleys replaced most of the cable cars in the 1890s; buses with gasoline engines completed the job in the 20th century. Visible today from Aquatic Park, one of the few remaining cable cars continues to clank up Hyde Street to Nob Hill several times daily.

Another section of the City experiencing dramatic growth was the Barbary Coast, between lower Broadway and Pacific Avenue, inland now from the fishing pier, Pier 7. Named after the notorious coast of North Africa where pirates congregated, the San Francisco version of the Barbary well deserved its name. Some writers and filmmakers have romanticized this "colorful" era, but, in fact, some of the unsavory activities that took place here were anything but colorful. Today nothing remains of the Barbary Coast but the stories, both the romantic and the real.

China Camp State Park

Contemporary sailors exploring the Bay can relive another important change brought about in part by the Gold Rush and in part by the building of the transcontinental railroad. Chinese immigrants arrived in relatively small numbers to seek their fortunes in the gold fields; many more came to join those failed gold miners to work on the railroad. Upon completion of the railroad in 1869, the majority of the Chinese laborers returned to San Francisco. Chinatown is the best known result of the migration of these laborers, but for the sailor the Angel Island Immigration Station and China Camp in San Pablo Bay give further insight into the history of this group of San Franciscans.

A second economic boom lasting 20 years came to the Bay Area with the discovery of the Comstock silver lode in Western Nevada in 1859. San Francisco financiers provided the capital for the mining of this lode, and nearly all the supplies for both the mines and the miners passed through Bay waters before being transported overland or up the Sacramento River.

During this time, city leaders had the foresight to set aside land for a public park. Unfortunately, all the available land was sand dunes, and critics of the proposals to create a wooded haven in these barren dunes seemed justifiably skeptical. But Golden Gate Park, built on these dunes, stands today as one of the coun-

try's most accommodating and beautiful city parks, the park a long rectangle of green running for more than 3 miles (4, if the narrow Panhandle between Fell and Oak is included) through the heart of metropolitan San Francisco down to the Pacific Ocean.

A few blocks north of the Pacific end of Golden Gate Park, Adolph Sutro, mayor of San Francisco from 1895 to 1897, opened a public bath house in 1896, the largest bath house in the United States at the time. Continuing in popularity well into the 20th century, the Sutro Baths finally closed in 1954, and then in 1966 fire destroyed the building, characterized by its 2-acre glass roof. Just south of the site of Sutro Baths, the Cliff House that today overlooks Seal Rocks is a greatly scaled down version of the Cliff House that Sutro erected there in 1896. The most significant legacy of Sutro for contemporary San Franciscans and visitors is Sutro Heights Park, the ocean property Sutro's daughter, Emma, left to the city in 1938.

The earthquake of 1906 brought a pause, though certainly not a halt, to the growth of San Francisco. The quake, or the fires that followed for three days after, destroyed many of the buildings, including virtually all those downtown. The filling in of Mission Bay with the debris left after the earthquake and fires is one of the other permanent changes to the coastline of San Francisco Bay.

The rebuilding of the City began immediately, and by 1909 San Franciscans were ready to share with the world their city's rejuvenation. City leaders bid for the international fair that had been discussed to celebrate the opening of the Panama Canal in 1904. To transform Harbor View (now called the Marina District, directly east of the Presidio), workers built a seawall and filled in behind it with sand dredged from the Bay. The Panama Pacific International Exposition opened on the site in 1915 with great aesthetic and economic success. The Palace of Fine Arts, rising majestically above West Harbor, is the only building remaining, though the Exposition did result in Marina Green and the Marina Small Craft Harbor, both of which continue to be recreational assets for the City.

Treasure Island Administration Building

The next exposition for San Francisco—and one that also changed the configuration of the Bay—was the Golden Gate International Exposition of 1939-1940 to commemorate the opening of the Golden Gate and the Bay bridges. Engineers created a site for this exposition by adding mud and sand dredged from the Bay to the north shore of Yerba Buena Island and using stone quarried from the tunnel through the Island connecting the two sections of the Bay Bridge.

Sailors are perhaps most impressed with the other resulting addition to the Bay: Clipper Cove, the excellent anchorage in the lee of Treasure Island, and the public marina on Treasure Island.

Two miles directly west of Treasure Island is another Island of historic interest, though, unlike Treasure Island and Angel Island, it has no dock or anchorage for pleasure boats. This Island, Alcatraz, is today a part of the Golden Gate National Recreation Area; visitors must come by ferry from the City Front. However, sailors can get a good view of the exterior of the buildings and "the Rock" on which they perch by navigating around the Island, being careful not to interfere with the ferry traffic.

One can readily understand why this rock was first a military fort, standing sentinel with an unimpeded view of the Golden Gate. One can also well imagine why someone thought its location would make it ideal for a prison. From 1859 to 1907 it was, in fact, both a military fort and a military prison, the latter being only a minor function at that time. Beginning in 1907, Alcatraz became solely a military prison; and between 1934 and 1963, in its most widely known role, Alcatraz was the site of a maximum security federal penitentiary. The Rock had one final spate of national attention in 1969, when Native Americans laid claim to Alcatraz and occupied some of the former penitentiary buildings until 1971.

The Bay Area has, since the Gold Rush, attracted a diverse population, with people coming here from not only around the United States but around the world to seek their fortunes. With the onset of World War II, this trend gained impetus. Because of its strategic location, the Bay Area became the center of the West Coast war effort, with several army and navy bases spread around the Bay and two major shipbuilding facilities, Bechtel Corporation's Marinship in Sausalito and the Henry J. Kaiser Shipyard in Richmond.

Men and women of many diverse backgrounds poured into the area to fill the thousands of positions newly created. After the war, great numbers of civilians as well as military personnel who had come to the Bay Area stayed on to call one of the surrounding communities home.

Rosie the Riveter Museum

Historic Fort Point

THE MILITARY

Once the Treaty of Hidalgo, signed in 1848, assured California status as a United States territory, the U. S. military began its continuing and often extensive tenure in the Bay Area. Fort Point, on the south side of the narrowest part of the only entrance into San Francisco Bay from the Pacific Ocean, was the obvious site for the first U. S. fortification. In the late 18th century, Spanish explorers had recognized the strategic importance of this point they called *Punta del Cantil Blanco* ("White Cliff Point") and erected a gun battery there.

In 1849 the U. S. Army mounted artillery in the remains of the old Spanish fort. Planning and construction of a major fort on the site began almost immediately, later to be officially designated as *Fort Winfield Scott*, though *Fort Point* has prevailed in popular usage. The masonry fort, from which a shot was never fired at an enemy, has been restored as the Fort Point National Historic Site, open to the public Friday through Sunday.

From that modest beginning the U. S. military went on to build various kinds of military installations on the San Francisco Bay shores, some, such as Fort Point, for securing the Bay from enemy intrusion, some for debarkation of troops and materiel, some for wartime construction, and others for the training of military personnel. The islands of the Central Bay—Alcatraz, Angel, and Yerba Buena, and the manmade addition to it, Treasure Island—have all been military outposts. Other military installations along the waters of the Bay, mostly historic now, are Fort Baker, the San Francisco Presidio, Fort Mason, Point Molate U. S. Naval Fuel Depot, Kaiser Shipyards, Oakland Army Base, Alameda Naval Air Station, Moffett Field, Hunters Point, Mare Island Naval Shipyard, Hamilton Field, and Marinship Shipyards.

BOATS, SHIPS, AND FERRIES

The earliest boats of which we have any record in San Francisco Bay were the canoes Native Americans made from tule reeds. Early Spanish explorers made drawings of some of these canoes used by the various tribes around the Bay to catch fish, to gather shellfish, and to hunt otters and seals. The buoyancy of the reeds assured good flotation, but apparently the reeds were not always woven tightly enough to render the canoes water-tight. These early inhabitants of the area were excellent basket makers, however, and did weave the tule reeds into waterproof containers to hold everything from acorns to water to steaming mush. These baskets presumably could also be used as bailers in the leaky canoes.

Ayala's mapping of San Francisco Bay in 1775 alerted the world to the enormous potential this well-protected bay promised for shipping. Still, its remoteness kept the numbers of shipping vessels coming in here low during the Spanish and Mexican eras. But the U. S. conquest of California in 1846 began an accelerating period of commercial shipping in and out of the Bay, much of that shipping in-

Sailing the Bay

volving, too, the plying of the rivers and estuaries on the shores of the Bay. Cargo and passengers came in, from the East Coast primarily, and agricultural and livestock products and seafood went out. The Gold Rush caused a decided spurt in that acceleration, with close to 1,000 ships in Yerba Buena Cove at times during the 1850s.

Besides the port of San Francisco, several other cities have figured prominently in commercial traffic on the Bay. Benicia, Martinez, Port Costa, and Vallejo thrived in the early 20th century as busy links between the Bay and the agricultural towns to the north and the east. The numbers of merchant ships coming into the ports of Oakland, Alameda, and Richmond rose steadily during the 20th century, with Oakland today continuing to be a prosperous port. Among the other less busy and thus less well known ports are Pinole, Hercules, Crockett, Port Chicago, and Antioch.

Between 1882 and 1908, San Francisco Bay was the whaling capital of the world. (The last whaling station in the United States, at Point Richmond, closed in 1971.) The fishing industry in the Bay had taken off during the Gold Rush, when many immigrants drawn here by the gold realized they could find much more profit in the rich waters in and outside the Bay. Italian and Dalmatian fishermen in their *feluccas*, lateen-rigged fishing boats common in the Mediterranean, found bountiful harvest along the coast, while the Chinese were the primary shrimpers inside the Bay, building Chinese junks and sampans for the purpose.

Before the construction of the seven major bridges that connect opposite shores of the Bay Area, ferry services around the Bay were big business, with at times more than two dozen routes crisscrossing the Bay. First to open in the late 19th century were services from San Francisco to Richmond, Oakland, and Alameda and from Benicia to Martinez. Soon to follow were routes from San Francisco to Marin County and Vallejo, with many additional routes established in the first four decades of the 20th century. Today, a few ferry services remain in operation on the Bay.

did the racing of working craft, such as barkentines and schooners. Competitive rowing in the 20th century attracted crowds of spectators who lined the banks from the starting docks to the finish line. The coming of gasoline-powered boats facilitated the even wider use of boats for sport hunting and fishing.

Sailors today can view remnants of San Francisco's maritime past at the Hyde Street Pier. On the pier are an array of historic ships, including the *Balclutha*, a three-masted square rigger built in Scotland in 1886; the *C. A. Thayer*, a three-masted lumber schooner built in 1895 in Eureka, California; the *Alma*, perhaps the only surviving scow schooner in the world; the ferryboat *Eureka* from 1890; the *San Francisco Bay Ark*, also called the *Lewis Ark*; *Eppleton Hall*, a paddlewheel tug built in England in 1914; the *Wapama*, a lumber schooner, the last of her kind, built in St. Helens, Oregon, in 1915; and the *Hercules*, one of the last remaining steam tugs, built in New Jersey in 1907. Replicas of *feluccas* complete the impressive panoply.

BRIDGES

The three major Islands of the Central Bay—Angel, Alcatraz, and Yerba Buena—form a pleasing natural pattern for those of us who look for patterns. The works of men and women—the Golden Gate, the Oakland-San Francisco Bay, and the Richmond-San Rafael bridges—form a no less pleasing triangle. Of course, these bridges are enormously important in the economic and recreational life of San Francisco and all the surrounding communities.

One immediate change upon the completion of the bridges was the dramatic drop in the number of ferry boats working the Bay. Sailors here must still be on the lookout, however, for ferries making several daily runs from San Francisco to Alcatraz, Angel Island, Sausalito, Tiburon, Corte Madera, and Vallejo and from Tiburon to Angel Island.

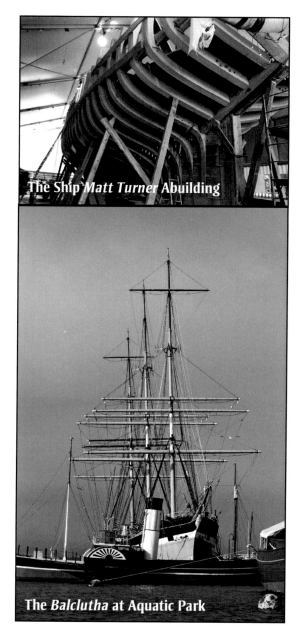

The Ship *Matt Turner* Abuilding

The *Balclutha* at Aquatic Park

Recreational boating on San Francisco Bay has no less an illustrious history than have the commercial marine enterprises. During the second half of the 19th century pleasure yachts began to populate the Bay. In 1869 the San Francisco Yacht Club was incorporated, with the Pacific and the Corinthian following over the next fifteen years. Yacht racing became popular, but so

Coit Tower, a Sailor's Landmark

For Bay sailors the bridges have another importance: they make ideal "fixed stars" for navigation, and, like those more time-honored fixed stars, the bridges lend unique beauty to the sky above the sailors. Unlike the fixed stars, however, these "stars" fascinate sailors by both day and night. At night the lights on the three bridges, like necklaces of diamonds, appear to be on chains looped above the dark water, all three bridges visible simultaneously from many positions on the water's surface. By day their intricate structures leave in awe Bay Area boaters who take time to contemplate these bridges.

The Bay Bridge, completed in 1936, was a marvel of construction with its eastern cantilevered-trussed section and western suspension span joined by a tunnel through Yerba Buena Island. (The largest public project in the history of California replaced this east section of the bridge with a suspension bridge completed in 2013, currently the world's widest bridge.)

The Golden Gate Bridge became the symbol of San Francisco upon its completion in 1937. The construction of this bridge on rocky shores along a tumult of water being pushed through the narrow opening between San Francisco Bay and the Pacific Ocean makes for a compelling story.

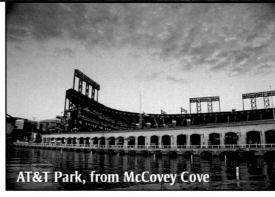

AT&T Park, from McCovey Cove

The newcomer among the Central Bay bridges, having been completed in 1956, the Richmond-San Rafael Bridge curves gracefully in a long, low arc to link the two cities giving the bridge its name. These three bridges circumscribe what most sailors know today as the *Central Bay*.

To the northeast of the Richmond-San Rafael lie two more bridges, the Carquinez and the Benicia-Martinez. Sailors venturing south of the Bay Bridge can view two more bridges that play major roles in the lives of Bay Area residents, the San Mateo and the Dumbarton. As do the bridges in the Central Bay, these four provide navigational landmarks and engineering interest to Bay sailors.

GEOGRAPHY AND GEOLOGY

> . . . and the next day before the dawn we were lying to upon the Oakland side of San Francisco Bay. The day was breaking as we crossed on the ferry; the fog was rising over the citied hills of San Francisco; the bay was perfect—not a ripple, scarce a stain, upon its blue expanse; everything was waiting, breathless, for the sun. A spot of cloudy gold lit first upon the head of Tamalpais, and then widened downward on its shapely shoulder; the air seemed to awaken, and began to sparkle; and suddenly "The tall hills Titan discovered," and the city of San Francisco, and the bay of gold and corn were lit from end to end with summer daylight.
>
> —Robert Louis Stevenson, 1879

The topography of San Francisco Bay is what makes this bay a premier cruising destination. Much of its some 430 square miles of surface is navigable by pleasure boats, both sail and motor, and its 276 miles of shoreline makes many turns and starts, including three embayments: Richardson, San Pablo, and Suisun. As a consequence, the Bay has dozens of suitable and varied spots for anchorages and marinas. While its ten islands and groups of islands—Angel, Belvedere, Alcatraz, Yerba Buena (and its extension, Treasure), Alameda, Brooks, Red Rock, the Marin Islands, the Brothers, and the Sisters—furnish additional attractions, only Angel, Belvedere, Yerba Buena/Treasure, and Alameda have reliable anchorages and/or marinas.

Nine California counties border the Bay shoreline—San Francisco, San Mateo, Santa Clara, Alameda, Contra Costa, Solano, Napa, Sonoma, and Marin. Each of these counties has unique features a boater can savor, in some cases only in passing, in other cases by anchoring or tying up and going ashore. Cityscapes and landscapes lend a constantly changing view. Coast Redwoods, Coast Live Oaks, Douglas Firs, Pacific Madrones, California Buckeyes, and several varieties of eucalyptus and pines grace the hillsides that are geometrically scored by lines of streets. Beaches and marshes are replete with egrets, herons, willets, stilts, sandpipers, and avocets pecking in the mud and sand at low tide.

Elephant Seals at Drakes Bay

Sea Lion Mothers with Pups at Drakes Bay

The marine influence determines, for the most part, the climate of the waters of the Bay and its shoreline, resulting in cool, wet winters and cool summers with frequent fog or wind. However, many boating destinations of the San Francisco Bay are quite near "banana belts," where the cold air drains away from the slopes. These bayshore sites get more heat year around.

Adding to this expanse of the Bay are the navigable rivers and sloughs that extend the potential destinations for boaters by many miles and in many directions. A cruise up one of these rivers or sloughs will take you past wetlands and grain fields, pastures and salt evaporation ponds. These rivers and sloughs generally have warmer, less windy summer weather and cooler, wetter winter weather than the Bay.

As rich as all this variety available in the Bay is today, we nevertheless like to imagine the appearance of the Bay in years, centuries, even millennia past. In 1775, when Juan Manuel de Ayala mapped the Bay, he observed a body of water quite different from the one we observe today. The bay he saw, however, almost surely closely resembled the bay the first indigenous people discovered when they migrated to these shores between 5,000 and 10,000 years ago. An almost identical bay also greeted the participants in the Bear Flag Rebellion who raised the United States flag above the Presidio in 1846.

Major changes to this bay began to occur only four years later, with the coming of the Gold Rush. Hydraulic mining sent millions of tons of sediment down the Sacramento River, silting in the Bay. At the same time, with the rapid growth in population in the Bay Area, the filling of the Bay proceeded unbridled in response to the demand from both commercial and private interests for waterfront property. Today, primarily as a result of these two factors, the Bay has only about 430 square miles of surface, rather than the over 700 square miles it had in 1846. Some coves, islands, beaches, creeks, sloughs, and wetlands mapped by Ayala in 1775 have disappeared altogether. Others have been altered drastically.

Alviso Boats Sit in the Mud

But change has ever been the nature of Nature, too. The San Francisco Bay we know today is in large part the product, though surely not the final product, of cataclysmic changes over millions of years. Some 200 million years ago, the Pacific Ocean Plate, one of several huge pieces making up the earth's fractured and dynamic crust, began to push eastward under the western edge of the Continental Plate. The vertical warping that resulted formed the land mass we now call the Bay Area.

About 30 million years ago, the Pacific Ocean Plate began to move northwest, sliding past the Continental Plate toward Alaska. This slide continues today along the San Andreas Fault, at the rate of one to two inches a year. The San Andreas Fault System, which includes the Calaveras and Hayward faults, extends from Point Arena in Mendocino County to the Mexican border, where it has formed the Sea of Cortés. This fault system continues to alter the topography of the Bay Area.

Volcanic activity beginning about 25 million years ago also contributed to the forming of what is today the Bay Area. These volcanoes combined with the folds, faults, and uplifts caused by the movement of the plates to form the Bay Area's mountains plus the Sierra Nevadas about 3 million years ago. With the rising of the Sierra Nevadas and the Coastal Range came increased rainfall and increased water flow into the Central Valley, creating the great river system of what is today called the Delta, so named because the three major cities of the Delta in the second half of the 19th century— Sacramento, Stockton, and Antioch—form a triangle, the symbol for the Greek letter *delta*.

The two major rivers, now called the *Sacramento* and the *San Joaquin*, carrying water down from the Sierras to the ocean then, as today, converged at Suisun Bay and passed through the Carquinez Strait. Exactly where the water then flowed into the Pacific Ocean geologists are unsure, but they believe the present outlet, the Golden Gate, dates from about one million years ago.

At about the same time the downward warping of the earth's crust between the San Andreas and

Hayward faults formed the basin where the Bay is now. The river funneling through Carquinez Strait began to carve out a valley in what we call the Central Bay, digging out a 350-foot canyon at the narrow gap in the Coastal Range, this gap to be named the *Golden Gate*. In the South Bay less boisterous rivers formed the Santa Clara Valley.

Tourists Watch Sea Lions at Pier 39

The present filling of this basin between these two faults began approximately 10,000 years ago. At that time the Pacific Coast shoreline lay about where the Farallon Islands are, now 27 miles offshore. Then, as the glacial melt raised the sea level, perhaps as much as 400 feet, the waters of the Pacific poured through the Golden Gate, filling the basin and the river valleys. The result is an extensive network of sloughs and wetlands draining into a large, shallow body of water, the present-day San Francisco Bay. Two-thirds of the water in the Bay is less than 18 feet deep, with only one-fifth more than 30 feet deep, the deepest places being the ancient river bed between Angel Island and Tiburon and the Golden Gate.

San Francisco Bay, which geologists say is really an estuary, "a closed embayment where fresh and saltwater mix," drains about 40 percent of California's water.

The Golden Gate. Think of all that has come about because of that rupture in the Coastal Range. The ocean has flowed in, giving us an exceptionally well-protected and extensive bay where we might have had a marshy lake after the last ice age. The fog and the sea breezes reach the Bay Area through this same entrance, tempering the heat that prevails to the east and making possible, some claim, the best sourdough bread in the world. Not to be neglected is the nautical result of the slenderness of the Golden Gate. Where the girdled water comes out of the Bay and into the ocean, a lively meeting of opposing forces occurs. Called the *Potato Patch*, as the legend goes because potato scows lost their loads here with some regularity but just as likely because the water looks like nothing so much as potatoes dug up and lying about in lumps and clumps, this interface has given many a sailor pause. A sailor can neither enter nor exit San Francisco Bay without being reminded of the enduring legacy of the Golden Gate.

Quiet Anchorage in South Bay

WIND, WEATHER, AND SEASONS

Point Bonita Light

WIND

> Gray-eyed Athena sent them a favorable breeze, a fresh west wind, singing over the wine-dark sea.
>
> —*The Iliad*

Of all its allures that draw men and women from around the world to sail on San Francisco Bay, the singing wind has the most persuasive voice. Those fortunate enough to get out on the Bay aboard a sailboat go home with glowing stories about these fabled Bay winds.

Of course, not every boater on the Bay desires the winds. On summer weekends, sails dot the Bay; powerboats add only an occasional accent. Those singing summer winds that sailboaters find so alluring elicit no enthusiastic responses from powerboaters.

THE CAUSES OF THE WIND IN SAN FRANCISCO BAY

San Francisco Bay is perhaps the only place in the world where boaters can, with relative assurance, expect to sail almost any afternoon from March

Carricklee in the Petaluma River

through October, confident the winds will blow at 20 knots or more. These consistent and dependable winds result from two primary causes. California's great Central Valley, the envy of farmers the world

Thick Fog on a Winter Day

over, produces bountiful crops because of the deep top soil and the 100-degree temperatures common during the summer months. That valley heat also siphons the cool marine air in through the Golden Gate, across the Bay, and toward the interior Valley. The hotter the Central Valley, the stronger the winds on the Bay.

The Pacific High Pressure Zone also plays a part in keeping the Valley hot and the Bay winds blowing. During the winter, the high moves south, allowing storms to push into Central California. Along about March, however, the high begins to move northward again and by spring has parked itself approximately 1,000 miles offshore northwest of San Francisco, blocking most storms at sea. If the high were not positioned off the coast, the storms could come through and cool the Central Valley. This cooling would result in comparable temperatures in the Valley and in the Bay, as is the case during the winter months; the winds on the Bay would then be gentle breezes.

As it is, the high pushes the storms to the north, giving Oregon and Washington summer rain, green grass, and light winds. The Central Valley remains hot, and Bay sailors gleefully listen to the "beat of the offshore wind" (Kipling, "The Long Trail"). These summer winds on the Central Bay are dependable, blowing with authority almost every afternoon between March 15 and November 15.

Winds on the Bay generally run in cycles. If the Central Valley is enduring one of its exceptionally hot spells when the temperatures exceed 100 degrees for several days, the winds will blow at 25 knots on the Central Bay. After a few days, however, the temperature in the Valley will gradually decrease, and the winds on the Bay will subside. When the temperature in the Valley drops to about 90 degrees, winds of 15 to 20 knots and warmer temperatures will prevail on the Bay. After a few days of this more gentle weather in both areas, the cycle of the hot Valley and the windy Bay will begin again. Some weather people and boaters claim a new cycle begins every six days.

Early spring and late fall bring milder temperatures for the Central Valley, so the winds in the Bay decrease somewhat. March, October, and November have a number of light air days on the Central Bay in some years. In other years, boaters find boisterous winds throughout November and even into December.

AVOIDING SAN FRANCISCO'S WINDS

But those boaters who don't care for heavy winds shouldn't despair. Those famous—or, for some, infamous—Bay winds don't typically blow 24 hours a day. In fact, the winds generally begin just before noon. Those who prefer to avoid the heavy winds of the afternoons can do so by being at their destinations before noon. For this reason, on a typical summer day many anchorages around the Bay begin filling up before noon.

Although many boaters choose to anchor or dock their boats before the heavy winds begin blowing across the Central Bay, others who want to avoid a rollicking ride can find sheltered areas to explore. For example, when most parts of the Central Bay have winds of 25 knots, the area close to the San Francisco shoreline south of the Bay Bridge will typically have 15-knot winds and calm water. Similarly, boaters can find light winds on the east side of Angel Island and the Tiburon Peninsula. And many other areas exist, of course, where boaters go when they don't feel like bashing into waves, for example, "up the river" to Napa, Petaluma, or the Delta.

Though the winds do occasionally blow strongly all night in some anchorages and marinas, the winds commonly die out to almost nothing at night. As in the day, any winds that do blow at night are generally westerly or northwesterly, with but an occasional east wind during the fall and winter months.

WINDS OUTSIDE SAN FRANCISCO BAY

Boaters who venture outside the Golden Gate past Point Bonita expecting to find the same wind conditions in the ocean as in the Bay often get a surprise. The heat of the Central Valley has little effect on the strength of the winds at sea. Rather, the winds at sea are an extension of those in the North Pacific Ocean on that particular day. We have seen days when the winds were blowing 25 knots on the Bay but were

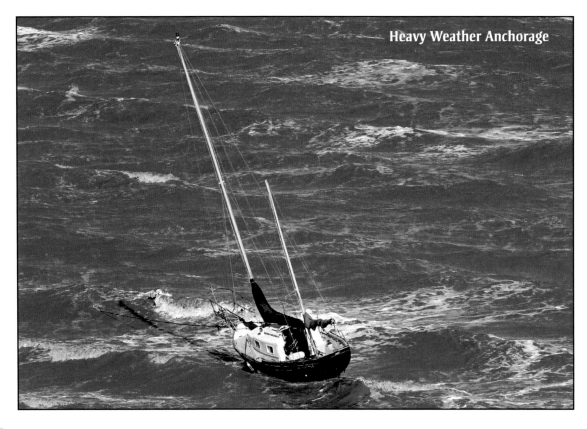

Heavy Weather Anchorage

flat after we passed Point Bonita. Conversely, we have seen days when the ocean was being blasted by gale-force winds and the Bay was experiencing nothing more than gentle breezes.

Typical ocean winds west of San Francisco blow from the northwest, but like all ocean winds, they vary. In the winter they might come from any direction and will generally be light unless a weather front is moving through the area. In the spring and summer, the northwesterly winds generally blow strongly during the late morning, afternoon, and early evening hours. Then during the late evening, night, and early morning hours the winds decrease, and sometimes cease altogether.

Because of these wind patterns in the Pacific Ocean off San Francisco, most who make an ocean passage watch the weather carefully before departure. If the winds are blowing strongly outside the Gate, boaters leave well before noon, using the motor until they clear Point Bonita. When they are a few miles offshore, they can adjust the sails and get serious about sailing.

Because the prevailing winds off the Northern California coast roughly parallel the coastline, northwest to southeast, the wind strength increases markedly near any point on the coastline that juts noticeably out into the ocean. Rounding such a point while heading into the wind can be treacherous, especially for small boats. Boaters heading north to Bodega Bay or Tomales Bay, for example, will find rounding Point Reyes in the afternoon difficult. To make this passage more comfortable, most north-bound boaters spend the night at Drakes Bay and round Point Reyes early the next morning.

SAN FRANCISCO BAY FOG

O the mutter overside,
when the port-fog holds us tied,
And the sirens hoot their dread!
—Rudyard Kipling, "The Long Trail"

Literature abounds with stories of the San Francisco Bay fog. Jack London began his novel *Sea Wolf* with

Tacking Toward the Presidio

a mid-bay collision caused by this heavy fog. In fact, however, fog inside the Bay is rarely the kind that results in zero visibility. What passes for a typically foggy day on the Bay is more commonly high fog, or a marine layer, that obscures the sun completely but leaves good horizontal visibility.

San Francisco's fog results when the Pacific Ocean winds encounter the coastal water that is cooler than the water mid-ocean. As the ocean meets the Pacific coast, the cold water that has been deep is forced to the surface. The warm winds that have traveled across the Pacific Ocean, carrying great amounts of water vapor, cross this area of cooler water and create coastal fog. Air travelers looking out the windows of the airplane see this thick, cottony fog as they approach San Francisco. The bottom of this fog may be no more than 200 feet off the water's surface, and it rarely extends more than 1,000 feet above the water. This relatively thin layer usually burns off inside the Bay by midday or shortly after. Above the Pacific Ocean outside the Bay, however, the fog may obscure the sun for a solid week at a time.

The typical San Francisco Bay fog dominates the weather picture between March and November at least part of each day. Often developing just before dark, this fog is more persistent in some areas than others. The fog rolls in through the Golden Gate and then moves down the City Front, enveloping Emeryville and Berkeley and sometimes Richmond. Later in the evening, it often covers the entire coastal Bay Area.

Every month the pattern of fog is different. March, which many local boaters consider the beginning of the boating season, typically has few foggy days. April has more foggy days. May, June, July, and August have many foggy days, with August usually having the most. September, October, and November, like the spring months, have fewer foggy days than the summer months have. In the winter months—December, January, and February—the occasional zero-visibility day may surprise boaters. We have been caught out sailing when a thick winter fog moved in, leaving us unable to see the bow of the boat from the cockpit.

This thick, zero-visibility fog rarely rolls into the Bay in the spring, summer, or fall, but you will occasionally find it around the Golden Gate in the summer. In early August 1982, Bob was making a voyage to Hawaii and departed the dock in Richmond at 0700 in bright sunshine. By the time he and his crew got within one mile of the Golden Gate Bridge, they sailed into a fog bank so thick they could not see the bridge, Fort Point, Mile Rocks, Point Bonita, Seal Rocks, or the buoys marking the ship channel. In fact, they could barely see the bow of the boat for the first 24 hours of the trip to Hawaii. While this anecdote illustrates that low, thick fog can form in the summer, happily such fog is rare.

STORMS

And I have asked to be
Where no storms come,
Where the green swell is in the havens dumb,
And out of the swing of the sea.
—Gerard Manley Hopkins, "Heaven-Haven"

Storms on San Francisco Bay occur almost exclusively during the winter months because of the Pacific High usually sitting offshore from mid-March to November. San Francisco seldom receives more than 15 inches of precipitation annually, and most of that falls during December, January, February, and March, with rain being unusual between May 1 and November 1. Fortunately, the Bay does not have real storms like those in most other areas of the world. A typical heavy-weight San Francisco storm might bring 40-knot winds and one inch of rain; considering the hurricanes and typhoons that strike other areas, that's not a storm.

SEASONS

The Bay really has only two seasons, winter and summer. Between come transition periods distinct enough to be called spring or autumn.
—Kimball Livingston, *Sailing the Bay*

Quiet Spring Day at Clipper Cove

The beginning of spring, March 21, roughly coincides with the beginning of the sailing season for most Bay sailors. Of course, a few boaters take to the water every weekend of the year, but between the middle of March and the last weekend of April, the date of the official Opening Day celebration, more and more boats appear on the Bay every weekend. Spring sailing is characterized by inconsistent winds, occasional days with light rain, and cool days and nights.

Summer sailing begins in early May, when winds are more predictable. Every afternoon between Alcatraz and Angel Island the winds generally blow in excess of 20 knots. And the high fog is predictable, too, covering the entire Bay from late evening one day until around noon the following day. The temperatures become warm enough so boaters can sleep overnight on their boats without a heater. All in all, this time of the year is blissful for boaters.

Fall sailing unofficially begins the first weekend after Labor Day. The weather commonly becomes more agreeable at this time of the year: winds become less boisterous; fog—if it forms—burns off early in the day; and temperatures rise, encouraging shirt-sleeve boating. In most years this gentle fall weather continues into November, ending only when the Pacific High retreats to the south and leaves the storm door open. When the rains begin to fall sometime in November and the temperatures drop enough to make being out of doors less than enjoyable, boating on the Bay decreases. After that, only the die-hard boaters take their boats out of their marinas regularly.

Most boaters use the winter months to work on their boats, making repairs and improvements for the next season. When a particularly warm weekend occurs in December, January, or February, some Bay boaters are once again out, but not in force. Winds typically are light and temperatures too cool for enjoying nights aboard in the deserted anchorages unless a heater is on the boat.

PREDICTING THE WEATHER

There is really no such thing as bad weather, only different kinds of good weather.

—John Ruskin

Boaters around the world pride themselves on being able to predict weather and thus stay out of trouble. This ability is necessary in most areas. San Francisco Bay boaters, however, have not gone out of their way to develop this ability because Bay Area weather presents few surprises during the most common sailing season—March through October. Even in November, the most noteworthy surprise the weather holds is an occasional rain shower. December, January, and February bring increased chances of heavy winds and rain, and they also bring a threat of the dense fog that hugs the ground and reduces visibility to zero.

~~~~~

TIDES AND CURRENTS

There is a tide in the affairs of men,
Which, taken at the flood, leads on to fortune.
—Shakespeare, *Julius Caesar*

Under Way from China Basin at First Light

San Francisco Bay boaters must understand tides or suffer the consequences. One friend had a frightening experience resulting from his inattention to the tide. He was sailing a Rhodes 19 inside the Bay near the Golden Gate Bridge, when the wind died about an hour before sunset just as a large ebb tide started to flow. Since his boat had no engine, he could do nothing more than watch as he and the boat were swept under the bridge and past Point Bonita into the Pacific Ocean. At slack tide, long after sundown, he was sitting in a dark ocean without food or drink on a boat without lights. Luckily, a light breeze came up, and he was able to ride the flood tide back to Sausalito. He arrived back at the dock after midnight, a hungrier and wiser man.

The lesson to be learned from his experience is simple: take heed of the powerful currents that result from the tides in the Bay.

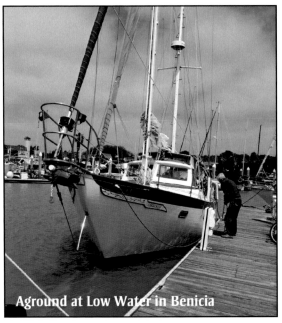

Aground at Low Water in Benicia

The more common nautical mishap resulting from boaters' not watching the tides in the Bay is a grounding. San Francisco Bay is but a shallow basin that the waters of the Pacific Ocean filled after the last ice age. Additionally, the rivers and streams continue to deposit sediment in the Bay. Many boaters have anchored their boats in protected coves or in the lee of the land, enjoyed dinner and one of the Bay's spectacular sunsets, and tucked into their bunks to get a good night's sleep, only to awaken during the night to find the boat aground. Particularly hard on the props on powerboats, going aground can also be serious for those aboard a sailboat because the boat may fall over on its side.

CAUSES OF THE TIDES

The moon and the sun have more to do with tides than anything else because both exert a gravitational pull on the earth, causing the waters of the oceans and bays to bulge toward them. The moon, though, has the greater effect on the tides because it is much closer to the earth than the sun. Yet, as the earth both rotates on its axis and orbits the sun, the same occurs but to a lesser degree. These gravitational pulls result in ebb and flood tides.

Every day the water ebbs (falls) and floods (rises) twice. The two highs and two lows each day differ significantly. Typically in the San Francisco Bay Area, one high tide will be as much as 3 feet higher than the other one every day, and the same is true of the two low tides on any given day.

Because of the moon's pull, we need to consider the moon's orbit of 27.3 days around the earth. Looking at the tide book, you will note that the high and low tides coincide with the phases of the moon. On the left margin of your tide guide are the symbols for the various phases of the moon. You will also see the letters **P and A in the left margins.**

The **P** represents *perigee*, meaning that on that particular day the moon is closest to the earth on its monthly orbit. On that day the pull of the moon on the water is at its strongest, and the difference between the highest high tide and the lowest low tide is greater than on any other day of the month. This tidal difference can be as much as 8 feet in San Francisco Bay.

The **A**, conversely, means that on the day the pull of the moon is at its weakest, the difference between the highest high tide and the lowest low tide is smaller than on any other day of the month. This tidal difference can be as little 3 feet.

Whenever the sun and moon get lined up on the same side of the earth, their pull on the earth's waters combines to create *spring tides*. These uncommonly large tides are, of course, not limited to the season of spring; rather, the word to describe them is believed to derive from either the German *springen* or the Anglo-Saxon *springan*, both meaning "to leap," or, in other words, "to spring." These extreme high and low tides occur every 13.6 days year around.

When the moon and sun are 90 degrees apart, the farthest from being lined up, the exertions cancel each other to some degree to produce *neap* tides (the word neap from the Old English *nep*, meaning "to become lower.") On those days, the range between high and low tides is small, sometimes no more than 2 or 3 feet. The average difference between high and low tides is 4.5 feet during neap tides. Both neap and spring tides are, of course, influenced most significantly by the moon when it is at perigee.

We all depend on our tide books to calculate for us the effects of these many and varied influences on the tide, and prudent boaters on the Bay keep a tide book nearby at all times.

CURRENTS IN THE BAY

As the tides rise and fall, the water moves in and out of the Bay, producing currents. The speed of these currents depends on the size of the tide. When the moon is at its perigee, the maximum ebb current at the Golden Gate Bridge will occasionally reach 6 knots. Aboard a sailboat with a top speed of 5 knots, which is fairly typical, you can end up seeming to be sailing at a great rate under the Golden Gate Bridge toward the Central Bay but in fact be slipping steadily out to sea. On those days when a large ebb is flowing, you will see boaters sailing backwards! Be familiar with currents in the Bay to keep yourself from being carried away by them.

The second reason to consider currents is to minimize the time required to get to your destination. Going against a current, you will clearly decrease your speed made good over the bottom. For instance, if you're going through the water at 6 knots against a 4-knot ebb current, your boat will actually be making good only 2 knots over the bottom.

Consider making the 20-mile trip from Sausalito to Vallejo as a typical cruise, and you can easily see how important knowledge of the currents can be. Assuming your boat averages 5 knots, this trip will take about four hours with no current. If you depart Sausalito during slack water before a large ebb current, however, you can easily add three or four hours to your trip. By contrast, leaving Sausalito on slack water before a large flood, you can cut your travel time by an hour. Using the current to help you can result in making a passage in much less time than you'd take if you went against the current.

Currents should also concern cruising boaters in the Bay because of the effects they have on anchored boats. A 5-knot current will put a tremendous strain on your anchor. If your ground tackle is not heavy enough or not properly set, your anchor will drag. To make sure you don't drag, begin with an anchor that is adequate for securing your boat. Do not make the mistake of cruising in the Bay with an anchor smaller than the size recommended. Go one size too large rather than one size too small.

Consider, too, that currents change direction. If you anchor facing north on the east side of Angel Island when the current is going out, you will be facing south when the current is coming back in. If you don't take into account this change in current, you can end up dangerously close to the shore, a pier, or a rock.

Current and wind work together to produce some curious results. We all know that a 10-knot wind can make an anchored boat hang back on the end of its anchor line—but not if a strong current is running counter to the wind. When you anchor at China Camp, for example, in a 2-knot current when a 10-knot wind is blowing over the hill ashore, the wind will often strike your boat abeam instead of on the bow: The 2-knot current has more effect on the direction your boat points than the 10-knot wind. This seeming anomaly can be disconcerting the first time you observe it.

If current and wind together produce disconcerting results, adding tide to the equation can produce even more dramatic problems. Many a boater has dropped anchor at low tide, let out a little scope, and settled in for dinner or a cozy night's sleep. A little later a flood tide lifts the boat enough to reduce the amount of scope on the anchor line, and the current and wind cause the anchor to drag. Bay sailors soon learn to take tide, current, and wind into consideration when they anchor.

The fact that 40 percent of all the water that runs off California's mountains—obviously a tremendous volume of water—drains out through San Francisco Bay suggests that river flow is another variable affecting currents. In fact, though, 80 per-

Aground at Low Tide

cent of all currents in San Francisco Bay result from tides and are thus remarkably predictable.

USING TIDE BOOKS

Most boaters use as their boating bible the small complimentary booklet titled *Tides and Currents: San Francisco Bay & Tributaries.* If you decide to anchor, you can use this little book to determine whether the tide is low or high so you can accurately estimate how much scope to let out.

Boaters anywhere outside the Central Bay of San Francisco Bay *must* rely on tide books if they wish to avoid sitting in the mud. At low tide many areas are simply unnavigable for a boat that draws 5 feet or more. South of the Oakland-San Francisco Bay Bridge and north of the Richmond-San Rafael Bridge, water depths outside the channel are less than 10 feet almost everywhere at low water. Before leaving the marina in that part of the Bay, study the tide book so you know the time of the high and low water as well as the state of the current.

Many boaters suggest that you should enter exceptionally shallow water areas only at low tide or on a flood tide so you can get off quickly if you do go aground. Aground at high tide, you can be in serious trouble when the tide ebbs. A 6-foot tide can leave your boat lying on its side. Even going aground during an ebb can create a serious problem because you may wait a long while for the incoming tide to float your boat off the ground.

Not all boaters consider the same parts of their tide books important. Many who do their boating in the Central Bay look only at the pages that show currents at the Golden Gate. They frequently care primarily about any current that will slow their progress but worry little about going aground. If the current is your concern, study the current page to determine the exact time the current will reach maximum velocity and what the speed will be at the Golden Gate.

If you're boating in another part of the Bay, you must add or subtract a correction factor to calculate the time of that maximum tide. The tables giving the correction factors for both tide and current are found in the beginning portion of the tide book. Once you

Mooring Buoys Show Current

find the correction factor, you simply need to add or subtract it to the figures from the tide tables to determine what time you can safely go into an area with shallow water. If your boat is in Redwood City, for example, you must add one hour and six minutes to the time of the high tide at the Golden Gate.

Using the tide book can make all your Bay sailing safer and more efficient. If you are going from the Central Bay to Napa, for instance, you want to know the time of the maximum flood current so you can use it to speed you on your journey. To lessen the risk of going aground, you also want to know the times of the high and low water since you'll be going through some shallow water. Your best option, then, as you make your way up the Napa River, is to leave Vallejo on a flood tide. Indeed, very few Bay Area boaters leave the dock for anything more than a casual day sail without first checking the tide book.

Westpoint Slough and Shallows

EQUIPMENT FOR SAFETY AND COMFORT

A ship of the best form will not show its good qualities, except when it is at the same time well rigged, well stowed, and well worked by those who command it.

—Chapman Piloting

For Bay cruising, you need little more than a sturdy boat to enjoy these waters. Many people we have known began visiting anchorages and marinas aboard a small boat with no frills. Over the years, they have bought larger, more comfortable boats and added equipment that has enhanced the enjoyment of their hobby. Although we all seem to add more and more equipment to our boats, little of it is required. The following presentation describes some of the essential equipment—anchors, lines, safety gear—as well as the non-essential equipment commonly found on boats cruising San Francisco Bay.

ANCHORING AND MOORING

First, equip your boat with four dock lines so you can tie up at the marinas you visit. If you normally keep your boat at a Bay Area marina, these dock lines should be in addition to the ones you use to tie up in your marina so you won't have to remove your lines from your dock every time you go out to enjoy the Bay. Be sure to have at least one extra long dock line to use for a spring. Guest berthing facilities in the marinas we visit are often end ties requiring one or more spring lines to keep our boat in place. To be prepared, we carry two 50-foot dock lines as well as a number of shorter ones.

A long line will also be handy when you visit Ayala Cove on Angel Island and want to tie up to the mooring buoys. We customarily use one 200-foot anchor line when we tie up to those buoys, tying off one end of the anchor line to a stern cleat, slipping the bitter end through the ring on the top of the buoy, and then tying off that end to our other stern cleat, forming a 100-foot-long vee between the stern of our boat and the buoy. We then motor ahead to the buoy we plan to tie our bow to and slip another line through

the ring on the top of that buoy, just as we did with the stern line. Since the buoys are often at least 100 feet apart, you'll need one medium-length line for the bow, at least 50 feet long, to tie up in this manner.

Assuming you'll also want to anchor out to enjoy some of the beautiful anchorages the Bay has to offer, you'll need good ground tackle. Most cruising boaters equip their boats with a primary anchor that is at least one size heavier than the recommended size. For recommended sizes for your boat, consult your local chandlery or look in the West Marine catalog.

Boaters have favorites when it comes to anchors, so you can expect them to have widely divergent opinions when you ask what type of anchor you should buy. If you were to check the anchors on cruising boats in the Bay area, you would almost certainly find that a majority of them have a CQR for a primary. The second most common anchor is likely to be

Long Lines Needed at Ayala Cove

At Anchor at China Camp

a Danforth style (including the West Marine Performance and the Fortress). The third is the Bruce, and the fourth is probably the Delta. The apparent popularity of each of the types above should not dictate the type you put on your boat. Rather, you should consider what type of cruising you plan to do. If you plan to cruise only in the San Francisco area, you would be well advised to put a Danforth-type anchor aboard. It will hold particularly well in the mud bottoms found most often in the Bay and Delta.

You will most likely choose a secondary anchor that is quite different from your primary. Looking for a primary anchor that will hang conveniently over the bow, many boaters choose the CQR or Bruce for a primary. However, because neither stows well in a locker or on the stern rail, these same sailors choose something else for a secondary anchor. The most common secondary anchor aboard Bay Area cruising boats is probably a Danforth-type anchor because it stows easily under all the normal equipment in lockers.

An apparent contradiction exists: most boats have a CQR or Bruce for a primary anchor because they stow most easily on a bow roller, even though a Danforth-type anchor would probably hold better in most Bay Area situations. Few boaters wish to dig their anchor out of a locker every time they want to anchor.

Once you've chosen an anchor, you'll need to select a rode. You can use either an all-chain rode or a nylon and chain rode. An all-chain rode is best if you plan to do any long distance cruising in the future. Many anchorages in Mexico, the Caribbean, and the South Pacific have coral patches on the bottom that will make short work of a nylon rode, so Bay cruisers who are making plans to visit these areas generally equip their boats with all-chain.

If your plans focus on only Pacific Coast cruising for the next few years, you can outfit your boat with a rode made up of 35 feet of chain and 200 feet of nylon. The advantages of the nylon/chain rode over the all-chain are many. First, the nylon/chain rode is lighter. Too often a cruiser puts 400 feet—and thus 400 to 600 pounds— of chain in the bow of the boat, causing the boat to hobby horse

in rough water. The second advantage to a nylon/chain rode becomes apparent when you weigh anchor. With a nylon/chain rode, you can use your muscles to get your anchor aboard.

On the other hand, if you have an all-chain rode and a 66-pound anchor, as we do, you'll have no choice except to use a windlass. And putting a windlass on your boat is expensive—*very* expensive if your boat is large. Another economic advantage to the nylon/chain rode is that chain costs three times as much as nylon. A final advantage is that you'll enjoy more quiet with nylon. Chain seems invariably to rub against the bobstay on a boat at anchor.

Despite the advantages of a nylon/chain anchor rode, we have an all-chain rode for cruising to such destinations as Central America and the South Pacific. We also have a nylon/chain rode aboard, but it is not as convenient as using the all-chain that is at the ready.

Many cruising boats have windlasses on the bow. A windlass is virtually mandatory if you have a large boat with an all-chain anchor rode. We do know some cruisers with boats under 30 feet with one-quarter-inch chain who pull their anchors up without a windlass, but they are the exception. And they have strong backs.

If you decide you need a windlass for your boat, you can choose between an electric and a hand-powered model. The hand-powered models are, of course, less expensive. Not only is the initial purchase price about one-half that of the electric, but the installation costs of the manual are much less. The electric windlass requires, at a minimum, two heavy battery cables, often as much as 35 feet long, a solenoid, and a foot-operated switch. And installing an electric windlass is much more involved than installing the manual. But bringing in 150 feet of chain with an electric windlass takes less time and requires far less effort than with a manual windlass.

Stowing your anchor as you sail around the Bay also deserves some forethought. If you leave your anchor on a bow roller, as most Bay cruisers do, be sure it is securely locked in place. You can secure it by putting a pin through the anchor

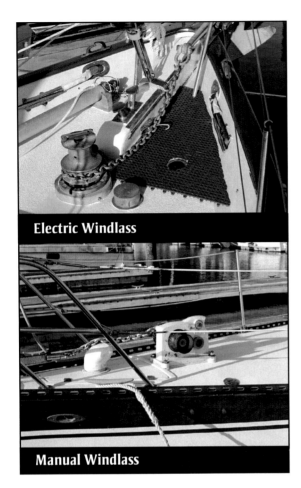

Electric Windlass

Manual Windlass

CLOTHING

You can easily pick days that are not rainy to cruise the Bay since rain in the area between May 1 and November 1 is rare. But the lack of rain shouldn't suggest that you'll need to bring along only a pair of shorts and a tee shirt to be comfortable cruising the Bay in the summer. As legendary as is the San Francisco fog are the cool summers on the Bay.

The secret to being comfortable while sailing in the San Francisco Area is layering. A few days a year are warm enough to wear shorts and a tee shirt, but generally you'll want to wear long pants and a long sleeved shirt, at the very least. When you're under way, plan to wear a layer over that long-sleeved shirt whenever the winds are blowing. And if the water is flying, particularly on a sailboat, you'll be comfortable in foul weather gear. Those who don't put that foul weather gear on often end up with wet clothes, a "zero at the bone" experience when a 20-knot wind is blowing on San Francisco Bay.

If you're planning to do some coastal cruising or extensive Bay cruising in the winter months, you should buy clothes designed especially for this weather. The layer next to your skin should be made of polypropylene or some similar man-made material. Do not use cotton, because it will get damp and only add to the chill. Most cruisers buy Patagonia or REI long underwear for this purpose. REI offers several weights of long underwear, some available with a zipper turtleneck that many find much warmer than underwear with a tee shirt neck.

The second layer for cold weather should be made of some sort of polar fleece. You can wear a bunting jacket with or without a windbreaker outer layer. If you wear foul weather gear over the bunting jacket, you probably won't need the windbreaker, and you'll feel less bound up when you try to move quickly. Many cruisers on the Bay prefer wool sweaters or sweatshirts under their foul weather gear. The "best" choice depends on you, but be prepared for the chilly weather on the Bay.

The top layer should be a good quality foul weather suit. You can buy quality equipment at

mount and the anchor, if your anchor mount has such a hole. Many cruisers have cruised for years without such a pin, however; they simply tie the anchor securely to the anchor mount before they make a passage during which their boat might be banging into waves.

Remember to protect your boat by seizing the pin in the anchor shackle. Because the pin in that anchor shackle is so hard to remove when you want to take it out, you may be tempted to say that you don't need to get out the seizing wire and take care of it, but ask someone who lost a boat when that pin backed out in the middle of the night; you will immediately get an emphatic recommendation to seize the pin. We have never had a pin back out, but we know cruisers who have, so our anchor shackle has a pin held in place by seizing wire.

Layers of Clothing

any of the larger chandleries. Expect to pay $300 and more for a good set of foul weather gear. You can buy cheaper foul weather gear, but it may not keep the water out. Some say the one-piece suits keep them drier, but those we tried were uncomfortable. We can also tell you from personal experience that the two-piece suits with the bib overall tops are more comfortable in serious weather than the one-piece models, even though they are inconvenient when you are trying to use the head in a rush. Try a variety of foul weather suits on before you buy.

You can also buy foul weather gear that has a built-in safety harness and built-in flotation. We find these not only expensive but bulky. When we want a safety harness or a PFD, we simply put those items over whatever outerwear we have on. Still, if you don't have a PFD and a safety harness, you might be able to save money by buying a jacket equipped with harness and flotation.

We know people who go boating on San Francisco Bay in bare feet in the summer, but we aren't among them. Many boaters have found that bare feet and boating result in broken toes. We recommend wearing heavy duty deck shoes or boots.

Good deck shoes with non-skid soles will keep you from sliding around, especially when the decks are wet (which will be most of the time on the Bay). On a sailboat, you'll have a particularly hard time remaining on your feet if you don't have good deck shoes. Leather deck shoes look good and hold up longer than any of the others we have tried. We

have leather shoes made by Timberland and Sperry that we have worn for over ten years while boating, and, although they show the wear, they are still comfortable and effective. By contrast, the cheaper canvas shoes bought on sale for $30 have lasted for a season or two at the most.

Some boaters like the deck sandals that have non-skid soles. Most Bay Area boaters find that bare feet, or almost so, are cold feet, however, so sandals have only a minimum number of adherents among boaters around San Francisco.

In wet weather, sea boots can make an otherwise uncomfortable day a pleasant day. Sea boots are also a great idea when you are sailing on a boat that takes a significant amount of water over the bow. Sea boots also make cold weather sailing more enjoyable because you can put on layers of socks. Many boaters buy their boots a little extra large so they can wear two pair of socks, a thin pair made of a man-made fabric next to their skin and a heavier pair of either man-made or wool fabric over those.

DODGER

A dodger for your boat does exactly the same thing as foul weather gear does for your body: it shields the cockpit from the flying water and cold winds. Dodgers come in all shapes and sizes. Some small ones do little more than provide protection for the crew coming on deck through the companionway hatch. The advantages of these smaller dodgers are that they don't destroy the aesthetic lines of the boat and they tend to be relatively inexpensive.

Other dodgers, such as the one on our center cockpit boat, completely enclose the cockpit area, enabling us to sail in rainy weather without getting wet. These larger dodgers make the cockpit into an all-weather room. The primary disadvantages of these larger dodgers, as you might guess, are that they do not do much for the looks of the boat and they are much more expensive than the smaller ones.

Another concept in dodgers is the hard dodger. The most significant advantages of the hard dodger are that a crew member can stand atop the

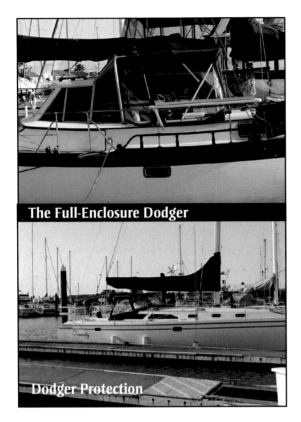

The Full-Enclosure Dodger

Dodger Protection

dodger to reef or furl the sail; these hard dodgers do not deteriorate in the sun as the fabric ones do; and they offer a more secure place to hold onto in rough weather on the Bay.

ELECTRONICS

You can put an endless amount of money into electronics, but for cruising the Bay you need but a few of the electronic marvels on the market.

• **A depth sounder** will give you confidence when you are entering anchorages. With a depth sounder, you can easily determine how much scope you need on your anchor rode. But the depth sounder also helps to avoid shallow areas when you sail up the Napa River or the Petaluma River or into the South Bay. Even as you enter a marina with shallow spots, such as Martinez Marina or Glen Cove Marina, a depth sounder can help you avoid going aground if you enter at a dead slow speed.

• **A VHF radio** is the second critical piece of electronic equipment every cruising boat in the Bay area should have.

The VHF radio is also a safety item. In case of an emergency, your VHF radio is your best resource. The Coast Guard monitors Channel 16 and responds immediately to life-threatening situations. If you call asking for help when the situation does not involve a life-threatening emergency, the Coast Guard will refer you to a private vessel assist company, but again your VHF radio will enable you to communicate with those who can help you.

Another traditional use of the VHF persists in harbors, particularly those outside the U. S., and that is for the daily cruisers' net, where those boaters in the harbor use a common VHF channel to share news and various kinds of updates among the cruising sailors who choose to turn to that channel.

Use VHF for Vessel Assist

• **The cell phone,** except for these two specific uses of the VHF, however, has taken over most other functions for boaters in U. S. harbors. In fact, for cruising on the Bay, a cell phone has also become an essential piece of equipment. As we interviewed harbormasters in marinas throughout the Bay for this revision, a number of them informed us they no longer use their VHF radios to accept calls from boaters, either those in their marinas or visitors seeking services there. They prefer to accept calls on the cell phone, while many of them also monitor an Internet address or website.

In emergencies, though, the VHF still has its uses. For example, if another boater anchored nearby but not acquainted with you needs your help, that boater would have no ready way of communicating

Three Communication Possibilities

with you other than with the VHF radio. The same thing is true, of course, if you experience an emergency and need help from another boater.

Beyond the depth sounder, the VHF radio, and the cell phone, most other electronic aids are non-essential items. But you, as do many other Bay boaters, may find the following optional electronic aids useful.

• **Radar** can help you find your way into an anchorage or a marina in foggy conditions or after dark. While we know many boaters who have radar units, we know few who use radar regularly inside the Bay. If you plan to cruise southward or northward along the coast, radar becomes much more desirable; for cruising limited to inside the Bay, you can probably spend elsewhere the $3,000 or more a radar installation costs.

• **Knotmeter and log** combinations are on most boats, but they aren't essential for cruising the Bay. Many boaters have enjoyed cruising for years without knowing how fast or how far they have gone. Even though non-essential, the knot-log will help you as you make your way to a new destination. For example, when we make trips up the river to Petaluma or Napa, we regularly watch our log and check the distance we've traveled against the chart so we can more readily identify the next landmark or buoy. If you carefully measure the distance beforehand on your chart, the log also helps you determine the location of a harbor at night or a not readily identifiable anchorage.

• **Electronic charts** are certainly helpful for boaters in the Bay Area. Some boaters are using electronic charting programs on their laptop computers; others have electronic charts on their chart plotters. If you decide to add electronic charting to your boat, do not throw out your paper charts when you do. For safety, plot a course on paper charts before getting under way, particularly for unfamiliar destinations in the Bay. Plotting on paper charts will reveal obstructions along your course--such as sand bars, sunken boats, and shallow water--that you might not see far enough ahead on electronic charts to avoid.

• **Autopilots** are, of course, not essential for cruising anywhere but especially not for inside the Bay. Considering that you'll rarely be making a passage to a destination more than a few hours away, the expense of an autopilot is difficult to justify. Again, though, if you plan to visit anchorages and marinas outside the Bay, you might consider installing an autopilot. When making the trip back to the Bay from Bodega Bay or Pillar Point, for example, you'll appreciate an autopilot, particularly if you're shorthanded. If you cruise as a couple, as we do, an autopilot allows one of you to relax or sleep more easily.

• **A GPS** is now considered an essential piece of equipment by many sailors on the Bay. Though for Bay sailing they are not, strictly speaking, essential to a safe passage, they are immensely valuable for finding locations identified by their coordinates, as, for example, are all the destinations in this cruising guide. Conceivably, too, you could use a GPS to assist you in making a passage under reduced visibility conditions, especially if you're unfamiliar with the approach to your destination. We regularly use our GPS when we make a trip to the Farallon Islands. Because of the marine layer that is common offshore, we can rarely see the Farallons until we're within 4 or 5 miles. By looking at the GPS from time to time, we can tell when we are being pushed off course by current or wind and arrive confidently at the island every time.

SAFETY EQUIPMENT

When the winds blow strongly and the waves are bouncing the boat around, boaters are only one moment of carelessness or one equipment failure removed from the water at any instant. You want to be especially careful not to fall overboard when boating in and around San Francisco Bay because of the cold water. The temperature of the water in the Bay, usually around 55°, makes it unlikely that you will survive for long swimming fully clothed.

Whatever other provisions you make for boating on the Bay, set up your boat to minimize the risk of anyone's accidentally falling overboard. Check lifelines and grab rails regularly, replacing everything that looks even slightly suspect. You'll fall against the lifelines and hang on to the grab rails many times when making sail changes, and you must be confident they will hold. Don't overlook your stanchions. Stanchions held to the deck with screws won't keep you on the boat. To be reliable, stanchions must be through bolted with backing plates on the underside of the deck. In addition, seriously consider the following safety items, some of which are required by Coast Guard regulations:

• **PFDs** (personal flotation devices) are required by the Coast Guard, and common sense also demands them. West Marine's newest categories describe the utility of each PFD. After studying the descriptions in each category, sailors can then buy PFDs designed for their specific needs. For instance, the least expensive PFDs, which many of us put on our boats in the past, are now sold as "Near Shore Vests." Boaters planning to use their boats for ocean cruising or racing can now clearly see they should purchase PFDs labeled "Offshore Sail" or "Offshore Power."

PFDs with a variety of features, including more buoyancy, have appeared over the last few years. The most promising of the new ones may be those that have inflatable bladders. Some have built-in safety harnesses. Inflatable PFDs recently received Coast Guard approval, so they count as part of the required equipment if they are wearable by the intended user and readily accessible. These inflatable PFDs are perhaps the most common new ones put on boats because they are far more comfortable and give twice as much flotation as do most other vests. The only drawback is these vests must be periodically checked and serviced and the expensive cartridges must be replaced each time the vest is inflated.

• **Safety harnesses** should be aboard every cruising boat. Although you'll not need to wear a harness every time you take your boat away from the dock, you should wear one whenever you're in heavy weather or working on deck at night. Too

Inflatable PFD

PFDs: Required for Children

• **Tethers** are just as important as safety harnesses. In fact, tethers and harnesses should be kept together in a location readily accessible from the cockpit. The most effective tether has a snap shackle on the end that attaches to the two D rings of the harness and a carabiner to attach to the jacklines or a padeye.

•**Jacklines** should run from the bow to the stern along each side of the boat. Attach one end of the jacklines to a solid padeye at the bow and the other end to a padeye or cleat near the cockpit or on the stern of your boat. Ideally, you should be able to snap your tether onto the jacklines as you get out of the cockpit and then be able to go from the cockpit to the bow and back without ever disconnecting your tether.

Good jacklines are made of either nylon or Dacron webbing or of the same covered wire that lifelines are made of. Jacklines made of webbing won't cause you to slip and fall if you step on them while working on deck as will the ones made of covered wire. The covered wire has a distinct advantage, however; it doesn't stretch as the webbing does.

Set up your jacklines before you depart if you have any notion you'll need them. For instance, in making a non-stop passage from Monterey to Marina Bay in Richmond, you will almost certainly arrive after dark; set up the jacklines before you depart from Monterey rather than waiting until you need them—after dark with the wind blowing 30 knots.

• **Overboard rescue systems** have become increasingly popular on boats in the San Francisco area. The Lifesling is the most common rescue system, perhaps because West Marine markets it so effectively. The Lifesling allows you to drag a line with an attached life-saving device to the person in the water and then to keep that person tethered to the boat until you can haul him or her aboard. All boaters who put these units on their boats would be well advised to practice using them before actual emergencies arise.

many cruisers go overboard from simple gear failures or mistakes. Since boaters who venture to distant locations—even those within the Bay—can get caught by heavy weather or darkness, safety harnesses, tethers, and jacklines are important safety items. These items should be mandatory for boats venturing outside the Bay.

Safety Harness

Always, One Hand for the Ship

EPIRB for Emergencies at Sea

• **EPIRBs** (Emergency Position Indicating Radio Beacons) could be a good addition if you plan to do a considerable amount of cruising outside the Bay. For destinations inside the Bay, we doubt you can justify the expense.

• **Life rafts** cause countless debates. Some boaters will not cruise the Bay without rafts aboard while other boaters sail around the world without them. We have made numerous trips to Hawaii, Mexico, and the Channel Islands without a life raft, but we brought one aboard when we began ocean cruising full-time a few years ago. Frankly, if you have a tender aboard, we can see no reason to purchase one if you plan to cruise only the Bay. If you expect to cruise offshore, however, we can see the justification.

•**Flares** are required on all boats. These may seem superfluous on boats that cruise only inside the Bay, but Coast Guard boarding parties will check for flares as routinely as they check for PFDs. The Coast Guard requires a minimum of three flares of any of the various types. If you choose destinations outside the Bay, carry more flares than this minimum specified by the Coast Guard: Six red meteor flares, six red handheld flares, and three parachute flares.

•**Radar reflectors** enhance your chances of being seen by ships and boats in the Bay, especially important if you are still underway after dark or if you get caught in the fog. However, do not count on radar reflectors because many radar operators on large ships cannot see small boats even if they have reflectors.

•**Fire extinguishers** are required by the Coast Guard on all boats with enclosed spaces. Boats up to 26 feet with enclosed spaces must have at least one B-1 extinguisher. Boats between 26 and 40 feet must have two B-I extinguishers or one B-II. Boats between 40 and 65 feet must have three B-I or one B-I and one B-II extinguisher. Several fire extinguishers strategically spaced throughout the boat are especially important for cruising sailors who will be cooking and using electrical devices out in remote anchorages. Make sure you can get to the extinguishers from every part of the boat. Don't just have one by the galley or in the engine room.

TENDERS

If you cruise only to marinas and tie up to a dock every time out, you obviously won't need a tender. But few cruisers can resist the temptation to anchor out at Clipper Cove, Paradise Cove, Westpoint Slough, or any number of other anchorages around the Bay. When they do, they need tenders to explore the area, to get ashore, or to go over to see friends on another boat.

When you tow a tender of any kind behind your cruising boat, you should always take the motor off when you move from one anchorage or marina to the next. In many instances cruisers have had their outboards damaged or lost when the winds have picked up suddenly, causing the tenders to flip over.

If you decide to get a tender, you will have three basic types from which to choose.

• **The hard dinghy** is the tender used by boaters for centuries. The hard dinghy has one outstanding characteristic: it rows well. Many boaters have gone to the hard dinghy after trying to row an inflatable in windy conditions. People who like tradition also choose hard dinghies because they can quietly explore an anchorage or a coastline without disturbing wildlife or other boaters. Hard dinghies have a couple of disadvantages that keep them from being widely used: they are difficult to get aboard and stow, and they are tipsy when being loaded or unloaded.

•**Inflatable dinghies** are chosen for weight and convenience. Lighter than RIB (Rigid Inflatable Boat) dinghies, the inflatable dinghy can be put into a bag and stored in a locker when not needed. The bag with the dinghy and pump weighs about 60 pounds, in contrast to, for example, our RIB that weights 158 pounds. One person can, with ease, roll up one of these inflatable dinghies and carry it to a locker on the boat.

The disadvantages of these inflatable dinghies are several. They are difficult to row in winds over 15 knots and almost uncontrollable when the winds reach 20 knots. Although many boaters buy small outboards for their soft dinghies to make them more usable when winds blow, the cruisers we've spoken with who use them almost universally complain that the inflatable dinghies are still too slow. Even when powered by an outboard, they will not make more than 6 or 8 knots.

In addition, some of these inflatable dinghies have serious loading limitations because of the soft floors. Anything heavy aboard one of these tenders, such as scuba tanks, is at risk of falling through the bottom. Furthermore, the soft bottom precludes your standing in it as you load or unload the dinghy, a serious disadvantage.

To make the inflatable boats more convenient to use, many now on the market have floors of firm air, aluminum, or light wood, some of these latter two types of floors removable for easy storage.

RIB Dinghy

• **RIB sport boats** have taken over the market. Although their most noteworthy feature may be their load-carrying capacity, sport boats also get high marks for their speed. With a 10-hp outboard on the transom, a 10-foot sport boat can easily plane and travel at almost 20 knots with two or three people aboard.

The speed of a sport boat makes long distance travel quite comfortable. We regularly range up to 5 miles from our anchored sailboat in our sport boat. For instance, when we were up the Napa River recently, we used our sport boat to explore the sloughs south of town and the river through the city of Napa because the shallow depths and low bridges prevented us from exploring these areas in our sailboat.

The major drawbacks of this sport boat are two-fold. Storage aboard a boat is the first of those. Because of its rigid bottom, it cannot be rolled up for storage; therefore, it must be placed on deck somewhere or on davits. The second problem if davits are not available is the weight of the RIB; ours, for example, weighs 158 pounds without the motor. This weight makes getting it up on deck a challenge, to say the least.

This weight leads to another drawback: pulling the heavy RIB, often with a motor to add to the weight, up on a shore we wish to visit. We have added easily removable wheels to our RIB to simplify this task, a particular challenge when the beach has a considerable incline.

RIB with Outboard and Wheels

Kite Boarder on the Bay

NAVIGATION AND SEAMANSHIP

NAVIGATION is the art and science of safely and efficiently directing the movements of a vessel from one point to another.

—*Chapman Piloting*

CHARTING A COURSE

Charting a course in the Central Bay is relatively straightforward. Often you can see a landmark—a bridge, an island, or a prominent building ashore—to aid in navigating to your destination, especially when you are going only a short distance. The farther you plan to travel, however, the more carefully you must navigate. Before you depart on a trip, lay out a course and consider how far the destination is and what hazards you will encounter. To lay out your course, you need only a pencil, parallel rules, and dividers. Then, at this stage of the planning, predict how long the trip will take. If you plan a trip to Suisun City, for example, you may decide to spend the first night en route at Benicia. Begin by plotting a course on your chart and measuring distances from one point to the next. Each leg of your proposed course should have the distance and the course written next to it.

During the trip, maintain an up-to-date DR position. That is, write on the chart the exact time you pass major landmarks. Heading to Benicia from a harbor in the Central Bay, you might write on the chart that you passed under the Richmond-San Rafael Bridge at 1015, around Point Pinole at 1225, and under the Carquinez Bridge at 1630. Keeping a DR will make you more comfortable if darkness should reduce your visibility before you reach your destination. With a good DR position marked, you need do no more than measure the distance to go and follow your predetermined compass course to arrive safely at Benicia for a good night's rest.

Do not rely completely on a GPS. As helpful as these devices are, they can fail. And only by drawing a course on your chart will you discover the hazards along the route to your destination before you are right on top of them.

As you travel toward your destination, you will simply follow the courses you wrote on your chart as you did your trip planning. Clearly, you must have an accurate compass in order to follow those predetermined courses. If you don't know whether or not your compass is accurate, have a professional compass adjuster come to your boat to check it.

B&B on East Brother Island

Transamerica Bldg. Rises Above City Front

The price of electronic navigation devices has come down quickly in the last few years. Everyone can now afford them. Furthermore, they are now so easy to use that virtually anyone can operate one within a few hours of purchasing it. As a result, boaters everywhere are becoming careless navigators. Many navigators now put in the coordinates of their destination before they depart from their marina and never use paper charts. If the coordinates they insert at the outset are slightly off or if their electronic instrument fails for some reason, they could be in serious trouble, particularly in low visibility, such as in the fog or in the dark.

On the other hand, experienced boaters employ both paper charts and electronic devices whenever they go to a destination outside the Bay, but they also maintain an accurate DR at all times. For example, after we lay out a course on paper charts or charts from a trusted cruising guide, we then turn to our electronic charts, where we enter the waypoints from the paper chart.

If we are making a passage from Ballena Isle Marina to Carquinez Strait, for instance, we might have eight waypoints, one for each of the landmarks: the Bay Bridge, the Richmond-San Rafael Bridge, the turn immediately after the Brothers Islands, Marker "P" off Pinole Point, the end of the pier at Davis Point, the Carquinez Bridge, Buoy "23" at the ruins of the old city wharf south of Benicia, and Buoy "1" at the entrance into Benicia Marina.

Boaters who take their boats outside Central Bay often use electronic charts accessed through an electronic navigation program such as Capn or Nobeltec. These programs display on the computer screen where a boat is in relation to the shore, bridges, rocks, and buoys. But no one should rely solely on electronic navigation. According to the electronic displays we've seen on our computer, we have sailed over hundreds of islands, peninsulas, rocks, and reefs as we have cruised during the past few years. This apparent feat results from inaccurate charts, many of which are based on hydrographic surveys done years prior to the advent of GPS. Although we turn on our electronic navigation program virtually every time we make a passage, we consider the locations of our boat and of land forms we see on our computer screen as approximate.

HANDLING A BOAT UNDER WAY

Good seamanship includes handling the boat correctly while under way. If you are going from a harbor across the Bay to Angel Island, for instance, you must steer the boat smoothly. A boat wandering from side to side confuses other boaters and could cause an accident. Steer the boat with a steady hand, carefully following a compass course or aiming the boat toward a fixed point such as a buoy or a building on shore.

People who take the helm on our boat and have trouble maintaining a steady course are generally those who don't focus on the chore at hand. Many people are unable to keep the boat on course while they're talking. On most race boats and some cruising boats, no one is allowed to speak to the person at the helm except about a boat-related matter. You might consider this rule if you can't both talk and steer the boat.

To keep the boat under control, the person at the helm must also understand the effects of the wind and current. Many a boat has collided with a buoy or a bridge tower because the person at the helm is not paying attention to current and wind. One sailboater we know was sailing near the south tower of the Golden Gate Bridge, enjoying being heeled over, when the current swept his boat up against the bridge, breaking his boat's mast. When out on the Bay, watch the current flowing by buoys, channel markers, and bridges to determine the speed and the direction of the current.

If you don't yet know how to read current when you look at a buoy or marker, practice by going out on the Bay at different tide/current states. First, look at your tide book under "Current." Pick out the day's date on the left margin and follow across horizontally. The first column will be headed "Slack" and will give you the time of the first slack water of the day. The second column will give you the time and speed of the maximum current during the first tide of the day; the speed will be followed by the letter E or F, indicating ebb or flood tide. Following the time of the flood will be the time of the second slack water. The remainder of the columns present the times of the alternating slack, flood, and ebb currents for that particular day.

Then go out on the Bay when the tide book predicts slack water and look at a buoy, preferably one out in the middle of the Bay that is clearly affected by current. Observe that the water around it is quiet. Come back three hours later when a strong ebb or flood tide is flowing and observe the buoy or marker once again. When a particularly fast ebb or flood is flowing, the buoy will be leaning over noticeably, indicating the direction of the flow. The water around the buoy or marker will be bubbling and forming little eddies and whirlpools. Observe the buoy repeatedly to understand what effects current can have.

When boating near a bridge tower, use particular caution. If your boat is moving slowly as you pass the tower, you can be sucked into the tower by the current. The same is true of buoys and channel markers. Many boaters who thought they had cleared a buoy have been swept into it by a strong current. Those boaters have too often discovered that buoys make holes in boats.

HANDLING A BOAT IN A HARBOR

Although handling a boat while under way can be mastered quite quickly, handling a boat in the close confines of a harbor or marina in San Francisco Bay is more challenging. As your forward motion slows, the effects of both wind and current become more noticeable. Observe both as you enter an anchorage or marina. For example, when you plan to pick up a mooring or a slip at Ayala Cove on Angel Island, prepare for wind gusts of 15 knots and currents of 1.5 or even 2.0 knots.

By observing other boats already moored in the Cove, you can determine if a cross current is flowing. If the boats are directly in line between the two buoys they are tied to, you shouldn't have to

Fast-Moving Ferries at Ayala Cove

Ferries a Threat for Small Boats

worry about being swept to one side or the other as you attempt to pick up your mooring. If the boats are to one side or the other of a line between the two buoys and the mooring lines are tight, a heavy cross current is flowing. In this case, picking up moorings is going to be challenging. When such conditions prevail, many boaters pick up the bow buoy first and then put a dinghy or sport boat in the water to take a line to the stern buoy.

Wind is the most common negative influence you will encounter when anchoring or entering a slip in the Bay Area. Experienced boaters would always design marinas so boats could enter and leave slips going directly upwind or downwind. Unfortunately, in many marinas the prevailing winds blow at right angles to the slips. In these marinas boaters are challenged to keep their boats under control as they enter slips. The strong winds that blow through some marinas in the afternoons during the summer require extra caution. Marina Bay, Berkeley, and Emeryville marinas, for example, experience especially strong winds.

To enter a slip in windy marinas, anticipate the effect the wind will have on your craft. As the speed of your craft slows, the wind will blow the bow of your boat off downwind first. The more freeboard on your boat, the more rapidly the wind will blow the bow off course. Large powerboats and sailboats alike are difficult to handle if a crosswind of 15 knots or more is blowing. When entering a slip in a crosswind, favor the upwind side of the slip, and enter the slip faster than you would otherwise, depending on a strong engine and reverse gear to slow the boat before it hits the front end of the slip.

As you practice maneuvering in a marina, you will find that in most cases the prop on your boat pulls either to starboard or to port when you use reverse gear. A left-hand prop will move your boat to starboard when you are backing up, no matter what you do with the rudder. A boat with a right-hand prop will try to move to port in reverse. Once you get your boat moving fast enough in reverse, the rudder will exert some control over the

direction you go, but most boats will have to be moving in excess of 2 knots for the rudder to counteract the pull of the prop. In the close confines of a marina, that speed is often not practicable. The alternative is to compensate for the pull of the prop, one area of seamanship that only practice will make perfect.

With more room to maneuver, anchoring is easier than entering a slip in a marina when the wind is blowing strongly. Before you stop the boat, make certain you have the bow headed directly into the wind. Even so, get the anchor down quickly because the bow will be trying to pass the stern as soon as the boat stops. As the bow slips off to one side or the other, let out anchor rode until you have an adequate scope and then run the engine in reverse at approximately one-half throttle for one minute to set the anchor. Adequate scope when you're using nylon rode is generally 7 feet of rode for every 1 foot of depth and 4 to 1 with all-chain rode. (The extra weight of the all-chain rode will prevent the boat from pulling out the anchor.) In heavy winds--25 knots or more--consider letting out more rode, the amount more depending on the strength of the winds.

Because most anchorages in the San Francisco Bay Area are in shallow water, you will almost never let out more than 200 feet of rode, even if you are using nylon. At Candlestick Point, for example, most boats anchor in 8 feet of water, so letting out 60 feet of nylon line will, in normal conditions, assure good holding. Since we have an all-chain rode, we let out only 35-45 feet of chain at Candlestick Point.

Whenever you anchor near other anchored boats, carefully observe how those other boats are anchored. If they are on single hooks and you anchor bow-and-stern, you run the risk of causing a collision. The other boats will swing freely in the wind and current. Your boat anchored bow and stern of course will not. Although the strong currents in Northern California discourage most boaters from anchoring bow-and-stern, you must be prepared to do so if you anchor near others who have bow and stern anchors down.

HANDLING A BOAT IN HEAVY WEATHER

Good seamanship in high winds and heavy seas calls for extra caution. Whether in heavy weather on the Bay or in the Pacific Ocean, you must throttle back if you're operating a powerboat or shorten sail if you're operating a sailboat. Pounding into the waves will make everyone aboard uncomfortable and put unnecessary stress and strain on your vessel.

We occasionally see a powerboat traveling at 15 knots across the Bay with water flying everywhere, pounding so badly we can hear the banging at a distance of a mile or more. When we get closer, we can see passengers inside holding on to whatever they can. Only the person at the throttle has fun in such a case. The same excess can be found aboard sailboats when the captain refuses to shorten sail and everyone ends up cold, wet, and terrified. A sailboat pushed so hard the rail is under water would not only afford

Smaller Boats May Be Obscured

the crew more comfort with a reefed main but also go faster. In the worst case, carrying too much sail can result in a torn sail or a broken mast.

When you're cruising in the ocean, don't challenge the sea. Banging into waves in the Bay makes little sense, but driving into huge waves in the ocean is crazy. If you attempt to drive directly into the steep waves en route to the Farallon Islands, for instance, green water coming over the bow will sweep the entire length of your boat. To avoid both the discomfort and the danger inherent in this situation, fall off and quarter the seas.

Handling a boat in heavy weather also requires special attention to avoid collisions. We all quite naturally want to get under cover when rain or salt spray begins to fly. Then the risk of collision increases. Sailboats present a special risk under such conditions because the headsail completely blocks a large area of forward vision. You must deliberately check for traffic in any blind areas on a regular basis. On some boats you can see under the genoa by getting down on the low side of the boat, but on other boats you must go out on deck to be sure you're safe from collision.

On those days when you get caught out by fog, be especially careful. A radar reflector hoisted in the rigging may help other boats and ships see you, but posting a lookout in heavy fog will also be necessary. A lookout on the bow can hear approaching traffic long before anyone in the cockpit can.

Reefed Main and Genoa in Central Bay

GOING AGROUND AND GETTING OFF

San Francisco Bay has many areas of shallow water, and most boaters who have enjoyed cruising the area for a number of years have gone aground at one time or another. We have been aground, either in our tender or in our ketch, in several cruising areas in the Bay. If you go exploring to get to know your cruising area, you, too, may find yourself aground, whether in a Swan 65 or an Avon sportboat.

Experienced cruising sailors consider going aground in San Francisco Bay, in most circumstances, merely an inconvenience. Most simply assume it comes with the territory in a bay with an average depth of less than 18 feet. Surely no one deliberately goes about looking for a good place to go aground, but it happens when boaters are adventurous.

When exploring areas such as the South Bay near Alviso or Redwood City, where you know you might go aground, use extra caution. Keep that chart nearby in the cockpit, and watch the depth sounder continuously as you move slowly into the suspect area. But even before you enter the area, know the tide state. If the tide is ebbing, don't go into an area where you know you might go aground. Boaters who go aground on an ebb risk having to sit and watch as their boats are left high and dry, often for many hours.

Before we explored Westpoint Slough, in the Redwood City area, we had been warned ahead of time that going aground was a definite possibility. Consequently, we timed our entrance into the Slough to coincide with the beginning of the flood tide. Sure enough, we did go aground, and we couldn't get our 35,000-pound boat off the mud bar by using an anchor as a kedge. We didn't worry, however, because we knew the incoming tide would float us off—as it did in a little over two hours. The ideal situation for those boaters who go aground is to have the tide on a flood.

Good seamanship requires not only that you plan ahead so that you risk going aground only on a flood tide but also that you have a strategy worked out ahead of time to get your boat off immediately if you go aground when the tide is ebbing. If a boat goes aground when it is barely moving, you can sometimes use reverse gear to get off. Be aware, however, of the danger to your engine if you do. When your boat is aground in mud and you use reverse gear, the prop will almost certainly kick up mud that may be sucked into your engine, destroying the impeller in your sea water pump. As soon as you lose your pump, of course, you can forget using your engine, even when you do float off, until you replace the impeller.

One alternative is to get a kedge anchor out immediately. If your boat is not too deeply embedded in the mud, you can often kedge off. We have done so many times. Keep a long anchor line, at least 200 feet, and an anchor at the ready whenever you know you might go aground.

Although some people try to kedge the boat out stern first, this endangers rudders and props, so we don't do it. The grounded boat should come out bow first, the way it went in. Typically, the water ahead of the boat is shallower than the water behind it. For this reason, we generally deploy the kedge from the bow and lead it aft off the quarter. We can pivot the boat, breaking the suction of the keel in the mud and then pull the boat almost 180° from the direction it was traveling when forward motion stopped.

Another practice we have successfully used is to move everyone aboard to the bow to lift the weight off the stern. If you have enough people aboard, the weight transfer can help lift the transom off the bottom and allow you to back off using the engine. Use this technique with caution if you are in the mud, of course, since you can easily suck the flying mud into your engine's impeller. Another option for sailboaters is to put up the mainsail and jib to create an angle of heel that may free the keel. Be cautious, however, that you don't drive your boat farther into the shallow area using this technique.

AVOIDING COLLISIONS

Perhaps no other aspect of seamanship deserves as much attention as avoiding collisions with other vessels. When two sailboats collide, of course, the risk to people on the boats is slight because the boats are generally traveling at less than 5 miles per hour. If

Ship Crew Often Can't See Small Boats

Wakes Reveal a Near-Collision

Choose Best Sails for Conditions

two fast-moving powerboats collide, however, people can be seriously injured. And if either a sailboat or a powerboat collides with a ship, the results can be disastrous. The ship will usually not sustain any damage; in fact, the crew members of a huge ship that collides with a pleasure boat are often unaware that the ship has been involved in a collision.

Parts of the Bay have heavy ship traffic. The Central Bay between the Golden Gate and the Bay Bridge, for example, has a surprising number of ships transiting every day. The Bay waters near Oakland frequently have container ships moving around. And tankers arrive or depart often from the Richmond pier just south of the eastern end of the Richmond-San Rafael Bridge. VTS (Vessel Traffic System) has established shipping lanes inside and outside the Bay. These lanes are marked clearly on your charts. Know where these lanes are. You can cross or travel up or down them, but recognize that ships have right of way in them.

Inside the Bay, you can be confident that a professional pilot is aboard any ship moving into or out of the Bay. These professionals have years of experience and know the shipping lanes inside the Bay and along the San Francisco coast. They know well where they cannot take the ship because of shallow water or Coast Guard regulations. In fact, their

options are few. Remember that those large ships can't stop for you. A 700-foot ship cannot even begin to slow down or turn in less than a mile. If you get in front of a ship traveling at 15 knots, all the pilot can do is sound the ship's horn to warn you.

Few pleasure boats collide with ships inside the Bay because visibility is generally good and because a professional pilot keeps watch at all times. A different situation exists outside the Bay. All of us who have sailed the ocean for years know of countless instances when we have encountered ships that apparently have no one on watch. For the safety of your boat and those aboard, assume no one aboard the ship sees you. You must stay alert to avoid ships.

The weather variable should also concern you. When the marine layer settles down, keep an especially vigilant watch. Don't assume that someone on the ship will be watching you on radar. We learned a frightening and valuable lesson once in a heavy fog along the coast. We could hear two ships' fog horns nearby and could hear the prop of one of them thumping as it cut into the water. Soon we heard crewmembers of the two ships talking by VHF radio, discussing their positions. They said they could easily see one another on radar. We made radio contact, asking if either of them could see our sailboat on radar. Neither could, in spite of the fact that we had

Quiet Day on the Bay

a radar reflector in the rigging. We were probably within a mile or two of one of the ships, a Standard Oil tanker, but we were invisible. In such a case, only keeping a good watch will keep you safe.

Not only does fog make it difficult for personnel aboard ships to detect you, but bridges also prevent radar from identifying your boat. Captain J. L. Shanower, a San Francisco Bar Pilot, told us he worries particularly about pleasure boats near the Golden Gate Bridge when he takes a ship in or out of the Bay in reduced visibility. He has had many near misses in the area because boaters assume their boats will show up on radar. Not so. The bridge makes a large image on the screen that blocks out all boats under it.

MAKING THE BOAT AND CREW SAFE

Coast Guard regulations and common sense require you to have PFDs, flares, a horn, and fire extinguishers aboard any boat you would take out for a Bay cruise. Having this safety equipment aboard is not of much use unless it is readily at hand. PFDs, for example, are typically stowed in the bottom of some locker to keep them out of the way, rendering them useless in an emergency. Yet falling overboard is perhaps the most serious threat to boaters on the Bay. Often the person who falls overboard has been boating for years. In fact, experienced boaters may be at greater risk than novices because experience on the water sometimes leads to overconfidence and carelessness.

Regardless of what you might have deduced from movies and news items, people who fall overboard are not in danger of being eaten by sharks. Rather, people who fall overboard are more likely to drown. Because they are usually fully clothed, they do not last long in the water. Just for the sake of knowledge, jump into a swimming pool sometime dressed in the three or four layers of clothes typical for a Bay area boater. As soon as all that clothing becomes waterlogged, probably in less than a minute, swimming or even keeping yourself afloat becomes nearly impossible. If you were to fall overboard in San Francisco Bay or the Pacific Ocean, the waves would wash over your face as the soaked clothes pulled you ever lower into the water. Add to that the 55° water temperature, and you have a fatal scenario.

More and more boaters on the Bay are wearing PFDs at all times. That makes sense. But staying aboard in the first place also makes sense. If the weather is rough, don't hesitate to rig your jacklines and put on your safety harness.

Fire at sea is a frightening danger for boaters. A chance always exists of a galley fire, so an extinguisher should be kept near the galley. But the danger from a fuel fire is even greater if your boat is powered by a gasoline engine. Many boats have fuel leaks at one time or another. A diesel fuel leak may create offensive odors and a terrible mess in the bilge, but if the fuel aboard is gasoline, a leak creates the potential for an explosion. When fueling the gasoline-powered craft, you are also at risk because of the build-up of static electricity. Be sure to keep the metal nozzle of the filler hose grounded on the fill pipe on your boat.

And while you are thinking about fuel and your boat, remember that you must avoid spilling fuel into Bay waters. When fueling your boat, block your scuppers so that the little fuel that does spill on deck as you fill your tanks can't run overboard. The fine you will be charged for spillage is high.

ANCHORAGES AND MARINAS

Carricklee Anchored at Winslow Cove

"One of the greatest fascinations that cruising holds for me is the landfalls."
—William Washburn Nutting

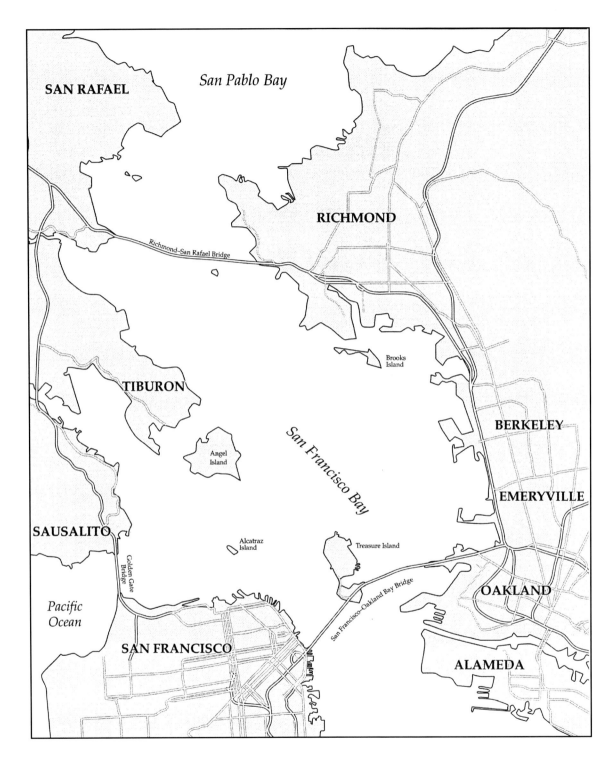

THE CENTRAL BAY

THE CENTRAL BAY

Bay Bridge, City Front, and Coit Tower

I left my heart in San Francisco.
High on a hill it calls to me
to be where little cable cars
climb halfway to the stars!
The morning fog may chill the air . . .
　　　—Douglas Cross, "I Left My Heart in San Francisco"

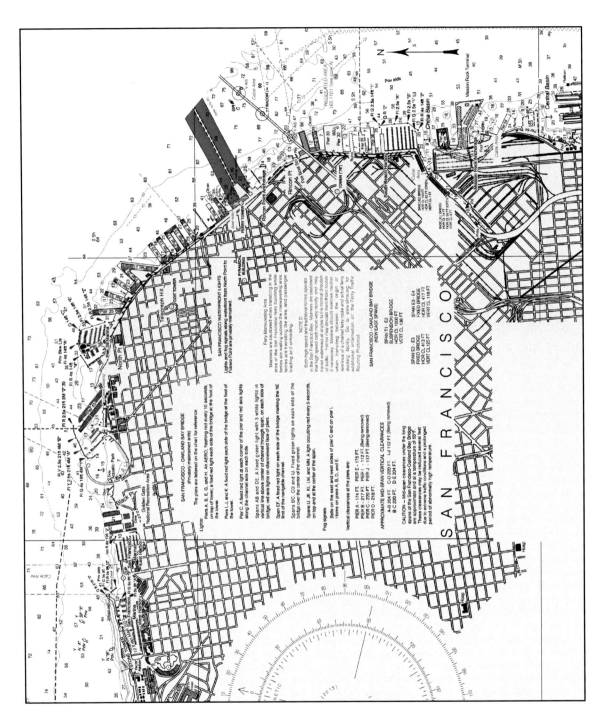

The City Front

SAN FRANCISCO CITY FRONT

CHART #18649, #18650, OR #18652
SAN FRANCISCO ENTRANCE (GOLDEN GATE)
37°49.19N, 122°28.71W

The San Francisco City Front, the waterfront from the south tower of the Golden Gate Bridge to just south of the west span of the Oakland-San Francisco Bay Bridge, is an ideal place to begin a cruise of the San Francisco Bay.

Along this stretch, much of San Francisco's colorful history has been played out. At the west end of the City Front is the Presidio, one of the first two European settlements in San Francisco. (The other settlement was *Misión San Francisco de Asís* at *Laguna de los Dolores*, now Mission Dolores.) In 1775 Spanish captain Juan Bautista de Anza planted a cross at what is today Fort Point to mark the site for a fortified camp, or a *presidio*. In 1846 the U. S. Army took over the Presidio and maintained it as a base for 148 years. Since 1994, the luxuriantly forested 1,000-acre Presidio has been a part of the Golden Gate National Recreation Area.

From the point where the Bay Bridge connects to land and northwest to Broadway was the pueblo of Yerba Buena, the commercial center from 1835 on for the Mexican land grant rancheros spread throughout the Bay Area. In 1847, the name of the village became *San Francisco*. During the latter half of the 19th century Yerba Buena Cove was filled in, and most of the forty-two wharves forming the hub of the city's waterfront were built.

Along the City Front are two yacht clubs, three public marinas, and four anchorages. Practically speaking, though, only the marinas and anchorages are realistic options for overnight visitors. The yacht clubs, St. Francis and Golden Gate, occasionally have guest berthing for members of other yacht clubs. The three public marinas--South Beach Harbor, Pier 39 Marina, and San Francisco Marina--on the other hand, typically have some guest berths available.

Mission Dolores

The anchorages and marinas between the Golden Gate Bridge and the Bay Bridge will give you unparalleled views of the three bridges (the third, the Richmond-San Rafael) linking the shores along the Central Bay. Alcatraz and Angel Island lie to the north of the City Front, and beyond the two islands are the hills of Sausalito, Tiburon, and Belvedere Island. To the east Yerba Buena Island, where the two spans of the Bay Bridge meet in a tunnel, and Treasure Island partially obscure the hills of Point Richmond and Berkeley and the Emeryville marina. And the jewel, the Golden City itself, rises in front of you.

South Beach Harbor and the three anchorages south of the Bay Bridge will not give you quite the same view, lying as they do on the east shore of the City Front rather than on the north shore. You will, however, have an excellent view of the Bay Bridge and, across the Bay, of Oakland and Alameda.

ATTRACTIONS OF THE CITY FRONT

The primary attraction for cruising sailors to the City Front is the ready access to the City itself, its multitude of pleasures requiring an entire guidebook to enumerate. And the public transportation in San Francisco gives you access to any of these pleasures. The top tourist draw in the City is Pier 39, attracting 10.5 million visitors annually.

After savoring the foods, sampling the wares, and admiring (as well as smelling!) the sea lions that have captured several docks in the marina at Pier 39, you may be ready for a bus or taxi ride to one of the country's most accommodating and beautifully landscaped city parks, Golden Gate Park.

Up until the 1850s, the site of this park, now dense with vegetation, was a windy sand dune so inhospitable that neither the native tribes nor the Spanish and Mexican explorers had permanent settlements here. Today, though, this site has something for every cruising sailor: the Japanese Tea Garden; two art museums, the M. H. de Young Memorial Museum and the Asian Art Museum; the California Academy of Sciences, including the Steinhart Aquarium, the Morrison Planetarium, and a natural history museum; Strybing Arboretum; lakes; and walking, biking, and skating paths throughout. In the summer and early fall, drama productions and concerts add to the allure of the park.

Other points of interest near the marinas and anchorages are, of course, the Embarcadero itself, where you can go aboard a restored Liberty ship or a three-masted square-rigger; Fisherman's Wharf; the Maritime Museum; museums at Fort Mason, the Presidio, and Fort Point; and the Palace of Fine Arts (housing the Exploratorium Science Museum, a wonderful hands-on exhibit for children and adults alike).

Chinatown remains one of San Francisco's colorful attractions, where you can experience the flavor of China in the architecture, the food, and the wares for sale along the narrow, crowded streets. From the waterfront, part of the adventure is in the getting there. Two of the three remaining cable car lines run from near Fisherman's Wharf up to Chinatown. Catch a

Golden Gate Bridge

car at either Hyde and Beach or at Taylor and Bay.

Alcatraz, since 1972 a part of the Golden Gate National Recreation Area, is another popular site for boaters. A ferry picks up passengers at Pier 41 and transports them to the island, where they may go ashore and wander around the buildings and through some of the cell blocks on a self-guided tour.

You can also take ferries from the Ferry Building to Alameda, Oakland, Sausalito, and Larkspur; from Pier 43 1/2 to Angel Island, Tiburon and Sausalito; and from Pier 39 to Six Flags Discovery Kingdom. While you can take your own boat to all but Alcatraz, Larkspur, and Six Flags, you may find the convenience of the ferries appealing.

Those of you wanting to enjoy the enticements ashore will be best off staying in one of the marinas, where you'll not worry about the security of your tender or your boat if you are away after nightfall. But some cruising sailors like to anchor out for a night on the City Front merely to partake of the spectacular views afforded of the bridges, the lights of the city, sunset over the Golden Gate, and the parade of other boats, ships, tugs, and ferries on the Bay.

BERTHING

SAN FRANCISCO CITY MARINA
East Harbor Entrance 37°48.48N,
    122°25.96W
West Harbor Entrance 37°48.48N,
    122°26.37W
Contact: 415-831-6322   VHF 16 or 68

This small craft harbor with 700 slips, the first public marina on the City Front inside the Golden Gate, is a legacy of the Panama Pacific International Exposition of 1915.

APPROACH

West Harbor, one of the two harbors of the San Francisco Marina, lies 1.85 miles E of the Golden Gate Bridge. The entrance, marked by a light, is 500 yards E of the cupola on the seawall. Visible among the trees ashore of West Harbor is the cream-colored octagonal rotunda of the Palace of Fine Arts, designed for the Panama Pacific Exposition of 1915.

The waters outside the harbor are popular for racing sailors and sailboarders, so be on the lookout for racing buoys, flotillas of sailboats, and dozens of colorful sailboards flitting about like butterflies.

The harbor has installed a floating wave attenuator, similar to a floating dock, midway between the end of the breakwater and the seawall to protect the marina from the heavy seas common along the shoreline. The attenuator--225 feet long, 15 feet wide, and 3 feet high above the water--is easy to locate. Because of the extreme shallow water near the E end of the breakwater, the harbormaster instructs all boaters to pass this structure on the S end only, that is, between the attenuator and the shore. Do not attempt to pass between the end of the breakwater and the attenuator.

Inside West Harbor, *Golden Gate Yacht Club* is in the first building to starboard. **Contact: 415-346-2618.** The clubhouse for *St. Francis Yacht Club* is at the W end of the harbor on the same side of the channel. **Contact: 415-563-6363.**

Rounding the South End of the Attenuator

Golden Gate Yacht Club

St. Francis Yacht Club

Entrance Sign, San Francisco City E. Harbor

Directly across the channel from the Golden Gate Yacht Club is a dock where boaters may tie their boats while they visit the Harbormaster's office to sign in for slips in either West or East Harbor.

The entrance to **East Harbor** (also called *Gashouse Cove*), the other of the San Francisco Marina docks, is 600 yards E of the entrance to West Harbor. A breakwater running W to E and another running N to S on the E side of the marina protect the docks from the wave and surge action. A light marks the end of the pier at the entrance. When abeam of the harbor entrance, you can readily spot the fuel dock at the back of the entrance channel.

FACILITIES AT OR NEAR THE MARINA:

Bus Stop
Fuel Dock
Hoist
Grocery Store
Laundry
Post Office
Pump Out
Restaurants

~~~~~~

PIER 39
Entrance 37°48.52N, 122°24.45W
Contact: 415-705-5436   VHF 16
info@pier39marina.com

Pier 39 Marina, with 350 slips, gladly caters to guest boaters, but call ahead because demand often outstrips the number of available slips, especially on weekends. Among the multitude of restaurants and shops that draw tourists by the thousands daily to Pier 39, the California Sea Lions that have homesteaded several docks at the west end of the marina have apparently made this site one of the busiest tourist spots in the country.

Of particular interest to sailors is the nearby *Jeremiah O'Brien*, a World War II Liberty Ship open to the public at Pier 45.

APPROACH

Approaching from the W, east of Aquatic Park is the Fisherman's Wharf area, which offers no facilities for boaters but is the site of a constant flow of ferry traffic. A short distance beyond, 0.75 mile from Aquatic Park, signs designate Pier 39, but it is also easily located by the sailboat masts on either side of the buildings on the pier. In the background, 0.5 mile SE of the marina, the 210-foot Coit Tower, a slender column built in 1937 as a monument to San Francisco firefighters, stands above the trees on Telegraph Hill. From Pier 39 to the Bay Bridge is another 1.55 miles.

Enter the marina on the E side of the buildings at Pier 39. A breakwater extends from the end of the buildings to the E and then to the S. Lights mark the position of the breakwater. The entrance is back near the shore and leads to the docks immediately below the harbormaster's office.

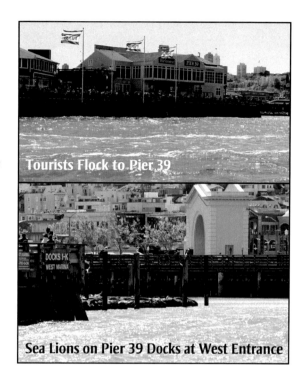

Tourists Flock to Pier 39

Sea Lions on Pier 39 Docks at West Entrance

Pier 39 also has a harbor on the W side of the buildings, but many of the docks in this harbor have been given over to the colony of sea lions that has taken up permanent residence here. Do not enter this harbor unless directed to do so by the harbormaster.

FACILITIES AT OR NEAR THE MARINA:

Bus and Cable Car Stops
Grocery Store
Laundromat
Pump Out
Restaurants
Shops

~~~~~

SOUTH BEACH HARBOR
North Entrance 37°46.91N, 122°23.10W
South Entrance 37°46.68N, 122°23.14W
Contact: 415-495-4911   VHF 16

South Beach Harbor gives one a wholly different feeling from the other marinas along the City Front. Near the southernmost extremity of the Embarcadero, this portion of the City Front has relatively little tourist activity and traffic. Yet handsome red brick commercial buildings grace this portion of the waterfront, and the marina itself attaches to a grassy park with trees and benches and a long fishing pier at the southern end.

Here you can enjoy the City experience in relative solitude from the City bustle, excepting, of course, the bustle on the days and nights of the Giants baseball games at AT&T stadium right next door to the marina.

You can walk to numerous fine restaurants, take public transportation to all points of San Francisco, or simply enjoy the view from this prime piece of real estate that can be yours for a night or so.

Visiting boats can tie up at the long guest dock at the N end of the marina or in any one of the 700 berths that is vacant.

The *South Beach Yacht Club* is located at the shore end of the guest dock, but it has no guest dock of its own. **Contact:** 415-495-2295

APPROACH

This modern marina is 0.5 mile SE of the City end of the Bay Bridge. As you are passing under the Bridge close to shore, shipping terminals obscure the marina. When you get closer, however, you'll spot the marina sign on the end of the warehouse on the NW pier of the marina, the masts of the sailboats, and the breakwater with navigation lights on it. Boaters can enter the marina through openings at either end of the breakwater.

Shipping terminal warehouses to the N of the marina protect boaters from the winds and waves, making South Beach Harbor an excellent destination.

FACILITIES AT OR NEAR
SOUTH BEACH HARBOR

Banks
Bike and Kayak Rental
Boat Maintenance and Repair
Grocery Store
Haul Out
Laundry
Post Office
Pump Out
Public Transportation
Restaurants
Shops

On the Approach to South Beach Harbor

ANCHORAGES

AQUATIC PARK
Entrance 37°48.65N, 122°25.42W
Contact: 415-859-6779 or 415-859-6807
bill_doll@nps.gov

To anchor in Aquatic Park, boaters must obtain permission from the Aquatic Park Ranger Station.

Aquatic Park has been a favorite location for swimmers and boaters from the Dolphin Swimming and Boating Club and the South End Rowing Club for over a century; hence, the Park is closed to power vessels as well as jet skis. Park regulations now specify that sailboats can enter the park slowly and cautiously with the use of a motor, being careful to give way to swimmers and row boaters. Check with the ranger at Aquatic Park for current regulations before entering. San Francisco Maritime National Historic Park rangers patrol the lagoon area.

Though moorings belonging to the Sea Scouts take up the south side of the anchorage, another 10 to 15 boats can anchor in this lagoon without crowding. Anchor in 7 to 14 feet in clay and sand in the center of the lagoon. The breakwater protects anchored boats from much of the motion of San Francisco Bay, but the surge may still keep your boat rolling.

The *Balclutha*

Signs at Aquatic Park Entrance

Anchored at Aquatic Park

The current in this anchorage is strong at times, causing boats to drag anchor and endanger the historic ships displayed at the Maritime Museum. To minimize the danger to these treasures from our maritime history, Park Service rangers urge visiting boaters to anchor as far away as possible, at least 200 feet, from the full-rigged ship *Balclutha*, the lumber schooner *C. A. Thayer*, the ferry *Eureka*, and the scow schooner *Alma*.

Landing a dinghy or sportboat on the inviting sand beach on the S shore of the anchorage is simple enough. However, you must row ashore, being especially alert for swimmers in the water. Also, you should not leave your tender unguarded while you're ashore.

APPROACH TO AQUATIC PARK

On the City Front 0.5 mile E of San Francisco East Marina and directly across from Alcatraz Island is Aquatic Park (the San Francisco Maritime National Historic Park). This anchorage stands out clearly because of the huge 19th century sailing ships at the Maritime Museum dock that occupies the east side of Aquatic Park Lagoon. Behind the cove about 200 yards, the Ghirardelli Square sign is prominent. A curved breakwater extending from Black Point protects Aquatic Park. The entrance into the anchorage area is approximately 200 feet wide, but set a course for the center to avoid the fishing lines that often seem to be in the water here.

FACILITIES NEAR THE ANCHORAGE:

Bus and Cable Car Stops
Grocery Store
Restaurants
Shops

~~~~

PT. RINCON ANCHORAGE
(BAY BRIDGE ANCHORAGE)
Anchorage 37°47.47N, 122°23.30W

Finding the Point Rincon anchorage is as easy as finding the Oakland-San Francisco Bay Bridge: The anchorage is immediately NW of the point where the bridge meets the City. The anchorage extends W from the bridge to the Ferry Building, a long, low terminal of gray sandstone dominated by a tall clock tower. The cove, easily spotted between the bridge and the clock tower when you're close to shore, once had mooring buoys, but the city removed them some years ago.

Carricklee at Point Rincon, SF City Front

Boats can anchor in 12-15 feet of water, with good holding, within 150 feet of shore. Though large enough for about 10 boats, this anchorage is rarely used by cruising boaters because of the wake caused by passing ferries and pleasure craft, especially during the daylight hours.

FACILITIES

Point Rincon anchorage has no satisfactory beach or pier for landing a tender. You can land at the inviting concrete ramps by the seawall, but your tender will be vulnerable to any of the thousands of passersby and the ever-present street people in the area. Your dinghy will also be at the mercy of the waves that will constantly throw it against the concrete. We would recommend having one crew member take those ashore who wish to explore and then return later to pick them up.

~~~~

City View from Point Rincon Anchorage

McCOVEY COVE
Anchorage 37°46.64N, 122°23.24W

The newest anchorage along the San Francisco waterfront, McCovey Cove is unique in that it is rarely used except when the San Francisco Giants team has home games. But when the Giants are playing, McCovey Cove is packed with nautical fans hoping to catch a home run ball hit hard enough to clear the wall and fall amid the boats at anchor.

Regulations require that motorized vessels must enter the Cove very slowly, leaving no wake, and that boats may not be anchored over night there.

The crowded conditions on game days and the anchoring limitations may make McCovey less than appealing for many cruising sailors. Yet the Cove can be an ideal destination for a lunch stop. When we recently anchored at McCovey Cove for a lunch break, the Giants were out of town, so we had the entire Cove virtually to ourselves.

McCovey Cove and AT&T Park

Anchorage at China Basin

CHINA BASIN (MISSION ROCK)
Anchorage 37°46.37N, 122°23.13W

Before it was largely filled in with the rubble from the 1906 earthquake, China Basin, also called *Mission Bay*, figured largely in the history of the San Francisco waterfront. In 1776, a few Ohlone villages were still clustered around a creek emptying into the bay. Mission Dolores, one of the first two Spanish settlements in the Bay Area, sat on the shores of the Bay. During the latter half of the 19th century the shores of this then large basin were the site of "greaseways," railways for moving boats into dry dock for repairs. Today you can see a later vintage railway on the southwest shore—a ferry terminal for transporting Santa Fe railroad cars between China Basin and Point Richmond, on the other side of San Francisco Bay. This facility closed several years ago.

At the turn of the century, San Franciscans lined the shores here to watch the rowers who competed in races from Fort Point.

The creek where the Ohlones lived, later called *Mission Creek* or *Third Street Channel*, was dredged in the late 19th century, and its banks became the site of hay and lumber wharves and brickyards. You can take your tender up this channel, today the location of several houseboats. The entrance to the creek is immediately south of South Beach Harbor Marina. You will pass under the old bascule bridge at the back of what is today McCovey Cove.

APPROACH

The China Basin anchorage is 0.2 mile S of South Beach Harbor. It is immediately S of the Mission Rock Pier, which protects the anchorage from waves that sweep across the Central Bay. The Mission Rock Pier is the largest on the City Front, extending out from the shore some 0.25 mile and having an end that is approximately 0.15 mile wide. Currently, large Navy ships are moored at the outer end of this pier, these ships aiding in the identification of the pier.

Enter the anchorage area just S of the pier, steering a course for the abandoned railroad ferry landing on the S side at the back of the anchorage.

You can see the Mariposa Hunters Point Yacht Club in the NW corner near the foot of the pier.

When we recently visited this anchorage, a yellow buoy was located in this anchorage area. Reluctant to anchor near this unmarked buoy, we later asked local boaters at the yacht club about the buoy. They explained it was a club racing buoy and assured us it did not denote a dangerous submerged object.

For good holding and excellent protection from prevailing winds, anchor in 15-25 feet of water in front of the Mariposa Hunters Point Yacht Club, but don't block the passageway for the launch ramp used daily by club members or for boats coming from the Bay View Boat Club dock in the SW corner of the basin. Additionally, "Duck" boats regularly use the City launch ramp between the two yacht club ramps. These commercial tour boats, converted ex-military amphibious vehicles, pick up 20-30 passengers on the streets near Fishermen's Wharf and drive them along the San Francisco waterfront to China Basin. Here, the Duck boats roll down this city launch ramp amid splashes and the squeals of the tourists. The Ducks then motor through the anchorage for a cruise in San Francisco Bay.

The anchorage area close to Mariposa Hunters Point Yacht Club accommodates only two or three boats, but you can also find good protection from prevailing winds to the S outside the abandoned ferry pier.

Members of both yacht clubs here are friendly and helpful. Tie up your tender at their docks and visit their clubs when they are open, though the locals caution against leaving either your tender or your boat unattended after dark. Yacht club members also caution visiting boaters to watch the weather carefully during the late fall/winter months, when E winds can make this anchorage dangerous.

Bay View Boat Club (415) 495-9500
Mariposa Hunters Point Yacht Club
(415) 495-9344

FACILITIES WITHIN WALKING DISTANCE

Boat Maintenance and Repair
Haul Out
Launch Ramps
Public Transportation
Restaurants

Mariposa Hunters Point Yacht Club

CENTRAL BASIN ANCHORAGE
Anchorage 37°45.96N, 122°23.12W

APPROACH

Approximately 0.3 mile S of China Basin Anchorage, still technically in the China Basin area, is the Central Basin Anchorage. Identify the anchorage area by the large ship repair facilities to the S. Floating dry docks face N, and at the back of the cove are two boat haul-out facilities and two restaurants.

Anchor in 20 feet of water off the fishing pier in the NW corner of the cove, with fair protection from prevailing winds. This anchorage has room for 10 or more boats. To the N of the anchorage area is an abandoned pier in an advanced state of disrepair. You can anchor close to the abandoned pier to be sure you are out of the way of the tugs bringing ships in or taking them out of the dry dock area (a relatively rare occurrence). Be on the lookout for debris in the water and under the surface in the anchorage.

On the water's edge is the small marina of San Francisco Boat Works. The docks in front of the Mission Rock Restaurant, immediately N of SF Boat Works, are easily identified by their state of disrepair. These docks are private, and visiting boaters are no longer encouraged to tie up their tenders there while going ashore for lunch or dinner.

Boaters wishing to visit the San Francisco Boat Works Chandlery can get permission to tie up their boats or tenders at the Boat Works dock if space is available by calling the office. **Contact: 415-626-3275.**

FACILITIES

Boat Maintenance and Repair
Chandlery
Haul Out
Launch Ramp
Public Transportation
Restaurants

Central Basin, San Francisco Boat Works

~~~~~

HORSESHOE BAY
Chart #18649 or #18652
Horseshoe Bay Entrance 37°49.90N, 122°28.57W

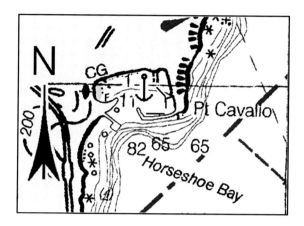

When you're entering San Francisco Bay through the Golden Gate, the first anchorage and marina you see will be in tiny Horseshoe Bay, 500 yards NE of the N tower of the bridge.

With this strategic location, Horseshoe Bay has had a long history of military presence. At the end of the Civil War, the U. S. Government purchased several hundred acres on the north side of San Francisco Bay and eventually established three forts here and equipped them with heavy artillery to guard the entrance into the Bay. The easternmost of these three, the former East Fort Baker, sits on the hill immediately above Horseshoe Bay. The batteries for guns and the platforms for missiles have now become historic landmarks, and the land is part of the Golden Gate National Recreational Area.

In Horseshoe Bay are a small marina and an anchorage for one or two single boats or as many as six or eight boats rafted together.

ATTRACTIONS

Directly up from the beach, shadowed by towering eucalyptus trees, is a row of trimly kept wooden buildings, formerly part of East Fort Baker but now housing the Cavallo Point Resort.

A short walk from the marina takes you to the old administration buildings that are now the Bay Area Discovery Museum. Those of you with youngsters (or the young-at-heart) aboard will want to explore this inter-active display of science and art. As well as exhibits, it has a carousel, a small cafe catering to children's tastes, and special presentations of music and dance on selected nights. The museum is open on Tuesday through Sunday, 0900 to 1700, and closed on Monday.

Horseshoe Bay is an ideal stop for hikers. From the beach area you can pick up trails heading E and N along the shore toward Sausalito, N toward Gerbode Valley, or W along the coastal headlands toward Point Bonita, with its 150-year-old Fresnel lens beacon still flashing a warning to sailors far out at sea. These trails take you past reminders of the 150 years of military history of this region, through the grasslands once the grazing pastures for the cattle of Rancho Saucelito, to the shores where Coast Miwoks fished. The miles of trails crisscross the Marin Headlands, velvety green in the winter and spring and, in the spring, laden with wildflowers—blue lupine, yellow mimulus, white Queen Anne's lace, orange California poppies. And year around, hawks, egrets, terns, and pelicans soar above this shoreline.

From Horseshoe Bay on a clear day, you have an unobstructed view of the city of San Francisco. By night the lights of the city and of the Bay Bridge sparkle like the jewels they are. But perhaps the single greatest attraction of this spot is, finally, the magnificent view afforded one of the fabled Golden Gate Bridge. Late in the afternoon you'll watch the coastal fog pushing its way into San Francisco Bay, gradually enveloping all the Golden Gate Bridge except for the tops of its two towers pushing their way toward the heavens, bright orange above the white fog. No sight is more quintessentially San Francisco.

Approach at Horseshoe Bay

APPROACH

When you approach Horseshoe, turbulent winds often exceeding 25 knots in this area can cause problems if you don't lower your sails before entering.

An additional problem is the sometimes 5- or 6-knot current at the entrance. If your boat speed is slow, you can easily find yourself slipping out under the Golden Gate Bridge before you can get into the harbor. Therefore, plan to enter this harbor on slack water or with a small ebb or flood tide.

The third serious problem with Horseshoe Bay is also weather related: fog. When a thick fog slides in under the bridge, your best plan is to choose another anchorage. Even if you could find the harbor and get anchored safely inside, the beauty of the anchorage would be lost in such weather.

As you enter Horseshoe Bay, a fishing pier is on your port. Choose a course midway between the end of the pier and the breakwater on the starboard. The harbor is quite shallow; the average depth at low water is about 8 feet.

BERTHING

Contact: 415-332-2319

Inside the breakwater, Travis Marina, a small facility, rings the S and E perimeter of the harbor. Guest slips are available; however, most slips here are relatively small. Call first to be sure a slip long enough for your boat is open.

ANCHORAGE

37°49.94N, 122°28.53W

Leave plenty of space around the Coast Guard docks on the W side of the harbor because CG boats arrive and depart regularly on an emergency basis. Although the depth and holding vary little from one part of the harbor to the next, that portion toward the E side near the docks is best because it will keep you comfortably away from the departure routes of emergency craft.

Anchorage and Marina at Horseshoe Bay

Coast Guard Boat Departs Horseshoe

Holding in the harbor is good, but not outstanding. Silt covers the bottom, and some anchors do not hold well in such loose material. After your anchor is down and you have let out an appropriate amount of rode, test the anchor's holding by running up your boat's engine in reverse to about one-half its normal cruising speed, keeping it there for at least 45 seconds. If your anchor drags, hoist and drop it again and again until you are confident it will hold if the wind increases.

FACILITIES

Travis Marina has staff on hand daily to assist visitors. The facilities are minimal: a lounge and bar on the second story of the large building on the N side of the marina in the NE corner of Horseshoe, open to the public and visiting boaters in late afternoons and early evenings. This facility includes restrooms and a shower. In the NW corner of the bay is a public boat launching ramp.

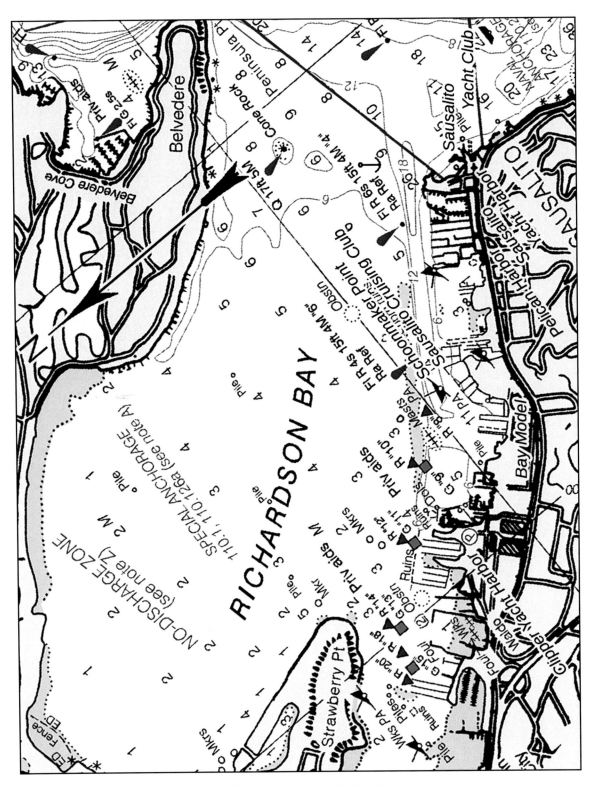

Sausalito Marinas and Anchorages

SAUSALITO

Chart #18649, #18652, or #18653

ENTRANCE LIGHT #2 (RICHARDSON BAY)	37°51.30N, 122°28.28W
SAUSALITO YACHT CLUB ENTRANCE	37°51.41N, 122°28.68W
ANCHORAGE (RICHARDSON BAY)	37°51.67N, 122°28.55W
SAUSALITO CRUISING CLUB ENTRANCE	37°51.69N, 122°29.15W
SCHOONMAKER MARINA	37°51.89N, 122°29.38W
CLIPPER YACHT HARBOR	37°52.29N, 122°29.77W

Sausalito as a cruising destination is a mixed bag. The anchorages tend to have either frequent turbulence or precarious water depths, and the marinas with guest docks are few and expensive. Yet in other ways it's extremely boater-friendly. All the marinas and the anchorage are essentially in the town of Sausalito, so boaters have access to all the usual facilities of any small city. In addition, Sausalito has a major terminal for both bus and ferry service of the Golden Gate Transit system. Then there's the small town of 7,100 residents itself, a town with a large personality and an impressive history.

Sausalito (or *Saucelito*, as Juan Manuel de Ayala reportedly named this site, presumably for the "little willows," or tule grass, growing here) has a long history of human occupation, having been home to perhaps as many as 2,500 Miwoks. Ayala, the first European to explore San Francisco Bay from the sea, anchored his ship in the protected cove near Sausalito in 1775. The first permanent European settlement here began in 1838, when William A. Richardson, an English seaman, obtained a Mexican land grant for Rancho Saucelito. With the coming of statehood, Richardson eventually lost all his holdings; we mark his legacy in the naming of Richardson Bay, the first large bay inside and to the N of the Golden Gate Bridge.

This coastal town has long been a much favored tourist attraction, yet it retains much of its unique flavor. True, its main street, Bridgeway, sports dozens of art, crafts, and toney clothing shops you'll immediately recognize as appealing to those on land tours. Nevertheless, the many businesses offering services necessary for a boating community, from chandleries to machine shops to sail lofts, attest to its nautical orientation. And in the hills above the tourists, and the traffic congestion they bring to Bridgeway Boulevard, lies the other Sausalito with its turn-of-the-century houses, its churches, its commercial enterprises like those of other communities, and its streets lacing through the year-round lushly green cliffside on which the citizens have built their homes.

Sausalito Channel, Marinas, and Anchorage

ATTRACTIONS

In the 19th century wealthy San Franciscans built elegant summer homes on the hills overlooking Richardson Bay. Though you can see some of these Victorian beauties from your boat, you may want to get a bit of aerobic exercise by hiking up the hill to get a closer look.

As you walk along the waterfront, notice the huge barn-like buildings left over from Sausalito's boat building days. As early as 1890, boat building was an important enterprise here. This enterprise boomed in the early 1940s with the opening of Marinship, the shipyard that built 93 of the Liberty ships as well as tankers and landing craft during World War II.

From Sausalito a fairly competent hiker can walk to the Marin Headlands of the Golden Gate National Recreation Area. Follow the shoreline south of Sausalito Point for about a mile to the Recreation Area, where a hiking trail veers off to the left just before the "Y" in the road. This trail connects with the numerous trails of the Marin Headlands. (See the section on Horseshoe Bay for more details.)

Save an hour or two out of your sightseeing and hiking day to visit what may be Sausalito's premier attraction for many boaters: the Bay Model Visitor Center, located in the Marinship area. Operated by the U. S. Army Corps of Engineers and free to the public, the Bay Model is a one-acre scale model where visitors can view the complete San Francisco Bay-Delta system. With the use of hydraulic pumps, the model simulates the ocean tides and Delta river flows to demonstrate the effects on the Bay. You'll walk along the shores of the entire Bay and Delta region—in miniature, of course—as the waters slowly rise and recede in imitation of the ceaseless rhythms of this intricately balanced water system.

APPROACH

Sausalito is easy to identify because of its proximity to the Golden Gate Bridge. From the N tower of the Golden Gate Bridge, go N 1.5 miles, and you'll see the residences of Sausalito on the hillside. In the early hours of the day, the morning sun--when the fog doesn't shield it--reflects off these structures.

On summer afternoons the fog rolls inland over the mountains behind the town, engulfing the streets and houses but rarely the boats in the harbors. Both the morning sunshine and the afternoon fog may help you identify the town as you approach.

If you are approaching from the E, 1.3 miles separates Sausalito from the Tiburon Peninsula. Halfway between Peninsula Point, the S point of land on the Tiburon Peninsula, and Sausalito, Buoy "2" marks the entrance to the Sausalito channel, which proceeds in a NW direction. Keeping the channel markers to your starboard and the town of Sausalito to your port, you will have plenty of water. **Do not stray to the starboard of the channel.** Examine your chart closely before entering Richardson Bay because shallow water covers much of this large bay.

Be cautious, too, of the winds in Richardson Bay. Local sailors often refer to the area just S of Sausalito as "Hurricane Gulch," where winds roar down the canyons in the afternoon hours. Sailboats can be sailing along under full sail in 10 knots of wind one minute and can suddenly be hit with a 30-knot gust, leaving the boat on her beam ends. The closer you are to shore, the greater the impact of these gusts on your boat.

Ferry to Sausalito

BERTHING

Sausalito is undoubtedly one of the most popular destinations for boaters in San Francisco Bay. Consequently, few accommodations for visiting boaters are available. The Sausalito Yacht Harbor, Pelican Yacht Harbor, and Richardson Bay Marina do not have any accommodations for guest boaters. All the slips in Sausalito Cruising Club, Schoonmaker Point Marina, and Clipper Yacht Harbor are generally filled, but the harbormasters of each of these three clubs will provide guest berths as availability permits.

SAUSALITO CRUISING CLUB

Entrance: 37°51.69N, 122°29.15W
Contact: 415-944-9950
portcaptain@sausalitocruisingclub.org

The Sausalito Cruising Club is a private yacht club with facilities for a few visiting cruising boats belonging to members of other yacht clubs. One of the appeals of this small club, as well as of the two other marinas this far up inside Richardson Bay, is the water: Unlike that in the anchorage areas by the Sausalito city front, the water in these marinas is delightfully calm.

APPROACH

From Entrance Marker "2", proceed up the Sausalito Channel, carefully keeping the red channel markers to starboard. At Marker "6," or slightly more than 0.5 mile beyond the Spinnaker Restaurant, turn to port toward the Sausalito Cruising Club. This club, as do many facilities in Richardson Bay, has a problem with shoal water. Because the depth of the entrance into the marina is 4 feet or less at low water, enter only at close to high water.

To avoid going aground, stay close to the "F" Dock of Schoonmaker Point Marina until you reach the guest dock at the Cruising Club. Then go slowly as you turn toward the main dock of the Club, beyond which lies the clubhouse of the Sausalito Cruising Club. Do not turn into the basin until you can see the Club facilities directly ahead of you. For more specific instructions, call the port captain at the club before getting under way.

The guest dock at the club exceeds 100 feet but is often full. Call ahead to be certain space exists for your boat. The club is open after 1600 on Fridays and Saturdays. If you are planning to arrive at a time when the club office is not open, call the port captain ahead of time to get permission to enter and tie up at the guest dock. You can also get permission to leave your dinghy at this dock if you decide to anchor out. A 48-hour limit has been established for all boats and tenders on the guest dock here.

FACILITIES
WiFi (free)

Sausalito Cruising Club

SCHOONMAKER POINT MARINA
Entrance: 37°51.89N, 122°29.38W
Contact: 415-331-5550
info@schoonmakermarina.com
VHF 16

Schoonmaker is strictly an upscale facility, with 161 slips and all the amenities a boater could require, including beautiful, wide concrete docks. This marina commonly has berths available for guest boats. All this comfort and convenience come at a price, of course; but, if you can get a slip here, you'll surely find the price worth paying. Schoonmaker has depths inside the marina to accommodate boats as large as 70 feet long. As with the other marinas up inside Richardson Bay, you'll find the water in this marina calm.

APPROACH

On the port side of the Sausalito Channel 200 yards beyond the Sausalito Cruising Club and just after Marker "6" is the entrance leading to the harbormaster's office at Schoonmaker Point Marina. Call ahead to ask if guest berthing is available.

FACILITIES AT THE MARINA:

Kayak and Paddleboard Rental
Laundry
Pump Out
WiFi (free)

CLIPPER YACHT HARBOR
Entrance: 37°52.29N, 122°29.77W
Contact: 415-332-3500

Clipper Yacht Harbor, a well-run facility, is centrally located near marine repair facilities, restaurants, and chandleries. A large 600-slip facility, it has a specific guest berth area; but, even when those berths are filled, the harbormaster will attempt to accommodate guest boats if prospective visitors call ahead.

APPROACH

Almost a mile farther up the Sausalito channel beyond Schoonmaker, on the port side, you can identify Clipper Yacht Harbor by the Chevron sign marking the busy fuel dock. Again, as with all areas in Richardson Bay, be careful to stay in the channel.

FACILITIES AT OR NEAR THE CLIPPER YACHT HARBOR MARINA:

Fuel Dock
Launch Ramp
Laundry
Pump Out
WiFi (free)

Entrance to Schoonmaker

ANCHORAGES

Boats at anchor anywhere in Richardson Bay are limited to only 14 consecutive days.

The best anchorage for visiting boaters is in the S anchorage, across the Sausalito Channel from the Spinnaker Restaurant. Shallow water is a problem for those anchored farther N in Richardson Bay, but water depths in the preferred portion of the Bay are 10 feet or more.

Some instances of theft have been reported in this anchorage. If you plan to leave your boat unguarded while at anchor here, be sure to lock your boat and remove any on-deck items not locked.

To the E of Clipper Yacht Harbor, depths are about 5 feet at low water. Across from the Sausalito Cruising Club and Schoonmaker, the depths shown on the chart are generally about 4 feet at low water. Back down the channel toward San Francisco, however, the water deepens.

If you plan to stay for no more than a few hours to have lunch on your boat, you can anchor off the part of the city facing San Francisco. The holding in this area is good, and the scenery in every direction is spectacular. Anchor off *Old Town City Front* seaward of the Trident or Scoma's restaurant in 15-20 feet of water.

The *Trident Restaurant* has one mooring and a guest dock you may use free of charge while you have a meal at the restaurant. Call **415-331-3232** to obtain permission. While you and your guests will enjoy the beauty of the area, strong wind gusts and roiling waters keep this site from being anything more than a temporary destination.

If you plan to stay for more than a few hours, consider anchoring in the area between the *Sausalito Yacht Club*, adjacent to the ferry terminal on the N side, and the *Spinnaker Restaurant*. Sausalito Yacht Club also has ten buoys that visiting yacht club members can use. The club's buoys are frequently reserved months in advance on weekends, but they are normally free on weekdays. Call the yacht club at **415-332-7400** to see if one

Sausalito Anchorage

Dinghy Dock, Sausalito Cruising Club

Sausalito Yacht Club

of the buoys is available. The club is open Friday, Saturday, and Sunday, and it offers showers, a bar, and a restaurant.

Boats in both this anchorage and the buoy area will be subject to rolly conditions even though this area is somewhat protected by the ferry terminal. In spite of the uncomfortable motion, this location is a good destination because you can leave your dinghy at the club dock for up to two hours to go ashore for shopping and sightseeing.

Other docks for tenders are available:

Caruso's Seafood Deli (public access)
Sausalito Cruising Club
   (private; permission from the club harbormaster)
Sausalito Yacht Club
   (private; permission from the club harbormaster)
Schoonmaker Marina
   (public access)

~~~~~

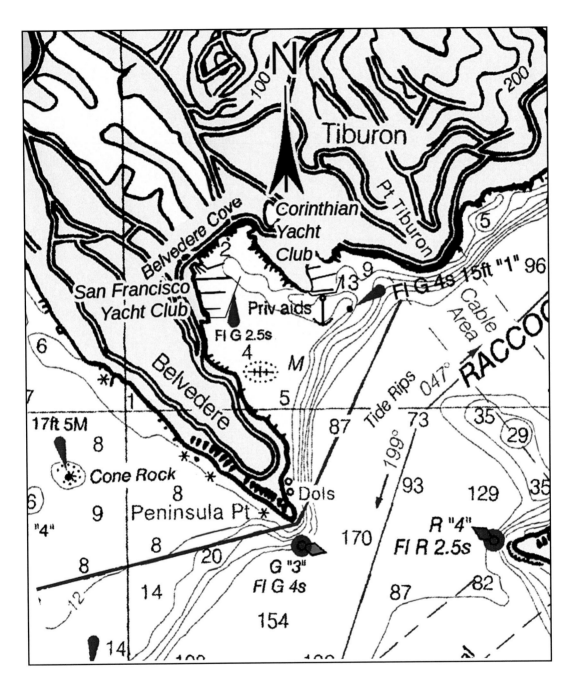

Raccoon Strait and Belvedere/Tiburon

TIBURON PENINSULA

Chart #18649, #18652, or #18653

The Tiburon Peninsula comprises two somewhat separate and, in many ways, wholly different cruising destinations. Tiburon (*Shark* in Spanish), a waterfront settlement and former railroad town, is a pleasant town of Victorian buildings, expensive private homes and condominiums, and a one-of-a-kind shopping area, Ark Row, which, along with the Boardwalk Shopping Center, sits on filled-in mudflats.

Belvedere, once separated from downtown Tiburon by a large lagoon which silting began to fill in the 1920s, is an exclusive housing area, where roads too narrow in places for two cars to pass wind around this *island* to houses tucked into the hills above or below the roads.

ATTRACTIONS

The event that changed Tiburon from an insignificant waterfront settlement to a prosperous community left behind few traces for the touring sailor to see. In 1884 the branch line of the San Francisco and North Pacific Railroad was completed, bringing passengers to Tiburon, where they could board a ferry to San Francisco. The old depot, now a historic landmark, is about all that remains. A well-used walking and biking path now covers the bed of the tracks.

This pathway through Shoreline Park provides a view of many of the major landmarks of the San Francisco Bay: to the north, Richmond, Red Rock, and the Richmond-San Rafael Bridge with San Pablo Bay beyond it; Sausalito and the Golden Gate Bridge to the southwest; the San Francisco skyline to the south; and Angel Island to the east.

If you're up for a hike of just under 3 miles, continue W along this path to Richardson Bay Park and the Richardson Bay Audubon Center and Sanctuary. This 900-acre sanctuary of tidal bay lands, grasslands, woodlands, and a freshwater pond is one of the few remaining San Francisco Bay wetlands virtually unaltered by human development. Here you might see up to 80 species of migratory waterfowl. A man-made treasure of this park, the Lyford House, is one of the Bay Area's oldest houses, having been built around 1876. This restored Victorian is worth a visit for both its authentic style and the art and nature exhibits it contains.

Another invigorating hike is the one up the hill to Old St. Hilary's Church, a simple wooden Gothic-style structure built in 1888. This site gives you an even more commanding view of the Bay than does the walk through Shoreline Park.

Back down at the waterfront, all you sailors will be intrigued by Ark Row, shops and offices in "arks" that were formerly floating homes in parts of Belvedere Cove now filled in. Some of these arks are over 100 years old. Nearby is another bit of sea history, China Cabin, the social saloon of the *SS China*, removed from the derelict ship in 1886. It is the only surviving social saloon from a 19th-Century passenger ship.

Even if you don't try the food, treat yourself to a drink on the deck at Sam's Anchor Cafe, where the gulls frequently swoop low over the tables in flocks of 30 or 40 and the waiters and waitresses rush to hide under the umbrellas sheltering some of the tables.

APPROACH

When approached from the water, Tiburon and Belvedere are hardly distinguishable from one another. Belvedere is that point of land 1.5 miles due E of Sausalito, its S tip, Peninsula Point, directly across Raccoon Strait from Point Stuart on Angel Island. From the buoy off Peninsula Point, go N into Belvedere Cove. Inside the cove, the San Francisco Yacht Club sits in the back of the cove on the port side, and the Corinthian Yacht Club sits on the small point in the center of the cove.

Except for some shallow water near the shoreline in the far back of the cove, the minimum depth here is 5 feet at low water. The entrance into the San Francisco Yacht Club is at the back of the cove.

San Francisco Yacht Club at Belvedere

BERTHING

No marinas in Belvedere Cove are available for the use of the general boater. However, the two yacht clubs accept visiting yacht club members, and Sam's Restaurant has two docks customers may use.

SAM'S ANCHOR CAFÉ
37°52.17N, 122°27.20W
Contact: 415-435-4527
info@samscafe.com

Any boater may tie up at Sam's Anchor Cafe, long a favorite destination for Bay Area boaters. Sam's has two large docks, one 100 feet long and the other 115 feet long for boaters to use on a first-come, first-served basis. Boaters may tie up on both sides of both the two docks. Commonly, 15-20 boats tie up here on weekend afternoons in the summer and fall. This dock is free for the use of boaters who have brunch, lunch, or dinner at the restaurant.

Check the tide when visiting Sam's. If your boat has a deep draft, you might come back from your meal to find the boat sitting on the bottom. The manager of the cafe reports that about 4 feet of water under the docks is typical at low water.

One other cautionary note: the heavy surge in Belvedere Cove mandates the use of strong dock lines and spring lines wherever you tie up in the Cove.

Guest Dock at Sam's

Breakwater Opening at Sam's

SAN FRANCISCO YACHT CLUB

Entrance 35°52.36N, 122°27.78W
Contact: Harbormaster: 415-439-3934
Clubhouse: 415-435-9133
harbor@sfyc.org

The San Francisco Yacht Club, founded in 1869 in China Basin, built the present clubhouse on this site in Belvedere Cove in 1937. This venerable club offers guest berths for members of other yacht clubs with reciprocal privileges, but be sure to call ahead to ascertain slip availability.

Corinthian Yacht Club

FACILITIES AT OR NEAR THE SF YACHT CLUB:

Banks
Bus and ferry service
Dry Haul Area
Grocery stores
Laundry
Library
Post Office
Restaurants
Shops
WiFi (free)

CORINTHIAN YACHT CLUB

Entrance 37°52.17N, 122°27.20W
Contact: 415-435-4771
ellen@cyc.org

Approximately 400 yards east of San Francisco Yacht Club, the Corinthian Yacht Club has almost as venerable a history, having been founded in 1886. This club is distinguished by its 1911 Colonial Revival clubhouse, the oldest clubhouse on the West Coast, sitting prominently out in the middle of the cove when you enter. Corinthian offers guest berthing only to members of other yacht clubs. Call ahead to inquire about slip availability, especially on weekends. If the guest slips are full, ask permission to use one of its mooring buoys.

FACILITIES AT OR NEAR THE YACHT CLUB:

Banks
Bus and ferry service
Grocery stores
Laundry
Library
Post Office
Restaurants
Shops
WiFi (free)

ANCHORAGE

In Belvedere Cove boaters can also find an acceptable location to drop a hook just S of Corinthian Yacht Club, being sure to anchor well clear of the permanent moorings. With depths of about 10 feet, you won't have to let out much anchor rode. The bottom in the cove is soft mud. You can leave your dinghy at the docks behind Sam's Cafe while you have dinner or go ashore.

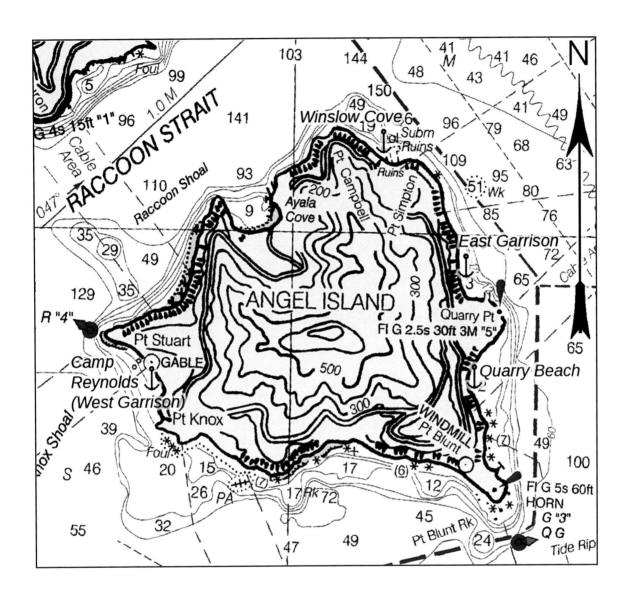

Angel Island

Oh! what a snug little island,
A right little, tight little island!
   —Thomas Dibdin, *The Snug Little Island*

ANGEL ISLAND
Chart #18649, #18652, or #18653

We can't know what vision Juan Manuel de Ayala might have had in August, 1775, that inspired him to name this largest of the islands in the San Francisco Bay *Isla de los Angeles*. Perhaps it was the Western Gulls circling overhead, their white wings glittering in the sunlight, or the Snowy Egrets "got up as angels" (from Elizabeth Bishop's poem "Seascape"). It could have even been the white pelicans skimming along just above the water in Ayala Cove with such grace and dignity in their pure white raiment.

This island may have looked heavenly to Ayala simply because the cove now bearing his name gave safe haven to him and his crew after a difficult nine-day passage from Monterey through gales and fog. Whatever Ayala's reasons, visitors to Angel Island today approve the name, and for boaters particularly this is indeed a celestial island.

For as long as 3,000 years previous to Ayala's charting of the Bay, Coast Miwoks occupied Angel Island. In 1775 they were living in four villages on the island, where apparently their idyllic life had not prepared them to resist the European intrusion that followed.

During the almost 200 years between Ayala's naming of the island and its designation in 1962 as a California State Park, Angel Island underwent many mutations: a Russian base for hunting sea otters, a cattle ranch, a rock quarry, a Civil War fort, a U. S. Army Cavalry headquarters, a vegetable farm for the inmates on Alcatraz, a quarantine station, a prisoner-of-war camp, an immigration center, and a Nike missile facility.

Today this island is once again clothed in green, though not all the flora is native, most visibly the gigantic eucalyptus trees but other trees and bushes as well brought here from around the world when Angel Island was a military base. This foliage gives shelter to numerous species of land and sea birds, to deer, and to raccoons.

As a cruising destination, Angel Island is for many sailors ideal. Its seven anchorages (one with

Camp Reynolds, Angel Island

buoys) ringing the island promise variety, availability, and at least one protected anchorage in any weather.

ATTRACTIONS

Many boaters settle into one of the anchorages off Angel Island and never go ashore, finding the natural beauty and wildlife activity to be all the entertainment they need. We have done just this many times. But for first-time visitors, we suggest you spend some time getting acquainted with this loveliest of islands.

Once ashore, you have three options for transportation: hiking, biking, or taking a TramTour. (You can rent bikes or take the tram daily April through October and on weekends between October and March.) Hiking will, of course, give you access to the

Ayala Cove with Moorings and Docks

most locations. On the dirt trails you can circle the island or ascend to its summit, Mt. Livermore (781 feet above sea level); a less strenuous hike along the paved perimeter road, at about 200 feet above sea level, will give you 5 miles of outstanding views of the Bay. If you have your own bicycle aboard, you can take it ashore and ride on the perimeter road. Visitors may rent bicycles or Segways at the Cove Café.

Whether hiking or biking, you'll be able to review the history of the previous 150 years on Angel Island. For an overview of the Island's geography and history, stop first at the Visitor Center, housed in the administration building of the San Francisco Quarantine Station (1892-1952) in Ayala Cove (formerly known as *Hospital Cove*).

The four primary sites of significance in U. S. history—Ayala Cove and North, East, and West garrisons—were also the sites of the four Coast Miwok villages noted by the first European explorers. You can take either direction from the Visitor Center to these other historically significant sites—the Immigration Station (North Garrison), Fort McDowell (East Garrison), and Camp Reynolds (West Garrison)—and to Mount Livermore, the island's pinnacle.

Ayala Cove and Quarry Beach at Fort McDowell both have sandy beaches protected from the cool afternoon winds and therefore are suitable for playing in the water or swimming, though the strong currents make venturing beyond the beach area risky. No lifeguards are on duty on the island.

APPROACH

Angel Island is nearly equidistant from the three bridges in the Central Bay. From the S the island is 4.0 miles from the Bay Bridge; from the N, 4.0 miles from the Richmond-San Rafael Bridge; and from the W, 3.0 miles from the Golden Gate Bridge.

BERTHING/MOORING

AYALA COVE
Entrance 37°52.10N, 122°26.20W
Contact   Angel Island State Park:
415-435-1915 or 415-435-5390

Ayala Cove, on the N shore of Angel Island facing Tiburon, is the first choice of most boaters who visit the island. Raccoon Strait, the body of water running roughly E to W between Angel Island and the Tiburon Peninsula, has depths in excess of 100 feet in most areas. Ayala Cove is located almost in the center of the S shore of the Strait on the N shore of Angel Island.

You can recognize Ayala by the ferry docks on the E shore of the cove, the pleasure boat docks on the SE shore, the green lawn and two-story white wooden administration building above the lawn, and the mooring buoys in the center.

Moorings and Docks, Ayala Cove

The docks in Ayala can accommodate 47 boats, up to 50 feet long. These docks, available on a first-come, first-served basis, may be used only between 0800 and sunset. Park rangers check daily to be certain all boats have been moved from the docks before sunset, and they patrol the docks again in the early morning to prevent boaters from tying up before 0800.

Rangers collect a fee for each boat using the docks; the fee can be paid at the kiosk at the top of the ramp leading to the docks or to the ranger patrolling the docks.

A cross current in excess of one knot will often be encountered around the docks as you are attempting to tie up. If you are unprepared, the current can slam your boat into the dock or away from the dock and into a nearby boat.

The State Park docks in Ayala Cove make going ashore convenient. Once ashore, visitors could spend several days exploring the beaches, the flora, and the fauna along the island's miles of hiking trails and bike paths, the visitor centers, and the numerous sites bearing testimony to the many eras of the island's history.

Boaters may use the mooring buoys in the cove during the day and night. Those who tie to a buoy may go ashore and pay the required fee at the kiosk at the head of the dock, or they may stay aboard, and a park ranger will collect a fee in the morning for all boats on buoys overnight.

Park personnel recommend boaters use bow and stern moorings because of the frequently changing currents in Ayala Cove. When you plan to use these buoys, bring long lines with you because many of these pairs of buoys are at least 150 feet apart. If your boat has good maneuverability, you can tie a stern line to a buoy as you pass by and then motor ahead to pick up a buoy for your boat's bow. Make allowances for the current in the cove, however, or you may end up being swept away from the buoy you want. Some boaters prefer to use their tenders to take mooring lines from their boats to the buoys.

The mooring buoys in Ayala Cove cannot possibly accommodate all who wish to visit the island. On busy weekends, another boater may tie the bow lines to the buoy you are using for a stern buoy and then tie the stern to someone else's bow buoy. All the boats on the moorings must be tied to face N.

Anchoring is a possibility at Ayala Cove, but the only room for boaters wishing to anchor is outside of the cove to the N. If you choose to anchor, be certain you are far enough away from the boats on moorings so you won't swing into them. Depths here are 20-60 feet, but holding is good. We cannot recommend this area because of the excessive wind and wave action. When Ayala Cove is full, the more prudent course is often to proceed on around the island clockwise to anchor in one of the other anchorages around Angel Island.

Winslow Cove with the Old Immigration Station (Commemorative Bell pictured below)

FACILITIES AT AYALA COVE:

Bicycle and Segway Rental
Ferry Service between Angel Island
      and Vallejo, Tiburon, Sausalito,
      and San Francisco
Restrooms
Snack Bar (April - October)
TramTour

ANCHORAGES

WINSLOW COVE (CHINA COVE)
Anchorage 37°52.25N, 122°25.55W

From Ayala Cove proceed E 0.4 mile to Point Campbell and then S for another 0.2 mile to Winslow Cove. The palm trees at Winslow stand out behind the beach, and the old two-storey faded white immigration station building appears on the W side of the cove about 200 feet inshore of the beach.

Winslow Cove has no docks or mooring buoys. However, boaters regularly anchor here in 20-30 feet of water and gain good holding in mud and clay. A strong tidal current runs through the anchorage, so you'll want to use plenty of scope and set your anchor carefully. The best anchorage area is between the beach below the old immigration station and Point Simpton.

This cove does not provide the protection that the moorings in Ayala do, hence the tremendous popularity of Ayala.

East Garrison Anchorage

Anchored at East Garrison

Quarry Beach Anchorage

ANCHORAGES

EAST GARRISON
Anchorage 37°51.86N, 122°25.26W

South from Point Simpton 0.5 mile, East Garrison anchorage is easily recognized by the buff-colored barracks, hospital, and mess hall remaining from Fort McDowell, the world's largest military induction center during World War I and World War II. Quarry Point marks the S extremity of the anchorage area.

The recently rebuilt ferry dock is just N of Quarry Point. Anchor well clear of this dock because ferries arrive and depart regularly on weekends. The best anchorage is in 20-35 feet of water on a mud and clay bottom that insures good holding. As with Winslow Cove, a strong tidal flow runs through this anchorage, so set your hook well.

QUARRY BEACH
Anchorage 37°51.57N, 122°25.13W

The anchorage at Quarry Beach is 0.2 mile S of Quarry Point. This anchorage is the largest on the island, extending 0.4 miles to the island's southernmost point, Point Blunt. The anchorage area is off the sand beach below the East Garrison buildings.

Anchor in 15-30 feet of water with a mud and clay bottom. Choose a protected spot as far inside the cove as possible to minimize the uncomfortable effects of the waves wrapping around Point Blunt. Although this anchorage can be uncomfortable, many boaters return again and again because it is so beautiful and so spacious.

SAND SPRINGS BEACH
Anchorage 37°51.28N, 122°25.72W

This anchorage is temporary only. Do not plan to go ashore from here or to anchor here overnight. If the winds are from the S or W, this anchorage should be considered untenable.

From Quarry Beach anchorage, go around the buoy at Point Blunt (0.4 mile) and then go W 0.5 mile. Stand at least 0.5 mile offshore when rounding Point Blunt because the area between the point and the buoy has numerous rocks above and just below the surface. A small white sand beach denotes the anchorage.

Anchor off the beach at Sand Springs in 20 feet of water with a mud and clay bottom. Use the Sand Springs Beach anchorage only when the N winds blow and render Ayala Cove, Winslow Cove, East Garrison, and Quarry Beach unsafe.

WEST GARRISON
Anchorage 37°51.49N, 122°26.59W

This anchorage is secure only when an E or S wind is blowing. When the prevailing W or NW wind is blowing, this anchorage is on a lee shore and must be avoided.

From Sand Springs proceed clockwise around the island 0.5 mile to Point Knox; West Garrison anchorage is 0.25 mile beyond this point. Only a few pilings remain from the old wooden pier, but they serve nicely as a landmark for the anchorage.

On the island 100 feet from the water's edge is a large two-storey brick structure that reportedly saw service as a schoolhouse and as an ordnance storehouse. This and the remainder of the buildings in the background here were part of Camp Reynolds, a U. S. Army installation built in 1864.

When you have identified the old pier and the brick building, proceed to a position 200- 300 feet S of the old pier and about the same distance from the beach. Anchorage is in 12-20 feet of water with good holding in a clay bottom.

POINT STUART
Anchorage 37°51.83N, 122°26.30W

Consider this anchorage temporary because of strong currents in the Point Stuart anchorage. Do not leave your boat unattended in this anchorage, and do not stay overnight here.

From the West Garrison anchorage to Point Stuart is 0.15 mile, and from the Point on to the anchorage is another 0.25 mile. The anchorage begins where the shoreline, which is basically E-W after Point Stuart, turns N for the 0.3 mile run to Point Ione. This anchorage gets overflow boaters from Ayala Cove.

Anchor 100-200 feet from shore in 15-25 feet of water with good holding in the typical mud and clay.

Moored in Ayala Cove

PARADISE COVE

Chart #18649, #18652, or #18653
Anchorage 37°53.72N, 122°27.37W

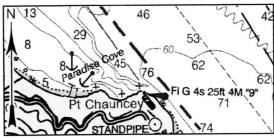

Paradise Cove

Paradise Cove, on the east side of Tiburon Peninsula and offshore of Paradise Beach State Park, has perhaps the greenest site above any anchorage in the Central Bay. The bright, manicured lawns framed by darker green oaks and redwoods coupled with this well-protected and generally uncrowded anchorage make it a particularly peaceful destination.

Paradise Cove was the site of the 1904 U. S. Navy coaling station, which closed in 1930 after oil superseded coal for powering ships. Several decades later the U. S. Navy had as many as 2,000 men stationed nearby during World War II. One of their primary functions was to set nets beneath the water's surface under the Golden Gate Bridge to snare any enemy submarines that might try to slip into San Francisco Bay. Some of the 2-ton concrete weights used to keep the nets submerged remain on the beach just north of the pier at Paradise Beach. The large iron rings on the tops of the weights, where the nets were attached, look like sturdy mooring rings. The Navy Net Depot closed in 1958.

ATTRACTIONS

Paradise Cove enjoys many beautiful warm, sunny days in the spring and summer, and it has a solid, if somewhat rocky, beach and sea bottom to attract both sunbathers and swimmers. Up the hill above the beach are dozens of picnic tables, many tucked in among the oaks and redwoods. A woodsy trail winds through these areas.

For a longer hike, go up to the paved road, turn left, and walk about a mile, past the Bay Conference Center and the Romberg Tiburon Centers on the left. After another 100 feet, a sign on the right points you to the Tiburon Uplands Trail, a 0.7-mile climb through woods and meadows.

Cruisers anchored at Paradise Cove can readily explore the surrounding areas by sportboat by going up Corte Madera Creek, then passing under the Highway 101 Bridge, heading into the lagoon behind the homes, and reaching almost as far as the campus of Marin Community College.

The trip to Corte Madera Creek is both challenging and long. Be sure to take plenty of fuel for the outboard and water for the crew. First, you'll go 3 miles N along the coastline to the channel used by the Corte Madera/Larkspur/San Quentin ferry. Be careful in the channel because ferries arrive and depart regularly; remember ferries cannot readily maneuver to avoid small boats in their path. When you reach the ferry terminal off to starboard, turn to port to enter the mouth of Corte Madera Creek.

The 4.5-mile trip up Corte Madera Creek offers an excellent adventure, but we recommend making the trip only early in the day to avoid a wet, uncomfortable ride back to your anchored boat. In the afternoons the NW winds often pick up to 20 knots or more; and, even though the return will be downwind, you're not likely to enjoy it in those winds.

Paradise Cove Fishing Pier and Anchorage

Rowing Ashore at Paradise Cove

Fishing at Paradise Cove

Another sportboat trip boaters anchored at Paradise enjoy is a 2.5-mile trip across the Bay to Red Rock, an uninhabited island immediately S of the Richmond-San Rafael Bridge. This island is privately owned, so you must take that into account if you decide to explore the island from the water. You should also consider that the island is totally undeveloped and has no vegetation worth mentioning. Having said that about Red Rock, we do know a number of boaters who have made the trip. Be sure you time your trip across the Bay shortly after daybreak. In the NW winds that prevail during the cruising months, you could be making a wet, uncomfortable return trip if you depart from Red Rock after about 1000 hours.

Another boater, Matt Morehouse, reports he has anchored his boat to the N of Red Rock a few times. He considers it a good day anchorage but not one for an overnight stay. The island does provide good protection from S winds, however, for boats anchored between the island and the Richmond-San Rafael Bridge.

APPROACH

Paradise Cove is on the E side of the Tiburon Peninsula, 1.5 miles NW of Bluff Point, the SE corner of the peninsula. When you approach the anchorage from the S, the Romberg Tiburon Centers will appear on the shore 0.75 mile NW of Bluff Point. Steel pilings where Navy ships were formerly tied remain 200 feet offshore. Therefore, stay at least 300 feet off-shore as you pass. You can easily identify the remains of the massive old concrete coal bunkers 150 feet inland of the seawall.

At Point Chauncey, 0.25 mile beyond the Romberg Centers, you'll have your first view of the green lawns at Paradise Beach County Park. Steer for a point just off the end of the concrete pier at the park.

Approaching from the N, set a course of 180° mag. from the center span of the Richmond-San Rafael Bridge. The anchorage is 2.5 miles from the bridge.

From Richmond, to the E, set a course of 240° mag. as you go past Buoy "4." You will first see the bright green lawn of the park shortly after you

Red Rock Island and Richmond-San Rafael Bridge

exit the Richmond Channel. From Buoy "4" to the Paradise Cove anchorage is 2.75 miles.

Paradise Beach State Park is heavily used on weekends. Swimmers often venture 400-500 feet out into the Bay, so you must be particularly careful when operating a boat in the Cove.

The T-shaped fishing pier extends 320 feet from the shore and has a 200-foot-long end. Boaters may not tie up any vessel, including dinghies, canoes, kayaks, and jet skis, at this pier. Nor may they take motorized vessels of any size inshore of the line of white buoys marking the swimming area. **Park administration rules prohibit operating any motorized vessel closer than 320 feet from shore. Park rangers strictly enforce this rule.**

You may row a dinghy, sportboat, or kayak ashore and land it on the beach. A park ranger from the Paradise Beach State Park will collect a fee for each person who goes ashore.

ANCHORAGE

The best anchorage is found at least 200 feet N of the end of the pier, but boaters also commonly anchor to the S of the pier when the favored area to the N is congested. The depth is about 10 feet, and the clay bottom provides excellent holding, although it also produces a muddy mess when you hoist anchor.

FACILITIES AND RESTRICTIONS

Restrooms
Showers (cold)

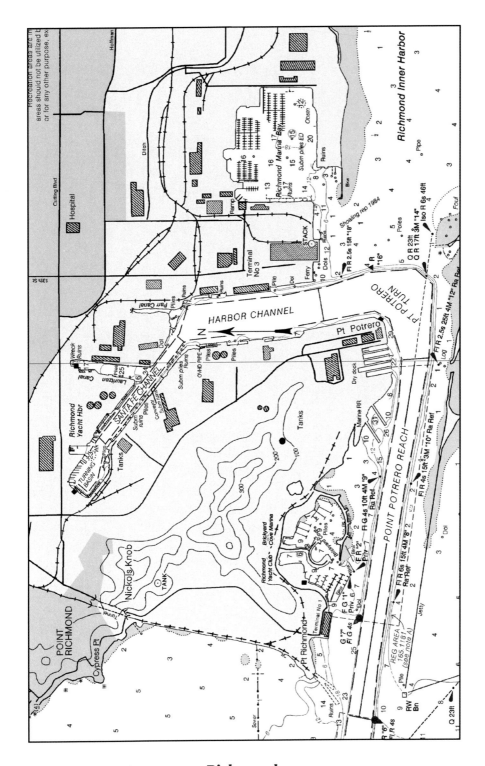

Richmond

RICHMOND *AND* POINT RICHMOND

Chart #18649, #18652, or #18653
Point Potrero Reach, G"5" 37°54.46N, 122°24.03W

Richmond and Point Richmond, though incorporated as one city, have maintained their separate identities. Richmond is a large industrial city especially prosperous during the first half of the 20th Century, through World War II. Point Richmond, which takes its name from the point about a mile south of the town, began the modern era as a small island and, in many ways, has retained its small, isolated status. Unlike the Richmond commercial district, which has spread out for miles beyond its Old Town, Point Richmond's downtown is still two or three blocks of businesses and services built around the original triangle.

Both communities were a part of Rancho San Pablo, a Mexican land grant given to the Castro family. Later, a U.S. citizen named Tewksbury bought 2,200 acres of the Rancho at Point Richmond. He built a dike and a road out to the point, and gradually the shoaling filled in to make the island and mainland one.

The Richmond-Point Richmond area will greet you most of the year with warmer and sunnier days than almost any other destination on the Bay. The fog, when it does get in this far, typically burns off early in the morning and comes in late in the afternoon. The wind here is usually more moderate than on other Bay waterfronts.

ATTRACTIONS

Brooks Island, just across Point Potrero Reach from Point Potrero, is part of the East Bay Regional Park District. This small, uninhabited island, once home for the Ohlones, is a short ride by dinghy from any of these marinas. However, you may not go ashore on Brooks Island unless you are among the members of a tour led by a guide from the East Bay Regional Park. Once ashore, you can watch some of the over one hundred species of sea and shore birds sighted here or hike around the approximately 2-mile-long island. Call 888-327-2757 to make reservations for this guided tour.

As you walk out of the Brickyard Cove Marina parking lot, notice the two large kilns in front of the condominiums. Many of the bricks used for the reconstruction of San Francisco after the 1906 earthquake were fired here and then taken by ferry to the City.

On Dornan Road, south of the tunnel that was built in 1915 to accommodate the traffic to and from the Richmond-San Francisco ferry at Point Richmond, is the Miller-Knox Regional Shoreline Park. It has paved walkways around a small saltwater lake seasonally populated by Canadian Geese, Snowy Egrets, Mallards, Wood Ducks, Phalaropes, American Coots, Sanderlings, and gulls of several species. At the north end of the park is a small swimming beach, heavily used on warm summer afternoons. Across from the park a nature trail climbs steeply to the ridge of the hill. (But watch out for the poison oak thriving in this sunny terrain.) Across the street, too, is the Golden State Model Railroad Museum, 10,000 sq. feet of operating model trains of all major scales.

On Garrard Street, immediately N of the tunnel, is the newly remodeled Richmond Plunge (or *Natatorium*, as it is named above the entrance), built in 1924-25. Turn W in front of the Natatorium, cross the railroad tracks laid down in 1895 by Santa Fe Railroad to ferry trains by barge from Richmond to San Francisco, and you'll be in downtown Point Richmond, where you will think you've taken a turn back in time.

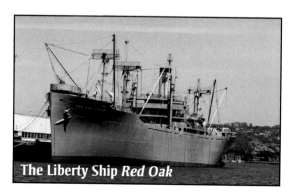

The Liberty Ship *Red Oak*

Entrance, Potrero Reach

Marina Bay, in the city of Richmond, has a history worthy of note. This complex of marina facilities and condominiums sits where once the world's largest shipyard sat, the Henry J. Kaiser Shipyard, which built over 747 ships during World War II.

The National Park Service and community volunteers have established a small but fascinating museum called the Rosie the Riveter/World War II Home Front Museum. Nearby, the *Red Oak Victory*, one of the Liberty ships built in Richmond, is being restored to represent the more than 500 Liberty ships the Kaiser Shipyard built in the early 1940s. On the site, too, is the old Ford Assembly Plant, where 49,000 jeeps were assembled and 91,000 other military vehicles were finished for use in WWII.

APPROACH

The channel into all the Richmond marinas, Point Potrero Reach, exits San Francisco Bay 2.5 miles SE of the E span of the Richmond-San Rafael Bridge. The channel is easy to spot when you approach from the N or W because channel markers and buoys outline it clearly for the large cargo ships that dock in Richmond.

Approaching from the S, set a course for the Southhampton Shoal light. From the light, proceed N for 1.5 miles, keeping a sharp lookout for the jetty extending W for 1.0 mile off Brooks Island.

To enter Point Potrero Reach, you must clear the W end of the jetty, which at night or in foggy weather is difficult to spot because it barely rises above the surface of the water. Identifying this obstruction are a marker on a pole at the end of the jetty and two range markers on poles, the closest only 350 yards SE of the end of the breakwater.

Inside the Reach, navigation aids designed for commercial ship traffic clearly mark the 35-foot-deep channel. Do not stray outside the channel markers on the starboard side, where water depths are as low as 2 feet in some areas.

The Richmond area has four possible destinations if you wish guest berthing, but it offers no anchorage area.

Marina Bay Entrance Buoys

BERTHING

BRICKYARD COVE MARINA
Brickyard Cove Marina Entrance 37°54.42N, 122°22.96W
Contact: 510-236-1933
info@bycmarina.com

Brickyard Cove Marina, with 250 slips, has long been one of the most popular marinas in the Central Bay, so popular indeed that it rarely can accommodate guests on its docks. Its location in this northern portion of San Francisco Bay gives it some of the best weather around, neither as cool and foggy as those sites nearer to the Pacific Ocean nor as warm as the marinas farther inland toward the Delta.

Three other advantages of its location are its proximity to the charming little town of Point Richmond, to the open waters of the Central Bay, and to Brooks Island, an uninhabited nature preserve.

Call ahead to inquire about guest berths.

APPROACH

Both Brickyard Cove Marina and Richmond Yacht Club are entered from Point Potrero Reach, on the port side 0.5 mile beyond the end of the jetty. You will pass Buoy "7" some 200 yards before you reach the entrance to the cove. The landmark for Brickyard Cove is the row of condominiums with green roofs snug in against the hillside inland of the marina.

Entrance to Brickyard and Richmond Yacht Club

FACILITIES AT BRICKYARD COVE MARINA

Hoist
Laundry
Restaurant

RICHMOND YACHT CLUB
Contact: 510-234-6949

The Richmond Yacht Club shares the Cove with the marina and thus offers the same advantageous location. The yacht club welcomes guests from other yacht clubs, space permitting. Be sure to call ahead.

RICHMOND YACHT CLUB FACILITIES

Hoist
Pump Out
Restaurant (Friday & Saturday)
WiFi (free)

RICHMOND MARINA BAY
Entrance 37°54.53N, 122°21.20W
Contact: 510-346-1013   VHF 16

With 850 slips, ranging from 28 to 120 feet long, this is the largest marina in the Richmond area and can generally provide guest slips. This marina has installed security cameras on all the docks.

APPROACH

One mile E of Brickyard Cove, Point Potrero Reach makes an abrupt turn to port. Five hundred yards after the turn, the entrance to Marina Bay exits to the starboard, proceeding E for 0.3 mile.

FACILITIES RICHMOND MARINA BAY

Bus Stop
Ice Machines (free; on D and F docks)
Launch Ramp
Laundry (on D and E docks)
Pump Outs (on G and D docks)
Restaurants
WiFi (free)

POINT SAN PABLO YACHT CLUB
37°55.28.64N, 122°22.35.83W
Contact: 510-233-1046
harbormaster@pspyc.org

Although the Point San Pablo Yacht Club is comparatively small, its friendly club members try to accommodate visiting boaters. Indeed, the Club advertises itself as the "friendliest yacht club on the Santa Fe Channel." Never mind that it's the *only* yacht club on the Santa Fe Channel.

APPROACH

The channel, at this point called *Harbor Channel*, continues N for 0.5 mile past the Marina Bay entrance, then bears off to the port and becomes the Santa Fe Channel. The **Point San Pablo Yacht Club** is on the port side at the far end of the Santa Fe Channel, 0.6 miles NW at the end of the Harbor Channel.

FACILITIES
POINT SAN PABLO YACHT CLUB

Banks
Boat Maintenance and Repair
    Chandleries
    Grocery Stores
    Haul-out
    Laundry
    Post Office
    Restaurants

~~~~

San Pablo Bay Yacht Club

BERKELEY MARINA

Chart #18649, #18652, or #18653
Berkeley Yacht Harbor Entrance 37°51.88N, 122°19.11W
Contact: 510-644-6376   VHF 16

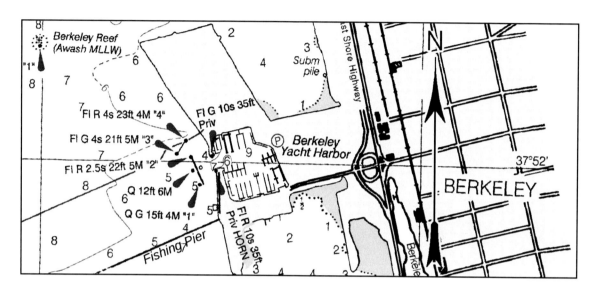

Berkeley Marina, with 1,100 slips for boats from 16 feet to 110 feet, is the jewel of the Berkeley Parks Recreation and Waterfront. Yet the city of Berkeley is undoubtedly better known for its location as the first campus of the University of California, founded in 1873, than for its marina. But it does also have quite an inviting marina, and certainly the opportunity to spend time wandering around this unique city adds to the appeal.

Some early citizens argued that the city should be named Peralta, for Luis Maria Peralta, whose 1820 Spanish land grant that he named *Rancho San Antonio* encompassed all this area, from San Leandro to El Cerrito.

Perhaps an even greater claim could have been made for naming the city for the Huichuins, earlier residents who spoke one of the eight Ohlone languages. After the scout Ortega saw these shores, he reported back to Portolá that he saw smoke rising from countless villages. In fact, one of the area's largest middens, 300 feet across and over 20 feet deep, lies buried under the site of Spenger's restaurant on the north side of University Avenue.

But some citizens liked so well the words of George Berkeley, an English bishop—"Westward the course of empire takes its way"— that *Berkeley* the city was named.

Anytime the fog comes into San Francisco Bay, it eventually comes to rest up against the Berkeley hills. Hence, Berkeley has an abundance of foggy days. Still, residents echo what Mayor Stitt said in 1911: "Any kind of a day in Berkeley seems sweeter than the best day anywhere else."

ATTRACTIONS

In the immediate vicinity of Berkeley Marina are three primary attractions: the pier, the 90-acre Cesar Chavez Park, and the Shorebird Nature Center. Berkeley has had a pier of some sort since Jacob's Landing, constructed in 1853. In 1926 the Golden Gate Ferry Company built a wooden automobile pier 3 miles long, where the ferries picked up vehicles and their passengers to take them across the Bay.

Busy Berkeley Fishing Pier

On the 0.5-mile concrete fishing pier that has replaced a section of the old wooden pier, anyone can fish without a license. Smelt, striped bass, perch, sharks, skates, and rays are common here. Or you can get your aerobic exercise by walking out to the end of the pier against the fierce winds that often blow from the Bay into the marina.

The Cesar Chavez Park has a large central green where you can watch the kites flying. Circling this green is a 1-mile paved shore walk, along which wild flowers bloom in profusion in the spring.

The Shorebird Nature Center comprises The Adventure Playground, where children learn to create using hammers, saws, and nails, and The Nature Center, which has a 100-gallon aquarium, a touch table, and a cormorant display. The Playground is open daily in the summer between 1100 and 1600. The Center is open Tues.-Sat. 1000-1600.

Adventure Playground

NO FOOD

Despite its relatively small size, the city of Berkeley has a large number of attractions because of the University of California campus. The campus itself is worth a walk around. Take a bus at the foot of University Avenue, ride about 3 miles, and you'll be at the campus. On this nearly 1,200-acre campus are a botanical garden, exhibits of art, anthropology, and science, and many striking and historically interesting campus buildings.

Berkeley Marina Entrance

APPROACH

If you approach Berkeley from the S, go around the end of the remains of the old Berkeley pier before setting a course for the marina. The 3-mile-long Berkeley pier now is a navigational hazard. The city rebuilt a section of the pier extending 0.5 mile from shore, but the more than 2-mile section remaining, abandoned for over 50 years, is now only a row of pilings with gaps in it.

Some boaters with local knowledge go between some of the visible pilings, but we strongly advise against this practice because other pilings may remain upright below the water's surface. The only relatively safe place to go through the remains of the old pier is to do so by passing immediately W of the end of the new pier.

Although the old Berkeley pier is a hazard, it is also an excellent navigational asset for first-time visitors to the Berkeley marina regardless of the direction of their approach. When you have identified the old pier and have taken up a position on the N side of it, run E, parallel to the pier. Stay at least 100 yards off the restored section of the pier, a well-used fishing pier, because of the numerous fishing lines in the water.

The only other navigational hazards are the unlighted racing buoys in the area and the Berkeley Reef. The nine unlighted racing buoys are easily visible during daylight hours but difficult to see at night except in bright moonlight. The location of these buoys is marked on your charts, of course, but essentially they are within 3 miles of the marina, extending from the Berkeley Pier almost to Brooks Island. Berkeley Reef is located 0.5 mile N of the entrance to the marina and 0.3 mile out from shore. It is marked by a lighted piling.

Local boaters often use Sather Tower, popularly called *the Campanile*, as a landmark when going to Berkeley Marina. The Campanile, on the UC Berkeley campus, is 3 miles almost directly E of the marina. From 5 miles away this tower stands out distinctly, and the marina is directly in a line between the SE corner of Angel Island and the tower.

Berkeley Marina has well-lighted breakwaters at the entrance to minimize the effects of the constant waves that pound the E shore of San Francisco Bay in this area. Local boaters enter and exit the marina on either side of the breakwater at the entrance, but the Berkeley harbormaster recommends visiting boaters avoid using the N entrance because shoaling often reduces depths there to less than 6 feet. Berkeley Yacht Harbor has no anchorage nearby.

The **Berkeley Yacht Club (510-843-9292)** has a guest dock at the Marina for reciprocal use by members of other yacht clubs. Otherwise, guest berthing is available from the Berkeley Marina Harbormaster. Boaters may also ask the harbormaster for the free use of a slip while they have lunch or dinner at **Doubletree Inn (510-548-7920)** or **Skates on the Bay (510-540-1900)**.

FACILITIES AT BERKELEY MARINA

Bait Shop
Boat Maintenance and Repairs

BERKELEY MARINA FACILITIES (cont'd.)

Bus Service
Chandlery
Fuel Dock (gasoline and diesel)
Grocery Store
Haul Out
Launch Ramp
Pump Out
Restaurants
Showers
Small Boat Hoist
WiFi (free)

All other services are available in the city of Berkeley, with excellent bus service from the marina.

Entrance to Emeryville through Breakwater

EMERYVILLE

Chart #18649 or #18652

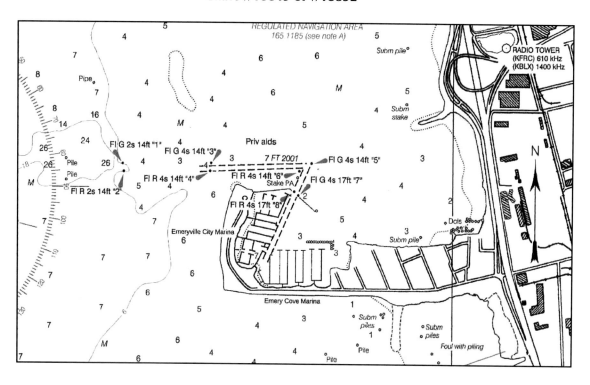

The two marinas at Emeryville—Emery Cove and Emeryville City—both welcome visiting yachts. Constructed between 1971 and 1974, the man-made spit of land sheltering these two has been turned into the national award-winning Waterfront Park, with a spectacular view of the San Francisco City Front and of sunsets over the City and the Golden Gate Bridge.

ATTRACTIONS

Emeryville provides a low-key, peaceful, and quiet spot within a few hundred yards of most of the services boaters might need. A paved and board walkway traces the shoreline from Interstate 80 out to the end of the spit and then back up the other side. Walk through the parking lot at Trader Vic's restaurant to gain access to the boardwalk behind the condominiums on the north side of the spit.

A sidewalk passes under the freeway at the frontage road. Take this walk for one block (on Powell Avenue); then turn left on Christie, and after one more short block, you'll see the old Pacific Linen building on the right. The ground floor is a public market, with about 20 international food merchants, several small shops, a large bookstore, and a popular night club featuring live jazz music. Across the street is a complex of 10 movie theatres.

Good bus service is available for Emeryville and the Bay Area in general.

APPROACH

The entrance to the marinas in Emeryville lies between the E span of the Bay Bridge and the old Berkeley pier. When coming from the W or N, approach to 100 feet or so of the end of the visible remains of the old pier, and then set a course of 088°

Emeryville City Marina

mag. This course will take you toward the channel into the Emeryville marinas, which begins 1.8 miles from the end of the pier.

When approaching from the S, steer to the E of Yerba Buena Island and pass under the span of the Bay Bridge closest to the island. After clearing the bridge, set a course of 026° mag. for 2.2 miles to arrive at the Emeryville channel.

The entrance channel into Emeryville requires caution. Stay carefully inside the clearly marked channel, which has a depth of 6.0 feet at low water. When you reach the last two buoys, "5" and "6," make a hard starboard turn. From that last buoy to the seawall of the marina is only 150 yards. Do not turn before Buoy "6," or you will almost certainly run aground.

Emeryville has no open anchorage area.

EMERYVILLE CITY MARINA
Emeryville Marina, Channel Buoy #1
  37°50.61N, 122°19.33W
Emeryville Marina, Channel Buoy #7
  37°50.54N, 122°18.64W
Contact: 510-654-3716   VHF 16
emeryville@marinasintl.com

Emeryville City Marina, with 404 slips, is on your right as you pass through the breakwater.

This marina is well run, with concrete docks and good facilities. Immediately W of the marina is an attractive breakwater with walking paths winding through the lush evergreen trees. This marina has a folksy, welcoming ambience.

FACILITIES

Fuel (gasoline and diesel)
Launch Ramp

EMERYVILLE CITY MARINA FACILITIES (Cont'd)

Laundry
Satellite TV (free)
WiFi (free)

All other services are available nearby.

EMERY COVE MARINA
Entrance 37°50.36N, 122°18.72W
Contact: 510-428-0505
info@emerycove.com

Ahead and to port as you pass the City Marina is Emery Cove Marina, with 430 slips. Observe the markers closely, and do not attempt to cut across from the breakwater to the marina as that area is shallow.

Everything at Emery Cove is up to date, from the modern office to the shiny cleats and abundance of large slips. The view from this marina is of the new E span of the Oakland-San Francisco Bay Bridge. This marina is located on Powell Street, with immediate access to the businesses of Emeryville.

FACILITIES AT EMERY COVE MARINA

Pump Out
Launch Ramp
Laundry
Fuel (gasoline and diesel)
WiFi (free)

All other services are available nearby.

Path Near City Marina

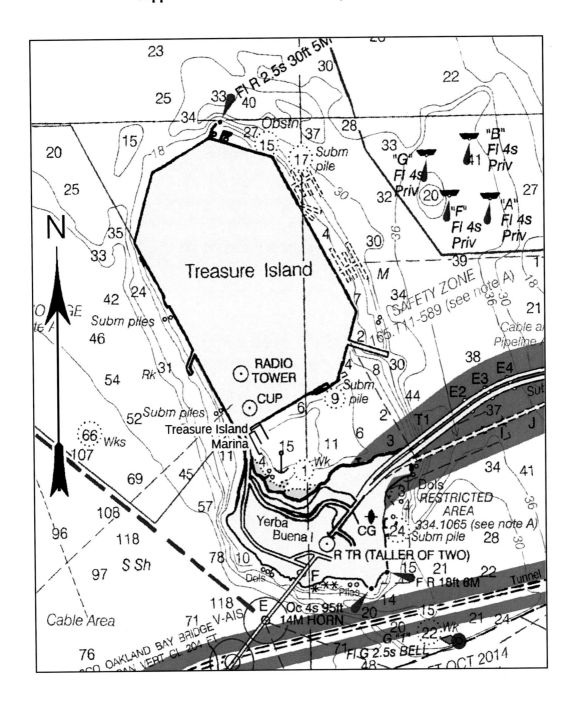

TREASURE ISLAND /CLIPPERCOVE

Clipper Cove lies between Yerba Buena and Treasure islands, directly below the NE span of the Bay Bridge as it disappears into the Yerba Buena tunnel. Yerba Buena (Spanish for *Good Herb*) is a natural island, called *Goat Island* on earlier charts. The name *Yerba Buena* was given first to the cove that lay across the channel to the S on the peninsula, in that part of San Francisco known today as the *Embarcadero*, bordered by Broadway and Harrison. The village of Yerba Buena became a busy landing, the settlement renamed *San Francisco* in 1847. This once important cove was largely filled in by 1851 by abandoned boats and the silting around them.

In preparation for the 1939-1940 Golden Gate International Exposition to commemorate the opening of the Golden Gate and Oakland-San Francisco Bay bridges, engineers created an island of rock, mud, and sand off the north shore of Yerba Buena Island. This artificial island, dubbed *Treasure Island* and connected by an isthmus to Yerba Buena Island, became the site of the Exposition.

Following the closing of the Exposition in 1940, the U. S. Navy took over the island and established the Treasure Island Naval Air Station. This base was one of the bases closed in 1996 as a result of the Defense Base Closure and Realignment Act, and the City and County of San Francisco assumed possession of Treasure Island. The Federal government continues to use about 40 acres of the island for the Job Corps, and some of the remaining buildings house a training facility and a fire station for the San Francisco Fire Department. Treasure Island is also scheduled for major development of housing and commercial facilities once the clean-up of contaminated soil is completed, though around 3,000 people already live on the island and sixteen wineries, with nine tasting rooms, have facilities there.

The marina, formerly for military personnel only, is now public and managed by Almar Management, Inc., which is planning a complete rebuilding of the marina in the next few years. Clipper Cove--the body of water protected by Yerba Buena Island, the connecting strip of land, and the man-made Treasure Island--was named for the PanAmerican China Clipper airplanes that were based here for transPacific flights between 1939 and 1946. Regional boaters frequently call this cove *Treasure Island* or simply *T. I.*

Yerba Buena Island is now the site of a Coast Guard station with an installation on the east end of the island. You can see rescue boats tied up at the docks there.

New and Old Spans of the Bay Bridge

ATTRACTIONS

Treasure Island, constructed for the 1939 Golden Gate Exposition, may derive its name from the title of Robert Louis Stevenson's adventure novel. Others say the name comes from the traces of gold in the landfill used to make the island, and still others claim the name refers to the treasures from the Pacific Rim that were on display for the Exposition.

One of the primary attractions for boaters in the marina or in the anchorage is a visit to this site of such a rich and varied history. Three art deco buildings and several pieces of statuary remain from the Exposition. A small but informative museum is housed in one of the historic buildings on Treasure Island.

More contemporary additions to the island that attract visitors are the wineries and tasting rooms, an active rugby club, and a flea market the last weekend of each month. Several of the sixteen wineries in operation on Treasure Island offer tastings of their products.

Another appeal of Treasure Island is the splendid view of the newly opened east span of the Oakland-San Francisco Bay Bridge and of the City, all particularly splendid when they're lit up after dark.

On the isthmus connecting the Yerba Buena and Treasure islands, you'll also have access to one of the few sandy beaches in San Francisco Bay.

If you're anchored in Clipper Cove, you may land a dinghy on the beach at the SW corner of the cove and then walk up the hill to the road leading onto Treasure Island. Do not take your dinghy to the marina dock if you want to go ashore without first checking with the harbormaster at Treasure Isle Marina. Because the gate providing access from the marina to Treasure Island is locked, you will need a key to get ashore onto the island as well as to get back to your dinghy.

APPROACH

The entrance into Clipper Cove is immediately N of the point at which the Bay Bridge meets Yerba Buena Island on the E side.

From the South Bay, pass under the bridge in the ship channel, which is below the first span E of Yerba Buena Island. The anchorage, approximately 0.25 mile wide and 0.50 mile long, will appear to port immediately after you pass under the bridge. Treasure Island Marina is at the far end of the cove on the N side.

From the N, pass E of Treasure Island, steering for the same Bay Bridge span. Clipper Cove opens to starboard just beyond the pier at the SE corner of Treasure Island. The isthmus connecting Yerba Buena and Treasure Island forms the W end of the cove.

The entrance to the cove appears to be approximately 400 yards wide, but, because of shoaling, you'll want to enter approximately 100 feet S of the end of the pier on the SE corner of Treasure Island. Water depths at this deepest part of the entrance are about 6 feet at low water, so go slowly as you enter.

The harbormaster recommends following a course on a line paralleling the pier until you are approximately halfway to where the pier attaches to the Treasure Island. Then you should change course and head for the end of the small pier in front of a small crane ashore used to launch small boats. Pass no more than 100 feet off the end of this small pier.

Once past the small pier, change course to head directly for the end of the closest marina dock. If you plan to anchor, go only about halfway the distance to the marina and then adopt a course taking you directly toward the beach in the SW corner of the cove.

Remember to go slowly as you enter the cove. These directions worked for us as we researched for this revision of the book, but, as the Bay continues to silt in, new shallow places will form. If you go slowly, you'll be able to get off with the changing tide.

BERTHING / ANCHORAGE

TREASURE ISLE MARINA
Entrance Channel   37°48.94N, 122°22.18W
Contact: 415-981-2416
slips@treasureisle.com

Almar operates the 107-berth marina, which has reciprocal privileges with all other Almar facilities. In San Francisco Bay, these include Ballena Isle, in Alameda, the five marinas of the Port of Oakland, and Martinez Marina.

Treasure Island Yacht Club has a clubhouse ashore of the marina. **Contact: 415-434-4475.**

FACILITIES AT THE MARINA OR ON THE ISLAND:

Deli
Grocery Store
Bus Service to San Francisco
Pump Out
Restaurants
Showers
WiFi (free)

Treasure Isle Marina

CLIPPER COVE
Anchorage 37°48.89N, 122°22.10W
Contact: 415-274-0382

Boaters may anchor for up to 24 hours in Clipper Cove without a permit; for 25-96 hours with a verbal permit obtained by calling 415-274-0382; for 96 hours-21 days with a written permit. No one is allowed on the isthmus beach after dark.

The best anchorage is on the SW side of the cove, where you will find some shelter from the strong prevailing winds that blow over the isthmus to windward. Avoid, of course, the very shallow water near shore. An added hazard to anchoring here is the debris, such as wire cables, left in the cove by the various entities occupying Treasure Island throughout its history.

Anchor in 10-15 feet on a blue-gray clay bottom, at least 200 feet from the marina to avoid interfering with the frequent movement of boats in and out of the marina. Lie to a single anchor.

If this favored spot is congested, you can anchor safely anywhere in the W half of the cove in good holding and still water under most conditions. However, no matter where you anchor in Clipper Cove, post an anchor watch if winds blow in excess of 30 knots. Many anchors may not hold well here, especially in the center of the anchorage area.

Fifty or more boats can anchor in Clipper Cove, upwind of the traffic noise from the bridge high overhead. Frequently, groups of as many as 8 or 10 yachts raft together in these usually calm waters.

Raft-Up at Clipper Cove

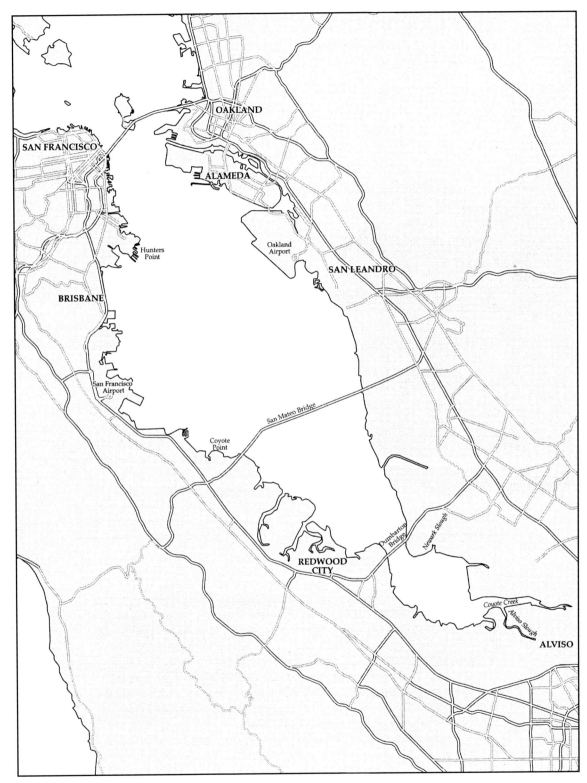

The South Bay

THE SOUTH BAY

Black-Necked Stilts Near Newark Slough

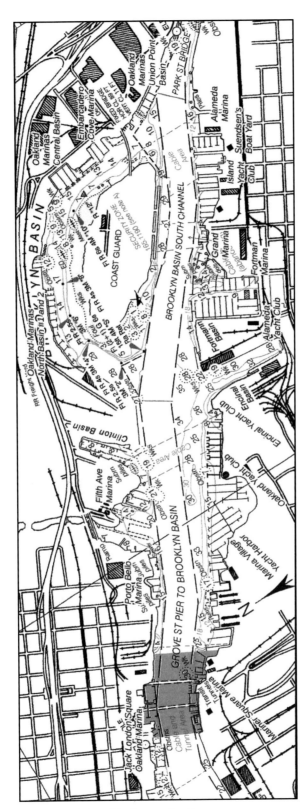

Oakland/Alameda Estuary

OAKLAND/ALAMEDA ESTUARY

Chart #18649, #18650, or #18652
Entrance Buoy R "2" 37°48.15N, 122°21.34W

As their names suggest, Alameda (*Poplar Grove* in Spanish) and Oakland attracted the attention of early European settlers in San Francisco Bay because of their abundance of trees. Redwoods covered the hills behind Oakland, and oaks, some reportedly spreading over half a city block, shaded the lower lands. Oakland's thriving lumber industry was made possible by the ease of transportation across the Bay to San Francisco.

After the trees were gone, long before the end of the 19th century, the waterfronts of Oakland and Alameda grew even more fiscally prominent. Passenger ferries, railroad ferries, whalers' docks, shipyards, and military installations figured largely in the prosperity of these two cities. Today, towering white gantries stand like skeletons of Trojan horses along the Oakland shore, and through their innards pass thousands and thousands of containers, making this the fifth busiest container port in the U. S.

Plenty of harbor space remains for pleasure boaters and fishermen. Along the Oakland shores of the estuary are six marinas, and the Alameda shoreline has seven marinas plus two yacht clubs, each with its own marina.

APPROACH

Getting to the Oakland/Alameda Estuary is easy: just follow the boats. The Estuary is home to more boaters than is any other area in the Bay. The entrance into the Estuary, or Oakland Inner Harbor, is 1.1 mile almost due E of the point where the West Span of the Bay Bridge joins the southernmost point of Yerba Buena Island. Buoys show the limits of the channel. The only possible confusion is in distinguishing the channel into the Estuary from the channels into the Oakland Outer and Middle harbors. Look closely at your chart, however, and the correct channel, the most S of the three, is easy to see.

For the first 2.5 miles of the channel, you will see huge ocean-going container ships loading and unloading. This is a busy harbor indeed. After that you'll find a continuous string of marinas. In the Oakland/Alameda Estuary are well over 3,500 public and private slips. Distinguishing one marina from another can be difficult, particularly when a single marina may have multiple sections of slips.

Line of Ships in the Estuary

OAKLAND ESTUARY MARINAS

Four of the seven public marinas on the Oakland side of the Estuary—Jack London Square, North Basin, Central Basin, and Union Point—are under the aegis of the Port of Oakland Marinas. The location of each offers access to a different part of the Estuary in the city of Oakland. All managed by the Almar Management group, these four marinas have reciprocal privileges with other Almar marinas; in the Bay Area these are Treasure Isle, Ballena Isle, and Martinez.

Guest berthing can usually be had in one of the four Port of Oakland marinas.

The three other marinas on the Oakland shore of the Estuary—Portobello, Fifth Avenue, and Embarcadero Cove—will probably be of most interest to boaters looking for permanent berths.

No recognized anchorage exists in the Estuary.

Jack London Square Marina

JACK LONDON SQUARE MARINA
Entrance 37°47.58N, 122°16.57W
Contact: 510-834-4591
slips@oaklandmarinas.com

Jack London Square, a 147-slip marina, is, as the name implies, at the center of the activities in Jack London Square. You can sit in your cockpit and watch the parade of boats on the Estuary or the parade of pedestrians on the sidewalks. Ashore, you can visit the relocated Jack London Klondike Gold Rush cabin. One of London's haunts in Oakland, the First and Last Chance Saloon, still welcomes patrons. Jack London Village, farther

south, has a small museum devoted to London memorabilia.

You can also see the *USS Potomac*, Franklin D. Roosevelt's presidential yacht that was rescued from the bottom of San Francisco Bay, restored to its former presidential but spartan style, and now permanently moored here. Another attraction for those who like boats is the largest Northern California boat show, held here yearly in April.

Early every morning produce vendors bring fresh fruits and vegetables to warehouses along Webster Street, just up from the waterfront. They sell primarily wholesale, although retail customers

Wholesale Market near Jack London Square

are welcome to purchase wonderfully fresh produce here. In Jack London Square is also a weekly Farmers' Market on Saturdays.

Numerous restaurants and shops occupy the waterfront, but if you want to venture farther ashore, you'll find public transportation to both Oakland and San Francisco. If you choose to wander even farther afield, Amtrak has a station close by.

You can tie up without charge at the 150-foot-long guest dock behind Scott's Seafood Restaurant for a maximum of 4 hours, on a first-come, first-served basis, without permission from the Port of Oakland Marinas harbormaster. The harbormaster also frequently puts visiting boaters in the berths behind the Waterfront Hotel while they go on a 4-hour tour ashore. The harbormaster may also assign boaters to these slips overnight.

The 4-hour stay is free of charge but carefully monitored. The Port of Oakland Marinas charges a reasonable fee for overnight accommodations.

APPROACH

Jack London Square is the first marina in the Estuary, 3.5 miles from Marker "2 A," at the entrance into the Estuary. This marina begins immediately after the last of the large gantry cranes on the port, or N, side of the Estuary.

Another excellent identifying feature is the huge American flag behind Scott's Seafood Restaurant that can be seen for 2 miles. Scott's is located in the middle of Jack London Square Marina.

FACILITIES AT OR NEAR JACK LONDON SQUARE MARINA:

Bank
Boat Maintenance and Repair
Fuel Dock (gasoline and diesel)
Grocery Store
Launch Ramp
Public Transportation
Pump Out
Restaurants
WiFi (fee)

Portobello Marina

PORTOBELLO MARINA
Entrance 37°47.36N, 122°16.25W
Contact: 510-451-7000
trish.dannayachts@yahoo.com

Portobello Marina is a small marina (87 slips) immediately SE of Jack London Square as you proceed on up the Estuary. With only a few dozen slips, this marina is best described as "cozy." (No liveaboards are permitted at Portobello.)

Associated with and situated behind an upscale condominium development, it's an attractive marina alongside an extensive paved Public Shoreline walkway that is part of the San Francisco Bay Trail. Close by Jack London Square, this marina gives access to all the attractions of that section of Oakland.

FACILITIES AT OR NEAR PORTOBELLO

Boat Maintenance and Repairs
Fuel Dock (gasoline and diesel)
Launch Ramp
Mobile Marine Services
Public Transportation
Restaurants and Shops

Fifth Avenue Marina

FIFTH AVENUE MARINA
Entrance 37°47.25N, 122°15.86W
Contact: 510-978-1245
jwsilveiraco@yahoo.com

Fifth Avenue Marina is the funky little marina that is third along the Oakland side of the Estuary. The nearest neighboring marina of Portobello, Fifth Avenue would lead you to think you're in a different city altogether. Derelict boats and rows of rundown but occupied dwellings line the two narrow roads leading down to the marina. The marina is no less neglected, with docks that seem about to tilt a visitor into the Estuary.

But this marina and its environs have character: A clutter of found-art objects fills all available spaces in the tiny yards of the dwellings, created with obvious tongues-in-cheeks, bringing smiles to the faces of visitors. And the few people around are as friendly as can be. The marina has 107 slips.

FACILITIES AT OR NEAR THE FIFTH AVENUE MARINA:

Bank
Groceries
Fuel Dock (gasoline and diesel)
Launch Ramp
Public Transportation
Restaurants and Shops

North Basin Marina

NORTH BASIN MARINA
Entrance 37°47.23N, 122°15.09W
Contact: 510-834-4591
slips@oaklandmarinas.com

North Basin is one of two Port of Oakland Marinas facilities that are located in Embarcadero Cove, a half-moon-shaped body of water on the Oakland side of the Estuary, with Coast Guard Island sitting in the middle of the cove. The 107 slips of this marina are divided between two basins located on the NE shore of Embarcadero Cove.

Guest docks are available in both North Basin facilities. Visitors can receive free berthing for up to 4 hours at the North Basin Guest Docks. Those wishing to take advantage of this free 4-hour docking or to obtain an overnight berth in North Basin should contact the Oakland Marinas harbormaster.

The atmosphere of North Basin contrasts sharply with that of Jack London Square. It is small and secluded, away from all the bustle of the Square, with little traffic, either boat or foot.

Similarly, the same description applies to the two other Port of Oakland marinas in the Estuary: Central Basin, also in Embarcadero Cove, and Union Point, across from Coast Guard Island but just outside the SE end of the Cove. A picnic area ashore is in keeping with the less urban feel of these marinas.

APPROACH

To get to North Basin, proceed E up the Estuary for 1 mile from the fuel dock at Jack London Square Marina to Coast Guard Island, and turn to port into Embarcadero Cove. Proceed for 0.3 mile from the entrance into the Cove.

FACILITIES AT OR NEAR NORTH BASIN
Boat Maintenance and Repair
Fuel Dock (gasoline and diesel)
Launch Ramp
Public Transportation
Pump Out
Restaurants
WiFi (fee)

Quinn's Lighthouse Restaurant

CENTRAL BASIN
Entrance 37°46.98N, 122°14.68W
Contact: 510-834-4591
slips@oaklandmarinas.com

The 146 slips of this Port of Oakland marina are 0.35 mile beyond North Basin in Embarcadero Cove. This modern marina provides particularly good protection from the wind and surge. Visitors who stay at Central Basin can walk to West Marine, Quinn's Lighthouse Restaurant, and other businesses.

FACILITIES AT OR NEAR THE
CENTRAL BASIN MARINA:

ATM
Boat Maintenance and Repair
Fuel Dock (gasoline and diesel)
Laundry
Launch Ramp
Public Transportation
Pump Out
Restaurants
WiFi (fee)

EMBARCADERO COVE MARINA
Entrance 37°46.52N, 122°14.68W
Contact: 510-532-6683
raymond@jonesdevelopers.com

Embarcadero Cove Marina, not one of the Port or Oakland marinas, is situated 0.25 mile beyond Central Basin. This marina has no overnight guest slips. All its slips are rented on a monthly basis only.

On the same premises as the marina office is Quinn's Lighthouse restaurant and British Marine boat repair. Quinn's Lighthouse provides guest berthing on a first come, first served basis for lunch or dinner patrons at the dock on the E side of the restaurant.

FACILITIES AT OR NEAR THE
EMBARCADERO COVE MARINA:

Boat Maintenance and Repair
Chandlery
Deli
Public Transportation
Restaurants
Showers
Rental Cars

Union Point Marina

UNION POINT BASIN
Entrance 37°46.63N, 122°14.57W
Contact: 510-834-4591
slips@oaklandmarinas.com

The last of the Port of Oakland Marinas in the Estuary, Union Point Basin has 95 slips. Though this marina lies only 0.3 mile from Central Basin, it cannot be reached directly because of the causeway connecting Coast Guard Island to Oakland.

To get to Union Point Basin Marina, you must continue up the Estuary, past the entrance into Embarcadero Cove. Immediately after you have passed the SW side of Coast Guard Island, turn to port, and proceed 0.8 mile to Union Point Basin, on the Oakland shoreline E of Coast Guard Island.

FACILITIES AT OR NEAR THE
UNION POINT BASIN MARINA:

Chandlery
Fuel Dock (gasoline and diesel)
Launch Ramp
Public Transportation
Pump Out
Restaurants
WiFi (fee)

~~~~

ALAMEDA ESTUARY MARINAS

Alameda, in 1795 a grove of trees in the southern portion of Contra Costa County, was part of Rancho San Antonio, the enormous Luis María Peralta rancho that covered much of the *contra costa,* that is, the coast opposite San Francisco. Like all the *contra costa,* Alameda was first a source of wood for the San Francisco market.

The hamlet of Alameda began in 1850 when two men leased 160 acres for peach orchards. Two other hamlets, Encinal and Woodstock, arose to become eventually one with the city of Alameda, by the end of the century a popular resort area because of its sandy beach and sunny days. San Franciscans rented cottages here for the summer, many of them spending their days at Neptune Beach, the *Coney Island of the West,* where they could swim in one of the country's largest swimming pools, thrill to carnival rides, or watch prize fights and baseball games.

Before 1902 Alameda had been a peninsula, its marshy eastern shore connecting to the mainland where the Estuary today flows into San Leandro Bay. The opening of the Tidal Canal between the Estuary and San Leandro Bay elicited a two-day carnival. A number of contemporary boaters now circumnavigate Alameda each New Year's Day.

The Island of Alameda is particularly accommodating for cruising sailors. In addition to its seven marinas, six of which are on the Estuary, and five yacht clubs, Alameda has a wide array of marine shops and chandleries. The compactness of the city facilitates a visitor's getting about on foot to visit one of the city's many parks, marvel at some of its 3,500 Victorian homes, or patronize some of the inviting shops along Park Street.

Ten 19th century "Red Train" stations scattered around the island are commercial centers today, housing shops and service centers of various sorts. The "Red Trains" circled the island, taking commuters to the ferry boats on the west end. The surviving stations vary from several buildings at an intersection to twenty buildings comprising two blocks.

Landmark Estuary Restaurant

MARINER SQUARE MARINA & DRYSTACK
Entrance 37°47.50N, 122°16.62W
Contact: 510-521-2727
andrea@johnbeery.com

Mariner Square Marina & Drystack, with its 50 slips, is the marina on the Alameda shoreline nearest the mouth of the Estuary and almost directly opposite Jack London Square Marina in Oakland. Locate the Mariner Square Marina by identifying the Pasta Pelican, a long-time favorite eating establishment with its name emblazoned on the N and W sides of the restaurant. The Mariner Square Marina docks almost completely surround the Pasta Pelican building.

The primary business of this marina now is storing as many as 100 power boats, up to 40 feet long, in the drystack, or dry storage, facility. It does, however, still have some guest berthing and a few liveaboard slips for boats up to 60 feet long. Pasta Pelican, the restaurant at the marina, also has two temporary slips available for lunch or dinner guests.

FACILITIES AT OR NEAR THE MARINER SQUARE MARINA:

Boat Maintenance and Repair
Grocery Store
Haul Out
Laundry
Public Transportation
Pump Out
Restaurants
Security Cameras
Shopping Center

MARINA VILLAGE YACHT HARBOR
Entrance 37°47.22N, 122°16.19W
Contact: 510-521-0905   VHF 16
scoong@marinavillageharbor.com

If you continue E 0.5 mile up the Estuary from the Pasta Pelican, you will come to Marina Village, its 750 berths making it the largest marina on the Estuary. The site of this marina has a long nautical history, having been occupied by the Bethlehem Steel Company, Shipbuilding Division, for many years. This extensive and attractive complex is now the setting for commercial establishments, apartments, and condominiums. A shoreline park with good hiking and biking trails is nearby.

Guest berthing is available.

FACILITIES AT OR NEAR THE MARINA VILLAGE DOCKS:

Boat Maintenance and Repair
Grocery Store
Laundry
Mini-Mart
Public Transportation
Pump Out
Restaurant
Showers
WiFi (free)

Storage for Powerboats

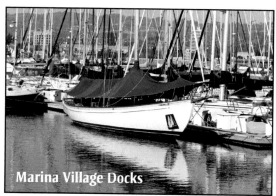
Marina Village Docks

PACIFIC MARINA
(OAKLAND YACHT CLUB)
Entrance 37°47.08N, 122°15.89W
Contact: 510-522-6868

Immediately E of Marina Village, Pacific Marina has 210 berths, all owned and managed by the Oakland Yacht Club. The club welcomes visiting members of other yacht clubs.

At the E end of Pacific Marina, *Encinal Yacht Club,* one of the oldest in the Bay Area, incorporated in 1890 to cater to the owners of boats smaller than those prevailing at the San Francisco Yacht Club, has a club building and dock. The club has no slips, but visiting yacht club members are invited to stay on the guest dock in front of the yacht club. **Contact: 510-522-3272.**

FACILITIES AT OR NEAR THE PACIFIC MARINA:

Bar and Restaurant

FORTMAN MARINA
Entrance 37°46.83N, 122°15.26
Contact: 510-522-9080   VHF 16
fortmanmarina@comcast.net

Eastward beyond Pacific Marina another 0.3 mile, past Encinal Basin, is Fortman Marina, with 486 slips. Fortman Marina has a history almost as lengthy as that of Encinal Yacht Club, though its inception was in response to the needs of commercial fishing boats rather than to those of pleasure boats. From 1904 to 1929 the Alaska Packers Association had a yard ashore of Fortmann (the earlier spelling) Basin and had laid up here between seasons the last great West Coast fleet of square riggers.

The marina provides guest berthing when slips are available.

Alameda Yacht Club is located in this marina, and the harbormaster of the Fortman will arrange guest berthing for visiting yacht club members if slips are available. On Wednesdays non-yacht club members are welcome to have dinner at the yacht club. **Contact: 510-865-KNOT.**

FACILITIES AT OR NEAR THE FORTMAN MARINA:

Boat Maintenance and Repair
Laundry
Mini-mart
Public Transportation
Pump Out

GRAND MARINA
Entrance 37°46.73N, 122°15.13W
Contact: 510-865-1200   VHF 71
marina@grandmarina.com

Grand Marina, with 400 slips, is 300 yards E of Fortman Marina. Grand has two easily identifiable landmarks for boaters visiting for the first time: The name *Grand Marina* has been painted on the warehouse and is clearly visible from the Estuary. The second landmark is the fuel dock with the two-story office extending over the water.

Alongside the marina facilities, the former tinned-salmon warehouse, the last surviving building of the Alaska Packers Association, reminds us of the grand and varied maritime past of the Estuary. This former warehouse today houses shops.

FACILITIES AT OR NEAR THE MARINA:

Boat Maintenance and Repair
Deli/Mini-mart
Fuel Dock (gasoline and diesel)
Haul Out
Launch Ramp
Laundry (restricted use)
Public Transportation
Pump Out
Restaurants
WiFi (free)

Svendsen's Marine Service Facility

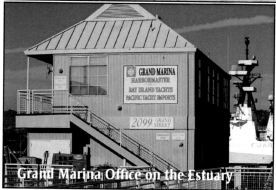

Grand Marina Office on the Estuary

ALAMEDA MARINA
Entrance 37°46.62N, 122°14.84W
Contact: 510-521-1133
info@alamedamarina.net

Since Alameda Marina, with 530 slips, is immediately E of Grand Marina, you can use the same landmarks that make Grand Marina easy to find: the fuel dock and the words *Grand Marina* on the warehouse. In addition, the name *Svendsen's* on another warehouse behind the Alameda Marina gives boaters one more landmark.

The slips in Alameda Marina accommodate boats up to 40 feet long. Some end-ties are available for longer boats, but these are primarily for the use of patrons of Svendsen's Boat Works. In any case, this marina discourages guests who are looking for accommodations for any visit there shorter than one month.

The office of the Alameda Marina harbormaster is in Building 25.

Island Yacht Club has facilities in Alameda Marina immediately in front of Svendsen's Boat Works. This club has no guest berths but will make arrangements for visitors from other yacht clubs who want to visit the club. **Contact: 510-521-2980.**

FACILITIES AT OR NEAR THE ALAMEDA MARINA:

Boat Maintenance and Repair
Grocery Store
Haul Out
Laundry (restricted)
Launch Ramp (public)
Public Transportation
Restaurants
Shops

Aeolian Yacht Club

AEOLIAN YACHT CLUB
Entrance 37°44.98N, 122°14.06W
Contact: 510-523-2586 or 510-523-0848
aeolianyc@aol.com

Aeolian Yacht Club, with about 70 slips, is unquestionably the most difficult destination to reach in the estuary. If you continue eastward up the Estuary approximately 2.5 miles, passing under the Park Street, Fruitvale, and High Street bridges, you will eventually arrive at Aeolian Yacht Club. Be very careful if you decide to visit Aeolian, however, because the channel shown on the charts must be followed exactly or you will certainly go aground. Club members recommend coming through this channel only at half-tide or more.

You can also navigate to Aeolian using the S entrance. A bridge tender will open the Bay Farm Island Bridge between 0800 and 1700 hours. The markers beyond the bridge are PVC pipes that are of questionable value, according to club members.

Aeolian normally has empty slips for visiting yacht club members with boats up to 40 feet long, with limited accommodations for larger boats on the guest dock.

FACILITIES AT OR NEAR THE AEOLIAN YACHT CLUB:

Grocery Store
Laundry
Public Transportation
Shops
WiFi

EAST SHORE DESTINATIONS

BALLENA ISLE MARINA
Chart #18649 or #18652
Entrance Buoy #1 37°45.81N, 122°16.94W
Contact: 510-523-5528   VHF 16
slips@ballenaisle.com

Ballena Isle Marina Entrance

Ballena Isle Fairway and Fuel Dock

Ballena Isle (*Whale Bay*), on the S shore of the Island of Alameda, today bears few signs of its namesake.

The whaling industry that figured prominently in the early settlement of European descendants in Alameda began in California during the mid-1850s, when two stations, one at Monterey and one at Crescent City, commenced operations. By the 1870s seventeen whaling stations were operating all along the California Coast.

Whaling ships laid up between seasons in the Oakland Estuary, on the opposite side of Alameda Island from Ballena Bay. Ballena Isle Marina, with 515 slips, is now under Almar management, and the harbor personnel are exceptionally accommodating. The guest dock is at the extreme W end of the harbor, adjacent to the fuel dock.

Boaters can get free guest berthing at the marina while they have lunch or dinner at the Pier 29 Restaurant, and those with a berth at another Almar facility can use reciprocal privileges to visit this marina if they arrange ahead with the harbormaster of their marina.

Ballena Bay Yacht Club has a clubhouse near the harbormaster office. The yacht club has no slips but will try to arrange slips for boaters from other yacht clubs at the Ballena Isle Marina guest dock. Contact: 510-523-2292

ATTRACTIONS

As was the Estuary for the whaling ships of the last century, sunny Ballena Bay is an excellent layover spot for cruising pleasure boats. Indeed, many boaters consider the weather at Ballena Isle the best in the Bay.

Ballena Isle Marina is far enough away from town to be relatively quiet, yet all the city facilities of Alameda are easily accessible by moderate walks or short bus rides.

Directly E of the marina are the sandy beaches of the Crown Memorial State Beach, formerly the site of Neptune Beach. The city restored the beach, badly eroded by wind and water, in 1982. You will spot people here several hundred yards offshore, walking in the warm, shallow water. This beach is a fairly easy and certainly a most pleasant walk from the marina.

Just inside Crown Memorial State Beach, the Crab Cove Visitors Center has some fine exhibits of both the human and the natural history of Alameda. On a low-tide Saturday in June, the Sand Castle and Sand Sculpture Contest takes place in front of the bathhouse on the beach.

The San Francisco Bay Trail runs for about 3 miles along the SW shore of the island.

APPROACH

Whether boaters approach Ballena Isle Marina from the N, S, or W, they should plan to come in on half-tide or more.

From all three directions of approach, the aircraft carrier *Hornet* and other large military-gray ships moored alongside it as well as large buff-colored buildings identify the site of the former Alameda Naval Air Station (NAS). Coming from the N or W, identify Buoy "2" at the entrance channel into the former NAS. From the buoy, set a course of 90° mag., and go 2.85 miles to the marina entrance.

On this approach, avoid getting too close to the shore. The area within 0.4 mile of the now closed NAS is no longer off limits, but the area close to the breakwater of the marina has shoal water.

Just S of the NAS base is a small boat launch ramp beside the Encinal High School ball field. South of the high school, a large housing complex with two- and three-storey beige-colored buildings stands out. The canal beside this housing complex is not the entrance into Ballena Isle, but rather the entrance into a canal for another housing development. The entrance into Ballena Isle is at the S end of the breakwater that protects the marina.

Those boaters approaching Ballena Isle from the S can use the Oakland Airport to help them identify the marina entrance, which is 4.5 miles NW of the airport hangars and towers. To avoid shoaling and underwater obstructions, boaters should stay at least 1.25 miles offshore when coming N from San Leandro.

A substantial breakwater protects the Ballena Isle Marina on the S side. A flashing green light atop a 17-foot piling in the water identifies the S corner of this breakwater. Pass between that piling and the red cone a short distance E of it. Continue through the narrow channel between the breakwater and the following three red cone buoys spaced along its E side. At the entrance into the marina, a green light marks the N end of the breakwater. Once in the fairway, note the white buoy to starboard, warning boaters to stay clear of a large pipe just below the water's surface at most tide states, but 3 feet or so above the surface at low water.

No reliable anchorage exists in the immediate area. Boaters do occasionally anchor in the small bay just inside the harbor, but shallow water and poor holding make this anchorage untenable. Recently some boats in here dragged anchor and were badly damaged or destroyed.

FACILITIES AT OR NEAR BALLENA ISLE:

Fuel Dock (gasoline and diesel)
Launch Ramp
Laundry (restricted to permanent marina residents)
Propane
Public Transportation
Pump Out
Restaurant
Tennis Courts

SAN LEANDRO MARINA
Chart #18651 or #18652
Channel Buoy "1" 37°40.16N, 122°11.21W
Channel Buoy "2" 37°40.15N, 122°13.20W
Contact: 800-559-7245 **VHF 16**
dsnodgrass@sanleandro.org

If hospitality is what you're looking for, you'll scarcely find a likelier destination than San Leandro. Named after St. Leander, an early 6th century Catholic bishop of Seville, this friendly city has retained many of its links to the past. Oyster shell mounds remind us of the Ohlones who were dwelling along these shores before the arrival of the Spanish and who hunted the once plentiful game, trapped fish in nets strung across the sloughs, and dug oysters in the mud flats.

Spanish explorers sent on an expedition to find a land route from Monterey to Pt. Reyes were the first Europeans of record to cross the broad, level plain that later was a part of the 1820 and 1842 Spanish land grants to José María Peralta and José Joaquín Estudillo, respectively. Estudillo called his vast holdings *Rancho San Leandro* to honor his patron saint, St. Leander. The heritage of the

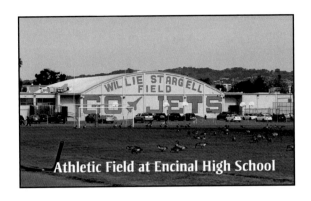
Athletic Field at Encinal High School

Spaniards remains throughout San Leandro, today a small city of 85,000 inhabitants, in the names of streets, parks, schools, historical landmark homes, and of course the city itself.

The designations of *Roberts' Landing* and *Mulford Point* signify the arrival of European-Americans who prospered here in the freight, grain, and oyster businesses in the latter half of the 19th century.

While today San Leandro has a well-run small boat harbor with 463 berths and two yacht clubs, this city also has a 15-year plan to remove all the docks and to convert this attractive setting in the South Bay into a multi-use facility of restaurants, shops, and townhouses. The harbormaster says the marina will continue to welcome boaters until at least 2017.

Both *Spinnaker Yacht Club* and *San Leandro Yacht Club* have clubhouses and guest docks and welcome visitors from other yacht clubs.

Contacts:
Spinnaker Yacht Club
510-351-7905 or
webmaster@spinnakeryc.org

San Leandro Yacht Club
520-351-3102 or
portcapt@sanleandroyc.org

ATTRACTIONS

The two public golf courses on the E side of San Leandro Harbor effectively constitute a greenbelt, lending the harbor a pastoral atmosphere despite

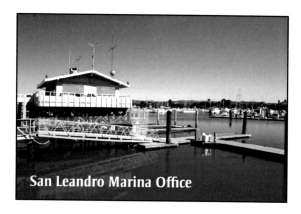

San Leandro Marina Office

its proximity to a busy city of 85,000 people.

On both the West Dike and the narrow grassy finger of land ending at Faro Point, at the S entrance to the harbor, are sections of the Bay Trail. On this S finger of Marina Park are a number of fitness trail stations. Hikers may walk for miles N or S on this trail. South along the shore past marshes filled with American Avocets, Black-necked Stilts, Snowy Plovers, and Forster's Terns, you can follow the San Lorenzo Trail to Roberts' Landing, in the late 19th century one of the South Bay's most important ports for scow schooners transporting hay and produce to San Francisco.

To the N the trail leads to Neptune Street, and then continues through the Oyster Bay Regional Shoreline, a 157-acre park atop a former garbage dump. Don't be put off by the site's past. The hillside now hosts fields of wild fennel and mustard, Swallowtail and Painted Ladies butterflies, and soaring Black-shouldered Kites and Red-tailed Hawks. Those fascinated by aviation can sit in the grass and watch the planes coming and going at Oakland International Airport.

A long walk, about 4 miles, or a short bus ride will take you into the heart of San Leandro, where you can stroll along a portion of the original El Camino Real and through a neighborhood settled by Portuguese immigrants who had cherry orchards here. Check out Little Shul, built in 1889, the oldest synagogue still standing in Northern California, and visit the Southern Pacific Railroad Station built in 1898, twenty-nine years after the

first transcontinental railroad went through San Leandro. You can also locate several other sites of historic interest—homes, parks, churches—clustered around the downtown area.

APPROACH

Boaters generally use three reference points to plot a course to San Leandro. Approaching from the N, identify Buoy "1" around 1 mile off the Central Basin on the San Francisco City Front, and set a SW course of 127° for 8.7 miles.

Another course is from the N buoy on the ship channel 1.5 miles S of Hunters Point Naval Base. From buoys "1" and "2" follow an E heading of 89° to the marina for 5.7 miles.

The third approach is from the entrance buoy at Coyote Point Marina. The entrance into San Leandro Marina is 6.3 miles away on a 030° mag. course. Any of these three courses should skirt the dreaded San Bruno Shoal.

Boaters have been going aground on the San Bruno Shoal for years. Its approximate location—as with all shoals, its location varies from season to season—is mid-way between the entrance into San Leandro Marina and the San Francisco International Airport. Identify its location on a chart, and keep a constant watch on the depth sounder.

A number of objects on shore help identify the marina. To the S of the entrance rise the buff-colored Coyote Hills; some boaters find them most distinctive and helpful. The huge hangars and control tower of the Oakland International Airport, 1.5 miles N of San Leandro Marina, are easily visible from 3 miles offshore, long before the channel markers. Watch the depth and the waypoints carefully. If you fail to identify the entrance correctly, you will almost surely go aground.

With the haze and fog that often obscure vision in San Francisco Bay, you may be unable to see any of the 14 channel markers into San Leandro Marina until you are within one mile of them. Not all the channel markers are lighted because of possible confusion with the lights of the nearby Oakland Airport: Only Marker "1" is lighted on the port side, and only "2," "6," "10," and "14" are lighted on the starboard side. (Channel Marker "14" is on the seaward starboard breakwater.)

Although the 2-mile-long channel into San Leandro Marina generally has a depth of 7 feet at mean low water, if you stray outside the channel, you will almost surely go aground. We saw one boater who had wandered out of the channel: he was standing alongside his seriously listing boat in ankle-deep water for a long while, waiting for the tide to come back in and float his boat off the mud.

The harbormaster warns visiting boaters that silting has become a serious problem near Channel Marker "8" and advises boaters approaching the marina to observe the range marker on the fishing pier straight ahead of the 14 channel markers. You will know you're in the middle of the channel as long as you are seeing a white light on the range marker, not a red or a green. If you stray too far to starboard, you'll see the red light; if you're too far to port, you'll see only the green light.

At the end of the channel, the *Spinnaker Yacht Club* is directly off your port bow. The San Leandro Marina is on the N side of the Spinnaker Yacht Club, to your port after you pass Mulford Point, on West Dike. The *San Leandro Yacht Club* is in the NE corner of the marina.

No anchorages exist in or near the harbor. The open basin to the S of the Spinnaker Yacht Club might appear to be an anchorage, but the depths are not adequate in this basin.

FACILITIES AT OR NEAR THE
SAN LEANDRO MARINA:

Bank
Bay Shoreline Trail with Fitness Trail Stations
Children's Play Area
Fuel Dock
   (accessible at high tide only; diesel and gasoline)
Golf Courses and Driving Range

Grocery Store
Hotel
Launch Ramp
Laundry
Post Office
Pump Outs
Public Transportation
Restaurants

Fitness Trail at San Leandro

Spinnaker Yacht Club

San Leandro Channel

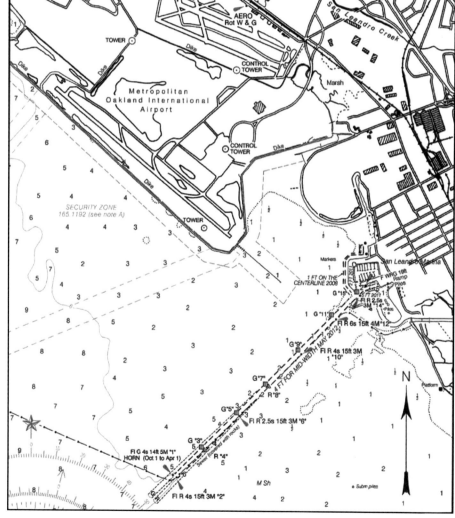

Entrance Channel at San Leandro

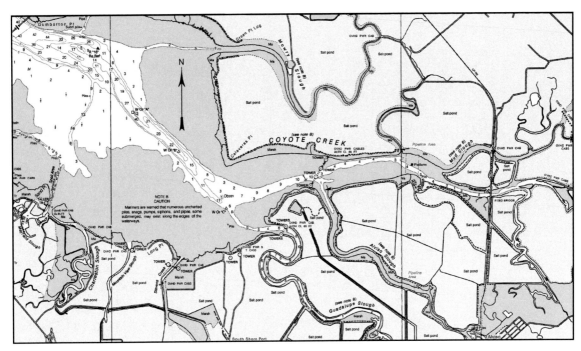

Newark Slough

NEWARK SLOUGH
Chart #18651 or #18652
Anchorage at Marker "16"
  37°29.44N, 122°05.12W
Newark Slough Entrance
  37°29.80N, 122°05.50W

Newark Slough, now part of the 23,000-acre San Francisco Bay National Wildlife Refuge, was during the 1800s an important access route for Mission San Jose and then later for the town of Newark. In the 1850s John Johnson built a system of levees through these marshes to contain the salty water from the Bay in evaporation ponds. He began what remains a thriving industry in the South Bay, the production of salt. Previous to Johnson's enterprise, salt was a precious and expensive commodity in this part of the world. The Refuge still leases some of these wetlands as salt evaporation ponds.

Newark Slough has long been a destination for adventurous boaters in the South Bay. However, as the natural sedimentation has continued, the water depths have become an increasing problem for boats with drafts of 5 and 6 feet. Consequently, for most boaters, especially those without local knowledge, the prudent option is to anchor outside the mouth of the slough and take a dinghy or kayak up the slough.

ATTRACTIONS

For many sailors from either the San Francisco Bay Area or outside the area, exploring these waters near the southernmost terminus of the Bay is a genuine treat. Little traffic passes this way now, though such was not the case when Moffett Field, across the Bay and south of Newark Slough, had a busy port where barges transported aircraft fuel up Guadalupe Slough. Pleasure and fishing boats that were moored in the Palo Alto Yacht Harbor--no longer accessible to boats because the city has ceased dredging the channel-- also kept these waters busier than they are today.

On the excursion up the Slough, you'll see seals by the hundreds, sunning in the cordgrass at water's edge, an unusual sight to those accustomed to seeing seals on rocks or sand beaches. Large flocks of Willets stand in the marshes nearby and fly up in dizzying M. C. Escher patterns of black and white as you pass. American Avocets, Black-necked Stilts, and Forster's Terns nest here. In the fall and winter, you'll see migrating water-fowl, such as Greater Scaups, Surf Scoters, North-ern Pintails, Ruddy Ducks, and Northern Shovel-ers. Dilapidated hunting blinds visible above the pickleweed attest to the popularity of this site for waterfowl hunting. (Waterfowl hunting is still permitted from mid-October to mid-January in Newark Slough south of the Hetch Hetchy aque-duct.)

APPROACH

After you pass under the San Mateo Bridge and then the Dumbarton Bridge (85 feet vertical clearance), you will pass through the old aban-doned railroad bridge, now locked in the open position. From the Dumbarton Bridge, 0.65 mile away, the passageway through the railroad bridge looks minimal, but it has a horizontal clearance of 125 feet.

After clearing the railroad bridge, set a course for Marker "16," approximately 090° mag., and go 1.1 miles. For easy access to the Slough, an-chor near this marker in 10-12 feet of water. Hold-ing is good, but you will be in a somewhat exposed position. If the winds pipe up, you could have a rough anchorage.

The channel from San Francisco Bay into New-ark Slough looks easily recognizable on the chart, yet you will find it invisible from the Bay except at extreme low water, when the mudflats on either side of the channel are exposed. And, at low water the entrance into the channel, with only 1 foot of depth, may be too shallow for you to enter in a din-ghy with a motor. You may choose to row your boat into the Slough.

The area on either side of the channel is under water so that at high tide the channel may appear to be almost a mile wide. But in fact the channel is no more than 50 feet wide in most places. The wa-ter depths increase as you go farther up the slough, while the width of the slough continues to narrow until the tule banks on either side are no more than 200 feet apart.

Local boaters have buried the end of a piece of 4-inch PVC pipe in the mud at the entrance to Newark Slough. This white piece of pipe was there when we recently visited the South Bay, but it may no longer be there when you visit.

Anchored in Westpoint Slough

Frank Nugent

WEST SHORE DESTINATIONS

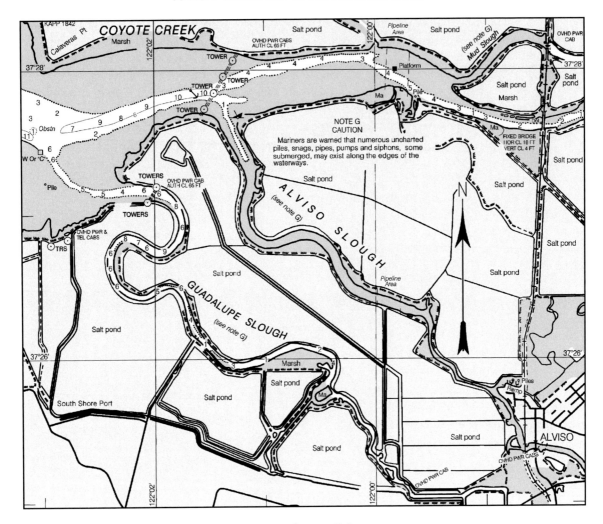

Approach to Alviso

This port, on the National Register of Historic Places and adjoining the extensive San Francisco Bay National Wildlife Refuge, certainly merits a visit, but some of you may elect to make that visit by land rather than by water. The slough leading to what was the port of entry to San Jose before the coming of the railroad, and therefore once one of the busiest ports on the Bay, is now a challenge for even the smallest of pleasure boats. A combination of natural sedimentation and the loss of industrial importance has rendered the Alviso waterfront a relic of its busy past.

ALVISO
Chart #18651 or #18652
Exit from Coyote Creek 37°27.20N, 122°01.36W
Contact: South Bay Yacht Club, 408-263-0100

In 1840 Ignacio Alviso moved from Santa Clara Mission to the site of the present day Alviso, then a part of his 6,353-acre Rancho de los Esteros. From this port beaver pelts, cattle hides, and tallow went to San Francisco. In 1851 four U. S. citizens purchased the land surrounding the port and named their nascent city "Alviso." For the next 35 years this active port supplied redwood, grain, and produce to Northern California. The railroad completed in 1884 between San Francisco and San Jose bypassed Alviso and thus effectively ended the commercial usefulness of the port. Between 1907 and 1936 the Bayside Cannery brought renewed prosperity to Alviso. By 1920 this cannery was the third largest in the country.

Many wells were dug near these shores of the South Bay in the late 19th century to irrigate the orchards and fields and to provide water for the burgeoning population. The result was land subsidence averaging 11 feet. Flooding became commonplace for Alviso. Today cordgrass and cattails surround the remnants of the docks and the derelict boats sinking into the silt at the defunct marina. The South Bay Yacht Club has a few docks along the Alviso Slough (though the boats sit in the mud at low tide) and continues with an active membership.

ATTRACTIONS

The history of Alviso lives on in the several buildings remaining from its glory days. And they're all within easy walking distance of the dock. Several buildings are reminiscent of this port's earlier prosperity, including the old Wade warehouse, cannery buildings, and the Tilden House.

The town, with a majority Hispanic population, has numerous seafood and Mexican restaurants to sample as you walk around the streets of Alviso.

Serious hikers will find a real treasure of a trail here: the 9-mile loop on levees along the E side of Alviso Slough, along the S side of Coyote Creek, and across Triangle Marsh back to Alviso. From this trail you can see Great Egrets, Blue Herons, White Pelicans, and Dark-crested Night Herons that nest here. Avocets, Black-necked Stilts, and Willets feed in the exposed mud at low tide. You can also get a good look at the geography of the area, with views of the salt ponds and salt "mountains," of the Santa Cruz Mountains to the W, the East Bay hills to the N, and tiny Station Island (or Drawbridge Island) to the NE. Pick up this trail at the E end of the marina parking lot.

You may prefer to explore with your boat's tender or the increasingly popular sea kayak. If you've brought your boat all the way up Alviso Slough, you can take the smaller boat back out the slough to Coyote Creek, turn to the starboard, and go over to Station Island, the setting for the ghost town of Drawbridge, where two hand-operated drawbridges built by South Pacific Coast Railway in 1876 were the seeds of a town. Hunters soon discovered this paradise of waterfowl; and hunting, along with fishing, swimming, and boating, led to the development of a small town by the turn of the 20th Century.

Today no permanent residents remain on the island. Ranger-led tours during the summer months provide the only access for visitors. You can see the town from Coyote Creek, but be aware that the water in the creek is too shallow for even a sportboat or sea kayak unless you stay in the channel or make the trip at high tide.

Another worthwhile destination for those who cruise to Alviso is the San Francisco Bay National Wildlife Refuge Visitor Center. The Visitor Center is a good place to get on the trails out into the Refuge. The Center is a healthy walk, almost 2 miles from town, but the naturalists there will willingly provide you with information about the wildlife in the area.

South Bay Yacht Club

APPROACH

A cruise to Alviso, at the S end of San Francisco Bay, offers all the adventure many boaters could ask for. To get to Alviso, pass under the Dumbarton Bridge, go through the old railroad bridge one mile E, and proceed down the Bay, carefully observing the channel markers. The first marker, "16," marks the entrance to Mowry Slough, to your port about 0.65 mile E of Marker "16."

From Marker "16," change course to approximately SE and proceed past markers "17" and "18" to Marker "20," where Guadalupe Slough exits from the San Francisco Bay. Water depths are 10 feet or more in the channel as far as Marker "20," where the Bay becomes Coyote Creek. Continue E for 1.3 miles to the intersection of Alviso Slough, which exits to starboard immediately after you pass under the overhead power cables. Local boaters state that Alviso Slough exits from Coyote Creek 50 feet from the last S tower in the creek. The area by the old

pier to starboard is shoal. Look carefully at your chart before entering.

If you decide to take your boat to Alviso, plan your trip to coincide with a high tide; some locals suggest making the trip only when the tide is 6 feet or greater. (Though plans are on the table to dredge the Alviso Slough, a date for the dredging has not been set, so don't postpone your trip, waiting for that date.)

Follow the Slough slowly, watching your depth. As if you were transiting a river, swing wide at the turns, which tend to silt on the inside. Going aground and getting off quickly are commonplace on this trip.

We recently spoke with members of the Peninsula Yacht Club in Redwood City about their club cruise to Alviso. Apparently, only one of the boats, a sailboat with a 6-foot draft, went aground on the trip. Club members reported they got the boat off the soft mud easily and continued on with their great adventure.

Alviso Slough at Yacht Club

Launch Ramps at Alviso Slough

Most boaters choose to anchor W of the intersection of the Alviso Slough and Coyote Creek and use their tenders to make the 3.3-mile trip to the town of Alviso. One member of the yacht club had had his 100-foot boat anchored in Coyote Creek for six months when we visited Alviso a few years back. This intersection is as far as we took our boat. In town boaters can tie their tenders alongside the new launch ramp 0.3 mile W of Alviso or at the South Bay Yacht Club dock.

BERTHING

If you wish to tie up to a dock, you can stay for two or three days at South Bay Yacht Club. The guest dock there has enough space for two or three boats, and many more can be accommodated by rafting up. Be sure to call ahead to reserve space.

ANCHORAGE

You can anchor along Alviso Slough almost anywhere between Coyote Creek and the town of Alviso, but expect to sit in the mud, particularly at low tide. South Bay boaters experience neither surprise nor alarm when they feel their boats settle into the mud at low tide when they are at anchor. The closer you get to Alviso, the shallower the water in the slough. For that reason many boats with deep drafts anchor a mile or more from the docks in Alviso.

FACILITIES AT OR NEAR THE YACHT CLUB:

Chandlery
Grocery Store
Launch Ramp (at high tide only)
Laundry
Post Office
Restaurants

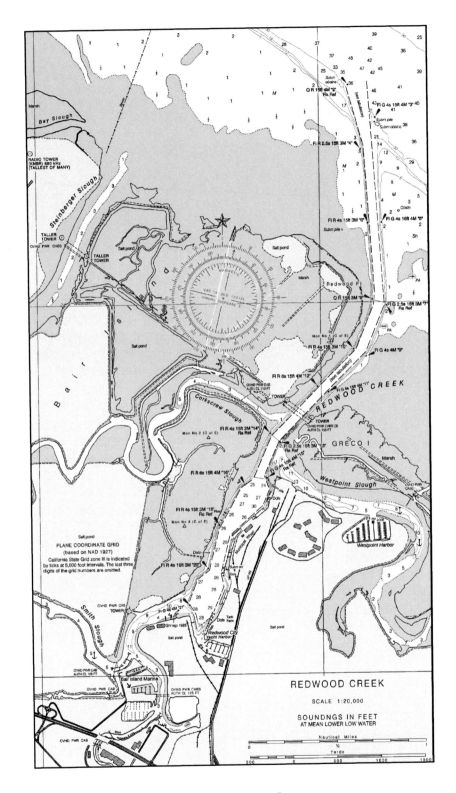

Redwood Creek

REDWOOD CITY

Chart #18651 or 18652
Channel Buoy "2" 37°33.06N, 122°11.67W

Bulk Ore Ship Loading

Rancho las Pulgas (*Fleas Ranch*), comprising the land between the Bay and the coastal range bounded by San Mateo Creek and San Francisquito Creek, was the Spanish land grant of Jose Dario Arguello. Cattle—undoubtedly with fleas that didn't always confine themselves to the cattle—cropped the grasses growing below the redwood forests on the mountainside. The redwood trees gave impetus to the building of the Port of Redwood City.

Redwood City continues to be the site of an important commercial port in San Francisco Bay. In fact, it is one of only four deep-water ports in the Bay. The earliest commercial purpose of the port was for the shipment of redwoods, initially to San Francisco and up the river to Sacramento and later to overseas destinations, primarily Japan. This port is also reputed to be the birthplace of shipbuilding on the west coast of North America, having as many as twelve shipyards during the second half of the 19th century.

Conditions here are ideal for the accumulation of salt: shallow salt water; flat, dense soil; meager rainfall; and abundant sun and wind. Long before the 1850s, when John Johnson built the first system of levees through the Hayward marshes to collect water from the Bay for salt production, the Ohlones had for generations gathered salt along the shores of these marshes.

Today the Port of Redwood City specializes in bulk, neo-bulk, and liquid cargo, including the historically prominent cargos of scrap metal and salt from the nearby evaporation ponds of Cargill, Inc.

The Port of Redwood City is also a busy place for pleasure boaters, where they have access to three marinas, two yacht clubs, and two sloughs. Westport and Smith sloughs both offer shallow-water but appealing rural anchorages.

Entrance to Westpoint Harbor with Dumbarton Bridge in Background

ATTRACTIONS

From any of the marinas and anchorages, you can take your tender up Smith Slough, then to Steinberger Slough, and to Corkscrew Slough to explore the shorelines of Bair Island. Most of Bair Island is a part of the San Francisco Bay National Wildlife Refuge.

For hikers, a 3-mile trail along the levee system E and N circles marshes rich with shorebirds. The E leg of this trail running parallel with Highway 101 connects with the Bay Trail on both the N and S. The Bay Trail in turn connects to numerous side trails.

Thus the Redwood City marinas and anchorages are an ideal destination for those of you wanting to experience some of the marshlands remaining in San Francisco Bay. The Refuge has protected these marshes, and the trails give you access to them.

APPROACH

Because ocean-going vessels enter this port, you'll find a well-marked wide, deep channel to navigate—a genuine treat in this region of the Bay, where water depths are often less than 6 feet at low water.

Whether coming from N or S, boaters will find an excellent landmark for Redwood City: a major bridge. Boaters approaching from the N will pass under the San Mateo Bridge and continue for 3.1 miles, staying in the ship channel on a SE course. The pairs of entrance markers into the Port of Redwood City begin on pilings at the starboard edge of the ship channel, where you'll find over 40 feet of water.

The few boaters approaching from the S will go under the Dumbarton Bridge and follow the ship channel for 4.5 miles, holding a NW course to the channel markers.

The dredged channel through Redwood Creek has excellent depths as far as the entrance into the Redwood City Yacht Harbor, but boaters who stray out of the well-marked channel may very well go aground. Beyond the Yacht Harbor the channel to Smith Slough and the marina in the S end of Redwood Creek is not regularly dredged and should be navigated with particular care.

BERTHING

Those wishing to explore ashore in and around Redwood City or simply to enjoy the security and conveniences of being tied to a dock can go into one of the three marinas. Though none of the marinas is in an area of the city that has a variety of markets and shops, *Bair Island*, the closest to commercial districts, is about 0.5 mile from a chandlery, a dive shop, a canvas shop, and movie theaters; 1.0 mile from service stations, banks, and a post office; and 1.5 miles from a mini-market and a laundromat. All three marinas have easy access to the San Francisco Bay Trail.

WESTPOINT HARBOR
Entrance Buoy "13"
  37°31.230N, 122°20.50 *W*
Contact: 650-306-0545
harbormaster@westpointharbor.com

This newest of the marinas along Redwood Creek is up Westpoint Slough, which is on the S side of the creek. Following the ship channel inside the Creek, turn to port at Marker "13." The entrance into Westpoint Harbor is 0.5 mile up the Slough. Water depths in the channel between Redwood Creek and the marina and inside the marina are generally a minimum of 9 feet at mean low water. The dockmaster at Westpoint Harbor nevertheless recommends boaters enter the shallow slough only on a making tide.

This thoroughly modern private marina with 418 slips is still in the process of development, with a fuel dock and a full-service boat yard in the offing. As part of a large planned development, this marina will be near restaurants, a hotel, and retail shops at some future time.

FACILITIES AT OR NEAR THE
WESTPOINT HARBOR MARINA:

Launch Ramp
Laundry
Pacific Shores Health & Fitness Center (fee)
Party Barges (free)
Public Transportation
Pump Out at Each Slip
WiFi (free)

REDWOOD CITY YACHT HARBOR
Entrance 37°30.20N, 122°12.88W
Contact: Spinnaker Sailing School for berths, 650-363-1390
or office@spinnakersailing.com

Continuing SW in Redwood Creek, just beyond the ship docks where cargo is loaded onto the freighters, you will come to the city marina, which has 183 slips. From the channel in the Creek, turn to port before Marker "21" and enter the fairway into the marina.

Harbor Office

Office for Sailing School and City Marina

**FACILITIES AT OR NEAR THE
REDWOOD CITY YACHT HARBOR MARINA:**

Launch Ramp
Laundromat
Pump Out
Restaurants

The *Sequoia Yacht Club* clubhouse sits on the NW end of this harbor and has some guest berthing, where the club welcomes visitors from other yacht clubs. **Contact: 650-361-9472 or portcaptain@sequoiayc.org.**

BAIR ISLAND MARINA
**Entrance 37°30.04N, 122°13.23W
Contact: 670-701-0282
iturner@greatslips.com**

Examine your charts carefully before attempting to go to Bair Island Marina. Because some depths in the channel can be as little as 3.5 feet at low water, the dockmaster recommends approaching Bair Island Marina within 2 hours either before or after high water. Proceeding slowly in case you do go aground (not at all unlikely), continue on down Redwood Creek beyond Westpoint Slough and past the ship loading facility. Then turn to starboard at the G"21" buoy.

The immaculately maintained condominium complex Villas of Bair Island lines three sides of this small marina that, according to the dockmaster, typically has a 99% occupancy rate of its 95 slips, though guests are welcomed when space

Good Wind Protection at Bair

is available. This full-service marina can accommodate boats up to 60 feet in length.

Within easy walking distance from the marina is the San Francisco Bay National Wildlife Refuge, with a three-mile hiking trail from which visitors can enjoy the variety of wildlife inhabiting the sloughs and creeks of the South Bay.

**FACILITIES AT OR NEAR THE
BAIR ISLAND MARINA:**

Gym
Jacuzzi
Kayak Rental
Laundry
Movie Theaters
Playground for Children
Pool
Pump Out
Restaurants
Shops

The *Peninsula Yacht Club* facility and docks lie 0.25 mile beyond Bair Island Marina. The club welcomes visitors from other yacht clubs on the weekends. Call ahead to ask about slip availability. If space is available, a yacht club member will meet you near Bair Island Marina and lead you into a waiting slip. Peninsula Yacht Club members advise against trying to navigate this 0.25 mile without local knowledge. **Contact: 650-369-4410, 650-669-1500, or 916-276-6266.**

Anchoring in a slough off Redwood Creek can be an absolute pleasure, as long as you are careful and watch the tides. Dick Honey, a long-time sailor in and around Redwood City, told us years ago, "When we're sailing this area, our tide books are our bibles."

The two anchorages can provide you two quite different experiences. In Westpoint Slough, you may choose to anchor fairly close to the new marina, Westpoint Harbor, though of course <u>not</u> in the marina basin.

However, if you desire a more private, rural atmosphere, you'll choose an anchoring site farther up Westpoint Slough. If you anchor a mile or so beyond the marina, you may never see another boat, instead seeing a spectacular shorebird show, especially when the tide recedes to expose the shoals extending into the slough on either side. We've seen American Avocets, Willets, Long-billed Curlews, Snowy and Great Egrets, Great Blue Herons, Dunlins, and Marbled Godwits feeding on the invertebrates in this slough. If you don't see all these species feeding alongside your boat, you'll be sure to see them if you take your tender farther up the slough.

The Smith Slough anchorage, on the other hand, will give you the sense of being in the middle of the activity of Redwood City Yacht Harbor. This anchorage will appeal more to those of you who want access to some of the appurtenances of civilization: restaurants, shops, theaters, and the like. This anchorage is in the middle of the marina activity and thus has many of the same attractions as the marinas.

WESTPOINT SLOUGH
Entrance Buoy "13" 37°52.08N, 122°20.50W
Anchorage 37°30.68N, 122°11.33W

After entering the Redwood Creek channel, continue SW 2.0 miles to Westpoint Slough, to port. This slough runs along the S shore of Greco Island, which is part of the San Francisco Bay National Wildlife Refuge. Turn to port 20 yards S of Marker "13," and set a course to take you between the red and green buoys leading into Westpoint Harbor. Proceed slowly as sand bars form in unusual places. Once past the entrance into the Harbor, you may anchor anywhere on up the slough wherever water depths are sufficient.

Westpoint Harbor has dredged the Slough as far as the Harbor entrance and has set buoys marking

the channel into the Harbor. But beyond these two channel markers, no other buoys mark the safe water.

On our recent visit, we maintained a course in the center of the Slough and found adequate depths for our 6-foot-draft ketch 0.25 mile beyond the Harbor entrance. Just beyond the PG&E pier on the N side of the Slough, we anchored in 8 feet of water at **37°30.870N, 122°11.500W**.

Our favorite anchorage, though, is another 0.25 mile from the PG&E pier at **37°30.700N, 122°11.350W**, where we have anchored in 15 feet of water on a mud bottom. Here, we see no boat traffic, and our boat sits motionless even when the winds pipe up.

A Fine Winter Anchorage

Boaters are limited to a 72-hour stay in the sloughs of Redwood City. Anyone wishing to stay longer than 72 hours must get permission from the Port Authority of Redwood City.

SMITH SLOUGH
Entrance 37°30.020N, 122°13.470W
Anchorage 37°30.11N, 122°13.64W

This anchorage is only for boats with under 5 feet of draft.

Smith Slough is off to starboard 0.40 mile SW of the turn-off into Redwood City Yacht Harbor. Boats anchor in Smith Slough in about 5 feet of water at low tide. We recommend entering sloughs in this South Bay area at low water or during an incoming tide. If you go aground, you want to be sure your boat will float off soon and not be there for a week while you wait for a tide high enough to float the boat off the mud.

COYOTE POINT MARINA

Chart #18651 or #18652
Channel Buoy "1" 37°35.62N, 122°18.75W
Contact: 650-573-2594   ehallett@co.sanmateo.ca.us

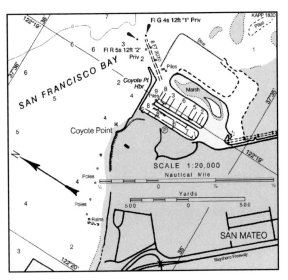

Coyote Point Marina

Coyote Point Marina is on the opposite side of Highway 101 from the city of San Mateo, yet so remote does it seem that it might as well be on the other side of the Bay from San Mateo. The marina is part of the Coyote Point Recreation Area of San Mateo County, with an expansive eucalyptus-tree-covered picnic area acting as a buffer between the city and the marina.

This marina, with 550 slips, including the new Dock 29 for large boats up to 60 feet, can offer guest berthing accommodations for many boats. While this marina allows no liveaboards, visiting boaters can stay on their boats for a few days.

Coyote Point Yacht Club has a long guest dock for members of other yacht clubs. The restaurant serves lunch and dinner Fridays, Saturdays, and Sundays for yacht club members. **Contact: 650-347-6730.**

ATTRACTIONS

The Coyote Point Recreation Area inland of the marina offers a variety of activities for visitors in the marina, such as swimming, sailboarding, surfing, and picnicking, including 4 large group sites near the marina. A volleyball court and a horseshoe pit are also nearby. A 2.5-mile hiking trail around the park leads to the CuriOdyssey, the natural history museum "devoted to the wildlife and ecosystems of the Bay Area." Farther along the trail are an elegant restaurant on the water, a sandy beach, and a well-equipped children's playground. The San Mateo Municipal Golf Course lies at the southern end of the park.

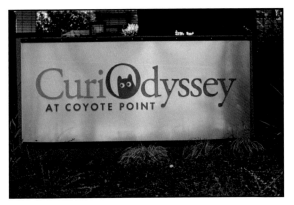

You can also hike or bike on another trail, part of the Bay Trail planned to follow the entire shoreline of San Francisco Bay. This trail has been completed for several miles in both directions, N and S, from Coyote Point Recreation Area, past marshlands alive with waterfowl and along the shores of some great windsurfing waters.

While none of the San Mateo city amenities are on the marina side of Highway 101, a pedestrian overpass on the other side of the park from the ma-

Trawler in Coyote Point Entrance

rina will take you across the freeway and onto Peninsula Street. Here, you can walk past immaculately kept homes and yards for about 0.5 mile, where you'll find a shopping center with a supermarket and other small shops.

To reach the overpass, take the path that traces the S perimeter of the park, above and alongside the golf course, for close to 1.0 mile. Though this walk will take you about a half hour each way, it's such a scenic trip you'll not mind the length.

APPROACH

Approaching Coyote Point Marina from any direction, use the San Francisco Airport as a convenient landmark. The tower, the beacon, the hangars, and the continuous flow of aircraft taking off and landing make this a great landmark. The entrance to Coyote Point is just over 2.2 miles E of the end of the runway. You can also use as a landmark the tree-covered Coyote Point, a cliff that rises well above the W side of the marina.

The 0.25-mile channel into the marina is clearly marked. Markers "1" and "2," on pilings 12 feet above the water, are easy to identify. Shoals as well as large rocks extend out to port from the channel, so be sure to remain safely inside the channel to avoid those hazards.

No anchorage area exists in or near the harbor.

FACILITIES AT OR NEAR THE
COYOTE POINT MARINA:

Fuel Dock (gasoline and diesel)
Launch Ramp
Pump Out
Restaurant

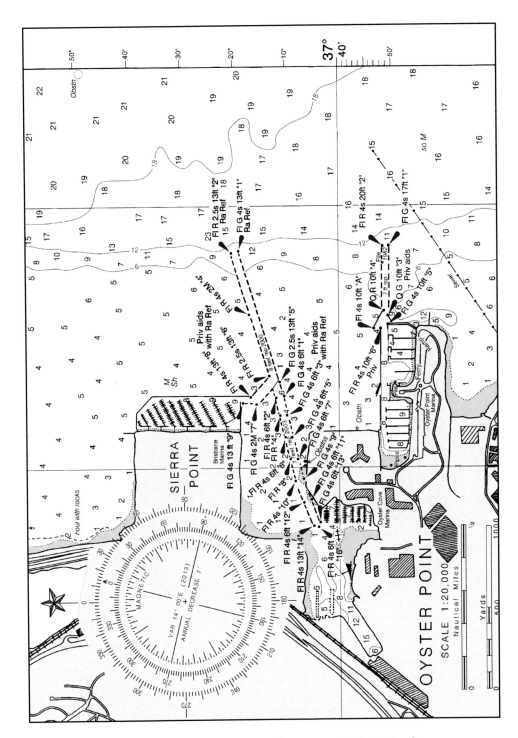

Brisbane, Oyster Cove, and Oyster Point Marinas

BRISBANE
AND SOUTH SAN FRANCISCO
Chart #18651 or #18652

The three marinas along the Bay shores of Brisbane and South San Francisco—Brisbane Marina, Oyster Cove Marina, and Oyster Point Marina—entice boating visitors with their modern docks and facilities, security, ease of access, and generally quiet isolation on the edge of the urban growth spreading south from San Francisco.

The shoreline where these marinas are located has been shaped by human intervention as much as any other shoreline in the Bay. Before the turn of the century San Bruno Mountain rose abruptly from the Bay shore to its 1,314 feet. Today, as a result of silting, it begins its ascent almost 3 miles west of the marinas.

For hundreds—perhaps thousands—of years, Ohlones harvested oysters and other mollusks here. The shell mounds testifying to this enterprise once lined the shores of both the Bay and the creeks; none of those mounds has survived the expansive urbanization and industrialization.

Catching on to the suitability of these waters for oysters, American entrepreneurs set up oyster beds at the end of the 19th century. Their enterprise was much shorter lived than that of the Ohlones: By 1905 polluted waters from raw sewage and insufficient tidal flushing caused by the diversion of freshwater streams for agricultural use had a deleterious effect on the oysters. By World War I Oyster Cove teemed not with boats harvesting oysters but with transport ships carrying pipes and steel from the heavy industries ashore and with ships newly built for service in the war.

Today you'll see little that is reminiscent of the oyster harvesting and/or cultivating that prospered for centuries or of the shipping industry that thrived for three-quarters of the 20th Century.

All three marinas sit on landfill, with office buildings nearby. The only activity on the water now is that of the pleasure boats, whose owners enjoy hearing the splashes of Brown Pelicans diving for dinner and the squawks of Forster's Terns sitting on the breakwater.

ATTRACTIONS

Bird watching, fishing, and walking are the primary activities in these somewhat isolated marinas. Segments of the Bay Trail have been completed both N and S of Brisbane. From Brisbane Marina, the trail to the S leads through an exercise station and continues through and beyond Safe Harbor. To the N the trail passes by a wooden fishing pier and along the western shore beyond Brisbane Lagoon for excellent viewing of shorebirds.

The Cabot, Cabot & Forbes Park, with 33 acres for picnicking, hiking and jogging, is close by Oyster Point Marina, as are a 2.5-acre sandy beach (with lifeguards from Memorial Day to Labor Day) and a 300-foot concrete fishing pier. With a walk of approximately 2 miles along city streets and across Highway 101, you can reach the San Bruno Mountain County Park from Oyster Point and Oyster Cove marinas.

Fishing Pier East of Brisbane

APPROACH

When you're approaching these three marinas from the N, Point Avisadero is the first major waypoint. Although it can be difficult to identify, Avisadero denotes a minor course change. You'll know you've passed Avisadero when you

Oyster Point Entrance/Breakwater

identify the Navy ships, ocean-going tankers, and huge cranes at Hunters Point Naval Shipyard on the starboard side approximately 0.25 mile beyond Point Avisadero.

Approaching from the S or E, you can use the San Francisco Airport for a landmark. From the N terminus of the airport, the entrance to Oyster Point Marina is 2.1 miles farther N, and to Brisbane and Oyster Cove, 2.85 miles.

The entrance channel into Brisbane Marina and Oyster Cove is 3 miles from the center of the Hunters Point complex on a course of 178° mag. Do not stray off course to starboard as the water shoals abruptly between Hunters Point and Brisbane. Notice on your chart that the water shallows from 20 feet or more to 4 feet just starboard of your course.

Channel markers "1" and "2" identify the channel into Brisbane and Oyster Cove. A series of 10 pairs of markers clearly outlines the boundaries of the mile-long channel. Stay carefully be-tween the markers as the water shallows quickly outside the channel. Turn to starboard just past Marker "6," 0.5 mile up the channel; the entrance into Brisbane Marina at Sierra Point, only 250 yards from the channel, is easy to see. For Oyster Cove Marina, continue up the channel for slightly more than 0.5 mile rather than turning right into Brisbane Marine.

Though Oyster Point Marina is adjacent to Oyster Cove Marina, the entrance is on a separate channel 0.75 mile south of the Brisbane Marina/Oyster Cove Channel. This channel into Oyster Point also has identifying markers numbered "1" and "2" that you will need to distinguish from the markers with the same numbers on the Brisbane-Oyster Cove Channel.

I know that grass beyond the door,
The sweet keen smell,
The sighing sound, the lights around the shore.
        —Dante Gabriel Rossetti, *Sudden Light*

BERTHING

BRISBANE MARINA
Brisbane/Oyster Cove Channel Entrance Buoy "2" 37°40.33N, 122°22.17W
Brisbane Marina Channel Buoy "6" 37°40.20N, 122°22.65W
Contact: 650-583-6975   VHF 16
harbormaster@ci.brisbane.ca.us

Brisbane Marina, with 580 slips, is the largest of the three marinas in South San Francisco. At only 7 miles from the Oakland-San Francisco Bay Bridge, it also offers the nearest access to the Central Bay. This marina has a 270-foot guest dock, and the berths can accommodate boats of 10-120 feet.

The *Sierra Point Yacht Club* facility is on the south end of the marina. The club will make arrangements with the harbormaster for cruise-ins from other yacht clubs. **Contact: 650-952-0651.**

FACILITIES AT OR NEAR THE BRISBANE MARINA:

Guest Dock
Laundry
Pump Out
Restaurant and Cafés
WiFi (free)

OYSTER COVE MARINA
Channel Buoy "2" 37°40.33N, 122°22.17W
Contact: 650-952-5540
contact@oystercovemarina.net

Oyster Cove Marina, the smallest of the three marinas in South San Francisco, has berthing for boats between 30-60 feet. Its landscaped promenade ashore makes for a pleasant walk or the beginning of an invigorating hike on the Bay Trail.

FACILITIES AT OR NEAR OYSTER COVE MARINA:

Cable TV
Chandlery
Guest Dock
Ice (free)
Laundry
Marine Services
Pump Out
Restaurant
Security Patrol (24 hrs.)

OYSTER POINT MARINA
Channel Buoy "2" 37°39.85N, 122°22.13W
Contact: 650-952-0808   VHF 16

The Oyster Point Marina, under the aegis of the San Mateo County Harbor District, has 455 slips that can accommodate boats 26-60 feet in length and welcomes guests. Of the three marinas, this one is the closest to the beach for kayaking, windsurfing, and swimming and to the ferry with service to Oakland and Alameda.

Oyster Point Yacht Club, near the ferry terminal, will arrange guest berthing for individual members of other yacht clubs or for cruise-ins from other yacht clubs. This club galley serves a Sunday breakfast during cruising season. **Contact: 650-873-5166**

FACILITIES AT OR NEAR OYSTER POINT MARINA:

Chandlery (1.5 miles)
Bait and Tackle Shop
Beach
Boat Maintenance and Repair
Ferry Service to Oakland and Alameda
Fuel Dock (gasoline and diesel)
Guest Dock
Launch Ramp
Laundry (tenants only)
Pump Out
Restaurants

Candlestick Point Anchorage

"The ship is anchored safe and sound, its voyage closed and done."
—Walt Whitman, "O Captain! My Captain!"

CANDLESTICK POINT

Candlestick Point   37°42.43N, 122°23.10W
Candlestick Point, East   37°42.58N, 122°22.39W

When the 49ers and Giants were still playing at the stadium ashore, Candlestick Point was one of the most colorful anchorages for local boaters in San Francisco Bay. Members of Peninsula Yacht Club in Redwood City refer to this anchorage as "Friday Harbor" because they regularly anchor here on Friday nights as they're en route to the Central Bay for the weekend. They report it offers good holding even though the wind often screams through the rigging during the night.

Enter the anchorage from the E 100 yards off the S side of the peninsula at Candlestick Point. Identify the two piers extending S from the shoreline. The best anchorage is S of the southernmost pier within 100 yards of shore in 6 to 10 feet of water.

Some boaters have anchored in the small cove directly E of the peninsula at Candlestick Point in 5 to 10 feet of water and reported having good protection from the heavy winds that roar across the Bay just S of old Candlestick Park.

San Francisco Bay boaters who sail the area regularly warn that the protected cove between Candlestick Point and Hunters Point, called South Basin, should be avoided because the bottom is shallow and fouled.

Boat Sailing North Near Candlestick Anchorage

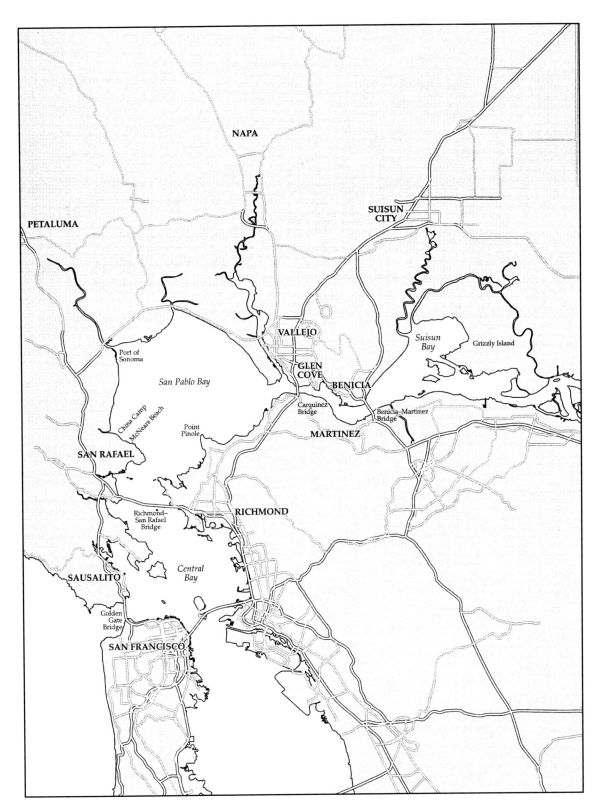

North Bay Destinations

THE NORTH BAY

Brothers Island Lighthouse

It was kind of solemn, drifting down the big still river, laying on our backs looking up at the stars, and we didn't ever feel like talking loud, and it warn't often that we laughed, only a little kind of a low chuckle. We had mighty good weather, as a general thing, and nothing ever happened to us at all, that night, nor the next, nor the next.

—Mark Twain, *Huckleberry Finn*

Opened Railroad Bridge, Petaluma River

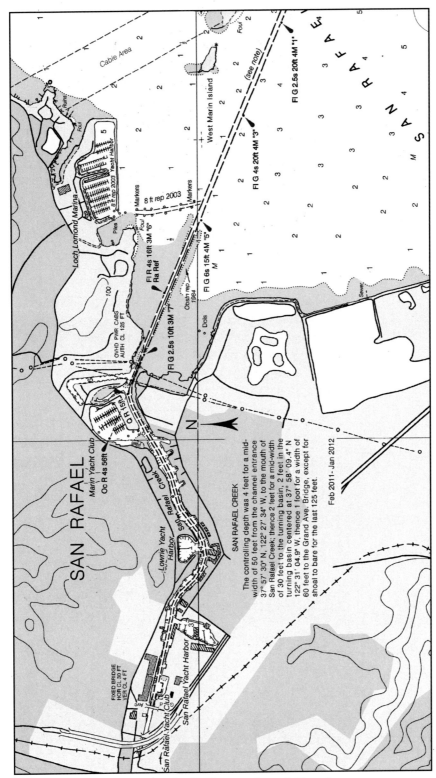

San Rafael Channel and Creek

SAN RAFAEL

Chart #18652, #18654, or #18649
Channel Entrance Buoy #17
37°57.44N, 122°27.41W

The oldest city in Marin County, San Rafael has today the same asset that attracted the first Spanish to settle here: In the lee of Mount Tamalpais it thrives in a Mediterranean-like climate, with warm, sunny days throughout a long summer. And we can safely assume the Coast Miwoks who lived here for thousands of years before the Spanish came appreciated this place they called "Nanaguani" for those same reasons. What a paradise it must have been! Antelope and elk grazed on the grassy hillsides made verdant by the combination of the sunny summers and rainy winters. Salmon spawned in the creeks, and mussels and abalones grew in abundance along the rocky shoreline. Sea otters were so numerous in the Bay they were said to form islands of fur over which canoes could skim.

The padres at *Misión San Francisco de Asís*--more popularly called *Misión Dolores,* the name of the lagoon on the shores of which it sat--had grown concerned with the mortality rate among the Costanoans at the mission. This rate of deaths from the diseases the Europeans had brought to these shores was higher than that at any of the other California missions. The padres began looking for a spot around the Bay with a climate less severe than that of San Francisco, where they could establish an *asistencia* (hospital).

In 1817, *Misión San Rafael Arcangel* became that site, having been named, appropriately, after the healing messenger of God, the archangel Rafael. With this new establishment, to become number twenty among California's twenty-one missions, the padres would also be able to attract a large number of new converts among the Miwoks living in what is now Marin County.

Establishing the *asistencia* in this part of the Bay Area also served a political purpose: It served as a warning to the Russians, who were begin-ning to look south of Fort Ross for new sea otter hunting grounds, that San Francisco Bay and all its contiguous lands belonged to the Spanish crown.

Mission San Rafael

The padres at Mission San Rafael apparently realized all their goals. The converts brought here from Mission Dolores were healthier, new Miwok converts flocked to the mission, and the Russians did not encroach on the Spanish territories. Succeeding far beyond their dreams, the padres, with the invaluable labor supplied by the converts, turned the mission farmlands into highly productive fields of wheat, corn, barley, beans, and peas. Later, after

San Rafael Creek (center); Highway 101 w/marina businesses (l.)

Mexico gained independence from Spain and, thirteen years later, secularized the missions, General Mariano Vallejo had a cattle and sheep ranch here. Mission San Rafael also became noted for the quality of its grapes.

During the Bear Flag Rebellion of 1846 John Fremont and Kit Carson used the mission as a barracks. The reconstructed mission standing today replaces the original adobe that was dismantled in 1861.

John Reed started up a ferry service in the 1830s to transport the padres and their charges between Mission Dolores and Mission San Rafael and also to take the whalers and seamen anchored in Richardson Bay in Sausalito to San Francisco. In 1907, the Northwest Pacific Railroad, bought by Southern Pacific in 1929, began to run trains down to the waterfront to meet the ferries.

ATTRACTIONS

San Rafael is a particularly satisfying cruising destination because it has a variety of attractions clustered within a few blocks. The heart of the downtown area is only four blocks from San Rafael Creek. You can take five walking tours through historic San Rafael, guided by a brochure available from the San Rafael Chamber of Commerce, 818 Fifth Street.

The *Downtown San Rafael* walk begins at Courthouse Square, where the Marin County Courthouse formed the "heart of the county" until 1969, when the county offices moved to the Civic Center, the last structure designed by Frank Lloyd Wright. Hotels, commercial buildings, and private residences remain from as early as 1859.

The *Mission and Early Mansions* walk will take you past the reconstructed mission and what is said to be the oldest building in San Rafael, the Coleman House, built between 1849 and 1852. One of

Marin Islands with sailboat in San Rafael Channel. Note Channel marks ahead of and behind sailboat.

the most interesting buildings on the third walk, the *Forbes Addition* walk, is one of the two remaining buildings from the 1915 Panama Pacific Exposition in San Francisco. The Victrola building that had housed the Victor Talking Machine Company was dismantled at the end of the exposition and barged across the Bay as a gift to Leon Douglas, who coined the slogan *His Master's Voice.* Southwest of the harbor is a fourth walking tour, *Short's Tract: The Gerstle Park Area.*

Finally, the Dominican tour is a bit of a distance from the harbor—10 or 12 long blocks—but well worth the walk. The Dominican College campus has long been renowned for the architectural excellence of many of its buildings. One of the most significant historically is the Mother House, the 1889 convent house built for the Dominican Sisters when they moved to San Rafael from Benicia. The tiles around the front entrance of the Mother House are by the Italian Renaissance sculp-

tor Luca della Robbia. On campus, too, dating from 1888, is Meadowlands, the summer house of Michael H. deYoung, one of the founders of the *San Francisco Chronicle*. The Dominican Order purchased the house in 1918 and added a dormitory wing in 1924.

If outdoor adventuring is more to your taste than historical walks, you can pick up a section of the Bay Trail at Pickleweed Park, on the S shore of San Rafael Creek near its mouth. Then walk along the Shoreline Park trail, with an excellent view of the Marin Islands just across San Rafael Bay. Take binoculars along to view the Snowy and Great Egrets and the Black-crowned Night Herons building nests, caring for their young, and feeding around the islands. You can continue south to Point San Quentin, named for Chief Quentin, who, along with Chief Marin (*el marinero*), led an uprising against the Mission in 1824. San Quentin State Prison is on the SW side of this point.

Loch Lomond Marina

APPROACH

BERTHING

Approaching San Rafael from either N or S, you will be in the ship channel. Enter San Rafael Channel at Marker "17," 1.4 miles NW of the Richmond-San Rafael Bridge. Boaters transiting San Rafael Channel must use caution because the channel suffers from chronic shoaling. Stay inside the 60-foot-wide channel that may be less than 5 feet deep at low water. The channel has large markers on pilings that identify the port side of the channel as you proceed from San Rafael Bay to San Rafael.

Visiting boaters should take their boats into this channel only at mid-tide or higher. If you wish to cruise to San Rafael and are not confident about the water depths in the channel, call one of the local marinas for an update on conditions and for advice on navigating the channel. Though shoaling is a continuing problem, the hundreds of boats moored in San Rafael furnish testimony that, with careful planning, you can find enough water in the channel.

If you plan to cruise to San Rafael and are a member of a yacht club, you can call ahead for a guest berthing at one of the two yacht clubs. If you're not a member of a club, call Loch Lomond Marina, Lowrie Yacht Harbor, or the San Rafael Yacht Harbor for guest berthing.

LOCH LOMOND MARINA
Channel Entrance   37°58.02N, 122°28.96W
Marina Entrance   37°58.28N, 122°29.00W
Contact: 415-454-7228

With 500 slips, Loch Lomond is the largest marina in the area. The new owners of Loch Lomond Marina are currently developing a condo-townhouse community north of the marina in what was once a parking lot and dry storage area. Boats continue to fill the marina, however, and the fuel dock is regularly busy.

Marin Yacht Club

APPROACH

The channel into Loch Lomond Marina exits to starboard from the San Rafael Channel 1.35 miles from the entrance marker. The secondary channel is, as is the San Rafael Channel, subject to shoaling and requires regular dredging. You should stay carefully between the pilings on the port and starboard marking the channel.

FACILITIES AT OR NEAR THE LOCH LOMOND MARINA:

Bank
Boat Maintenance and Repair
Dry Cleaners
Fuel
Grocery Store
Launch Ramp (fee)
Pump Out

MARIN YACHT CLUB
Entrance 37°58.18N, 122°30.00W
Contact: 415-453-9366

Marin Yacht Club, with 118 slips between 36-80 feet in length, has one of the most elegant facilities around the Bay. Although the slips are usually filled, the Club will try to accommodate members of other yacht clubs who wish to visit.

APPROACH

The San Rafael Channel continues 0.65 mile beyond the Loch Lomond channel, passing through mud flats before joining San Rafael Creek. When you join the creek, you will change course, coming about to a SW course. The entrance to the Marin Yacht Club exits to starboard from the creek 300 yards after the intersection of the channel and the creek.

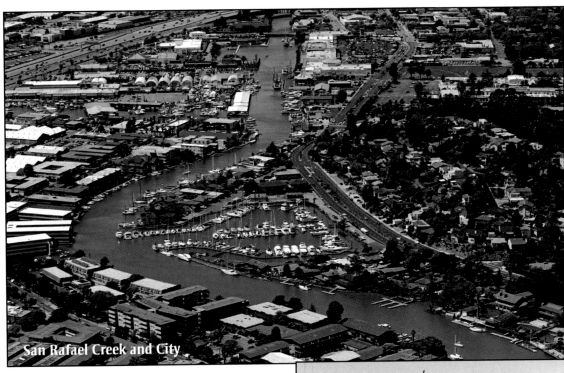

San Rafael Creek and City

FACILITIES AT OR NEAR THE MARIN YACHT CLUB:

Bait Shop
Boat Maintenance & Repair
Cable TV (free)
Grocery Store
Laundry
Pump Out
Restaurant and Bar
Swimming Pool
Small-boat Crane
Tennis Courts

LOWRIE YACHT HARBOR
Entrance 37°57.98N, 122°30.45W
Contact: 415-454-7595

One of the oldest marinas in the San Rafael area, Lowrie is still run by the descendants of the man who built the marina in 1948. The granddaughter of the builder is now training to become the manager. The excellent condition of the marina

today testifies to the pride of the family ownership.

This marina has 100 slips plus the end ties and can accommodate boats up to 65 feet long.

APPROACH

Up San Rafael Creek 0.4 mile beyond Marin Yacht Club, Lowrie Yacht Harbor is also on the starboard side of the creek. Because the creek has been dredged to 6 feet at mean low water, the personnel at Lowrie recommend that boaters come and go with a mid-tide or higher. Inside Lowrie the water is 8 feet deep.

San Rafael Yacht Harbor

FACILITIES AT OR NEAR THE
LOWRIE YACHT HARBOR MARINA:

Grocery Store
Pump Out
Restaurants

SAN RAFAEL YACHT HARBOR
Entrance 37°58.08N, 122°30.78W
Contact: 415-456-1600

The owner of San Rafael Yacht Harbor stresses the strong sense of community among those with boats permanently moored here. Of the 160 slips, approximately 20-25 per cent are liveaboards, although that percentage will decrease with the current policy of no new liveaboards accepted.

One of the extraordinary perquisites of this yacht harbor is the haul-out facility with a 30-ton crane, not a Travelift, and a do-it-yourself boatyard (formerly Garvie's). Svendsen's delivers parts to this yard so boat owners hauling their boats here don't need a car to obtain parts or supplies.

APPROACH

San Rafael Yacht Harbor is on the port side another 0.25 mile up San Rafael Creek beyond Lowrie Yacht Harbor. At the time of this writing, this yacht harbor had only 3 feet of depth at low mean water, so clearly those who come and go here will do so only at or near high tide. (Check with the harbormaster before planning a passage to San Rafael Yacht Harbor.)

FACILITIES AT OR NEAR THE
SAN RAFAEL YACHT HARBOR MARINA:

Boat Maintenance and Repair
Grocery Store
Haul-Out
Laundry
Post Office
Restaurants

~~~~

San Rafael Creek with San Rafael Yacht Harbor (l.)

SAN RAFAEL YACHT CLUB
Entrance 37°58.14N, 122°31.07W
Contact: 415-459-9828
infosryc@gmail.com

Founded in 1938, the San Rafael Yacht Club has good facilities for members of other yacht clubs, with 300 feet of dock space for visiting boats.

APPROACH

The San Rafael Yacht Club building is at the far W end of the navigable San Rafael Creek, immediately before the Grand Avenue Bridge. Again, be cautious because shoaling is particularly evident at the upper reaches of the Creek.

No anchorages exist in the San Rafael area. Boaters who want to anchor near San Rafael can proceed from the entrance channel for San Rafael 3 miles N to the anchorage at China Camp or 4 miles S to Paradise Cove.

FACILITIES AT OR NEAR THE SAN RAFAEL YACHT CLUB:

Boat Maintenance and Repair
Grocery Store
Laundry
Post Office
Restaurants

Blue Heron in San Rafael

MCNEARS BEACH AND CHINA CAMP

Chart #18652 or #18654

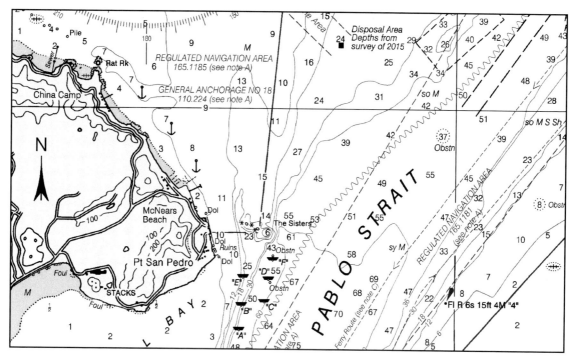

McNears Beach and China Camp

APPROACH TO MCNEARS BEACH AND CHINA CAMP

From San Francisco Bay, go under the Richmond-San Rafael Bridge to enter San Pablo Bay. Heading due N from the main span of the bridge for 2 miles, pass the Brothers Islands on your starboard, just offshore at Point San Pablo. You can clearly identify East Brother because of the refurbished lighthouse keeper's house. Directly off your bow about 2 miles are the Sisters Islands, which rise no more than 20 feet above the water's surface. These two islands have no buildings, though barges to haul gravel from the crushing plant are usually anchored nearby. Use caution when passing these barges: tugs are often moving them around.

You can safely pass on either side of the Sisters, with about 10 feet of water on the W and 50 feet on the E. Immediately beyond the Sisters, a pier just N of Point San Pedro marks the southern end of McNears Beach.

ANCHORAGES

Prevailing winds come over the land mass to the W during the afternoon, but winds frequently come from the S early in the day or even from the N during the afternoon. Even though the varying wind direction is unsettling, both anchorages are secure and comfortable in moderate winds from any direction but the E. A current, often in excess of 1 knot, runs through both anchorages.

Although the wind may blow 15 knots, the strong current can hold your boat beam to the wind. Despite these peculiarities of wind direction and current, both McNears and China Camp are comfortable anchorages. The two can accommodate 50 boats, but rarely will you see more than a dozen on a summer weekend.

McNears Fishing Pier

MCNEARS BEACH
McNears Beach Anchorage
37°59.64N, 122°27.09W

Most cruising boaters anchor at least 400 yards N of the pier and at least 600 feet from shore because of shallow water. Because of the current and the wind strength, be sure to let out sufficient scope and dig in your anchor by backing down before leaving your boat or settling in for the night.

ATTRACTIONS

You may land a dinghy or sport boat ashore on the rocky but accessible beach, where you can walk or swim. The rocks in the silt bottom make a pair of water shoes desirable. Above the beach are lush green lawns, picnic tables, and a snack bar. Farther up the hill is Point San Pablo Road, which will take you N to China Camp State Park or SW for a 3-mile jaunt into San Rafael.

FACILITIES

Beach
Fishing Pier
Picnic Tables
Restrooms
Snack Shop
Swimming Pool
Tennis Courts
Volley Ball

CHINA CAMP
China Camp Anchorage
38°00.10N, 122°27.38W

One mile N of McNears and less than 0.5 mile S of Rat Rock is the dilapidated 300-foot-long China Camp pier. Ashore here are several weathered wooden buildings from the days when China Camp was the site of a shrimp drying and packing plant and home to as many as 300 residents. As at McNears, the desirable spot for anchoring is at least 600 feet from shore—but S or E of the pier.

Going ashore here is a bit easier than at McNears, for you can tie up at the pier if the gate is unlocked, or you can land a dinghy or sportboat on the sandy beach. A few picnic tables are near the water on the N side of the pier, and the small restaurant/concession stand is open on weekends.

ATTRACTIONS

For many visitors the main attraction is the small museum chronicling the lives of the Chinese families who settled here in the late 1800s to harvest and process the plentiful grass shrimp in San Pablo Bay. Most of these shrimp were sold in China. The crumbling pier, the old processing plant (now the museum), the kiln and drying racks, and a handful of houses are all that remain today.

A paved road leading away from the museum will take you to numerous well-marked and well-tended trails in this 1,640-acre park. These trails wind through stands of oak trees (and healthy stands of poison oak!) and across the meadows, where Coast Miwoks had settlements until the early 19th century.

On the other hand, you can explore the area by sportboat. North of the anchorage and around Rat Island are a dozen or so duck blinds perched on stilts in the water. To the S and W of these blinds is a channel marked by pieces of PVC pipe stuck in the mud bottom; this channel leads to the mouth of Gallinas Creek, named for the Spanish ranch located here in the 19th century, *Rancho San Pedro, Santa Margarita y las Gallinas.*

Anchorage at China Camp

Boaters Anchor Far from Pier, and Shallow Water, at China Camp

From Rat Island to the entrance is about 1.5 miles. From the entrance to the first major fork is another 2 miles. At the fork you may go to the right for about 1.5 miles, ending up behind warehouses in east San Rafael, or to the left for almost 2 miles to the back of the Marin Civic Center, designed by Frank Lloyd Wright. Because the creek wanders among thick stands of swamp grass and pickleweed, the water remains fairly calm even on the windiest of days.

FACILITIES AT CHINA CAMP:

Fishing Pier
Outdoor Showers
Restrooms and Showers
Snack Bar (weekends)

~~~~~

PETALUMA RIVER

N

OVERHEAD POWER CABLE
AUTHORIZED CL 100 FT

2

3

5

PA

McNear Canal

Bridge under
construction
(see note)

SWING BRIDGE
HOR CL 54 FT
VERT CL 4 FT

Petaluma Marina

BASCULE BRIDGE
HOR CL 65 FT
HOR CL 52 FT (OPEN)
VERT CL 5 FT

D Street

2

Dol

6

6

7

(see note E)

Piles
PA

8

OVERHEAD CABLE
AUTH CL 70 FT

P

OVERHEAD POWER CABLE
AUTHORIZED CL 100 FT

*Pipeline
Area*

Obstn

8

6

8

Pipeline Area

8

9

Pi
A

Haystack Ldg

NWP

200

Southbound Boats Entering San Pablo Bay Channel from Petaluma River

PETALUMA

Chart #18652 or #18654
Channel Entrance Marker #5   38°04.25N, 122°25.70W

"Up the lazy river" captures exactly the ambience of a cruise up the Petaluma River. After leaving San Pablo Bay, you'll meander along with the river past housing developments, small marinas, undulating pastures dotted with oak trees, and dairy barns. Now and then you may meet a boat coming down the river.

The serenity today belies the busy past of this waterway, once the third most heavily used in the state. Beginning in 1775 with a band of sailors on a small boat from Juan Manuel de Ayala's ship, the *San Carlos*, looking for a route into Bodega Bay, the Petaluma was a much used waterway for the small boats of Spanish explorers as well as of Russian sailors and game hunters from San Francisco. Larger vessels--paddle-wheel steamboats, cargo sloops, and scow schooners--plied the river when the town of Petaluma was the supply center for inland gold camps and later a busy port for the shipment of manufactured goods.

Some of those San Francisco hunters settled in camps that became the town of Petaluma, which has gone from being one of California's largest cities in the 1860s to the world's egg basket in the early 1900s and the wrist (or arm) wrestling capital of the world for many years before the contest was recently moved to Las Vegas.

ATTRACTIONS

The adjective used frequently to describe Petaluma is "charming." The charm lies in its history, its architecture, its riverfront, but, even more than these, in its small-town atmosphere.

In 1830 General Vallejo built in Petaluma California's largest adobe, now called the Old Adobe. After viewing the Adobe, you can step forward in time a few years with a walking tour of Victorian homes in the "A" Street Historic District. A leaflet to guide you on this tour is available from the Petaluma Visitor's Program. Also of architectural interest downtown on Western Avenue is the row of commercial buildings

with cast iron fronts, these iron fronts mistakenly thought at the time to make structures fireproof.

Petaluma's riverfront is, of course, the reason for the city's existence. The Turning Basin, where pleasure boaters now dock or anchor, was an ox-bow bend in the river, dredged to facilitate shipping. This basin is today the centerpiece of the Petaluma River Walk, with many restaurants and cafes, a brew pub, and shops lining the banks of this wide spot in the river.

Save time to take a casual stroll through one of the town's 36 parks, two of which are quite close to the Turning Basin. Or you may want to wander about the town, talking with the friendly residents or enjoying the quiet of the residential streets.

Carricklee on Petaluma River

APPROACH

While the Petaluma is a placid river, navigating the channel to the river demands your full attention. On the approach from San Francisco Bay, the last easily recognizable point of reference is the Richmond-San Rafael Bridge. From the bridge, the Brothers Islands are easily visible 1.8 miles to the N.

Once abeam of the Brothers, follow a course of 346° mag. for 6.55 miles, passing buoys "1," "2," "3," and "4" en route to the Petaluma channel entrance, which is at Channel Marker "5," topped by a green dayboard. Change course to 327° mag. at Marker "5" and continue for 2.5 miles to Marker G "13" of the

Petaluma Marina and Winding Petaluma River

Petaluma Turning Basin and D Street Bridge

Petaluma Channel. The depth will decrease steadily on this course until you have only about 6 feet of water at the channel entrance at low water.

Approaching from the E, follow the ship channel 6.15 miles from the Carquinez Bridge. At Buoy "9," steer a course of 280° mag. for 4 miles to the Petaluma channel markers "5" and "6." Just prior to the channel, you'll find only 6 feet of depth at low water. If your boat has a deep draft, steer a more S course.

Stay carefully within the channel, well marked to the railroad bridge. The depth in the channel is 6 feet at low water. The depths outside the channel are in places no more than 1 foot. In the 4.7 miles from the entrance to the railroad bridge, the channel makes a number of course changes to port.

The railroad bridge remains open except when trains are crossing the river. If the bridge is closed, you may have to wait as much as 30 minutes.

Immediately beyond the railroad bridge off to starboard, you will see the docks and other structures remaining from the Port Sonoma Marina, now closed because of shoaling.

The Highway 37 overpass (70-foot vertical clearance) is 0.25 mile upriver from the railroad bridge. North of the Highway 37 overpass the river cuts through the countryside for 11 miles to the Petaluma Marina. Stay in the middle of the river all the way to Petaluma except for one section 0.7 mile above

Lakeville, at Cloudy Bend. Because of shoaling, steer wide to the port here to Buoy "5" at Cut B. Be sure to pass buoys "2" and "4" on the starboard. (This shallow water is clearly shown on Chart #18654.) After you pass Buoy "5," maintain a course up the center of the channel to Petaluma Marina.

To get to the Turning Basin, continue for just over 1 mile beyond the Petaluma Marina to the center of town. You must pass through another railroad bridge 100 feet N of the Petaluma Marina. This bridge, as does the previous one on the Petaluma River, stands open except when a train is passing.

Beyond the railroad bridge 150 yards is the Highway 101 overpass (70-foot vertical clearance). In 1 mile after this overpass, the D Street Bridge will block your entry to the Petaluma Turning Basin. You must make an appointment at least 4 hours (but preferably 24 hours) before you would like the bridge opened between the hours of 0800 and 1800. The bridge tender will then be waiting on VHF Channel 09 for a call at that appointed hour. You must follow this procedure for both entering and departing the Turning Basin.

If you wish to have the bridge opened between 1800h and 0800h, you *must* give 24 hours notice.

Contact: Bridge Tender: 707-778-4303 or online at publicworks@ci.petaluma.ca.us

BERTHING

PETALUMA MARINA
Entrance: 38°13.66N, 122°36.91W
Contact: 707-778-4489

The Petaluma Marina, with 196 berths, a fuel dock, and office buildings, is modern and inviting. The marina has plenty of guest slips for visiting boaters. Boaters here who are reluctant to walk the 1.25 miles into town can take their sportboats on an easy and interesting 1-mile trip to the Turning Basin. They can then tie up their sportboats at the end of the dock in front of the Petaluma Yacht Club.

Boaters who wish to dock their boats at the Petaluma Marina can do so without charge for a day during office hours. Call the office to inquire about this option.

The *Petaluma Yacht Club* has no docks but is an active club that will arrange cruise-ins at the Petaluma Marina for members of other yacht clubs. **Contact: 707-765-9725**

FACILITIES

ATM
Fuel Dock (gas and diesel)
Grocery Store (0.5 mile)
Laundromat (1 mile)
Launch Ramp
Pump Out
Restaurant

PETALUMA RIVER TURNING BASIN
D Street Bridge 38°14.08N, 122°38.12W

The Turning Basin provides both berthing and anchoring options. In the Basin is a dock with 875 feet of space for visiting boaters to tie up, most of this space with power and water. Boats may also be anchored in the Turning Basin. **Whether berthing or anchoring in the Basin, boaters must fill out an application, available in a box adjacent to the** Petaluma Yacht Club facility, and pay a fee of $24 a night per boat.

Petaluma is such a popular destination that on a summer weekend, more than 50 boats in the Turning Basin are not uncommon. Power boats generally tie stern to the dock or raft up. Sailboats typically raft up or anchor in the Turning Basin once the docks are full. As have other places in the channel, the Turning Basin has a depth of about 8-10 feet at low water.

FACILITIES

No facilities are available on the dock unless you can obtain reciprocal club privileges at the Petaluma Yacht Club. Since the public dock is in the heart of downtown Petaluma, you will be in easy walking distance of the following:

Banks
Grocery Stores
Laundry
Movie Theatre
Post Office
Restaurants
Shops
WiFi

ANCHORAGES

Anchorage opportunities abound along the Petaluma River. This river is wide enough in most locations for you to anchor safely out of the way of water traffic. Over the years we have frequently seen boats at anchor just N of the Highway 37 bridge. We assume boaters who anchor here go ashore at the remains of the Port Sonoma Marina. Farther N along the river, most of the anchored boats you pass are fishing boats. Essentially, boaters may anchor anywhere along the river that is not within the city limits of Petaluma

The only place within the city limits for boats to anchor, as well as berth, is the Turning Basin in downtown Petaluma. (See above under **Berthing** for details.)

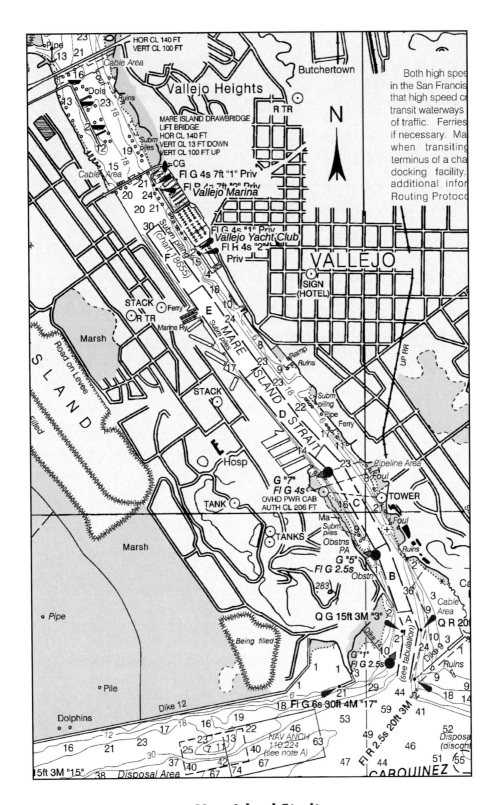

Mare Island Strait

VALLEJO

Chart #18652, #18654, or #18655
Vallejo Yacht Club Entrance   38°06.25N, 122°16.10W
Municipal Marina Entrance   38°11.01N, 122°26.70W

"Damn the torpedoes! Full speed ahead!"

David G. Farragut had the good luck to utter (in the presence of someone standing by to record it) one of those immortal lines that express the emotions of a people at a time of crisis, in this case the Civil War.

Scarcely remembered, though, is Farragut's naval role in the decade before the Civil War, when he served as the first commandant of the U. S. Government's first navy yard, and the first Pacific naval installation, at Mare Island. During the next 117 years, from 1853-1970, the Mare Island Shipyard built more than 500 Navy ships. Closed in 1996, the shipyard leaves behind the legacy of a prosperous community: Vallejo, with a population of 117,000.

The native Suisuns occupied these grassy hills and marshy shores before 1835, when General Mariano Guadalupe Vallejo came to colonize his land grant, which he called Suscol and which encompassed what is now Vallejo, Benicia, Napa, and Sonoma. In the 1840s the settlers called their new home "Eden."

The city of Vallejo was at one time, as was Benicia, a capital of California. Vallejo was the state capital for part of one year in 1852-53. Living and working aboard the steamer *Empire,* members of the legislature met in Vallejo in January, moved to Sacramento for four months, and returned to work in Vallejo until early 1853.

A cruise to Vallejo from the Bay or Delta makes a good weekend adventure. Those coming from the Bay can depart early in the day, slip under the Richmond-San Rafael Bridge before noon, enjoy the 13.4-mile run across San Pablo Bay, and arrive at Vallejo Marina mid-afternoon. They can enjoy the evening in Vallejo and return to the Bay early the next day. If you want a faster ride under sail, and enjoy making a fast passage, then plan to pass the Richmond-San Rafael Bridge early afternoon on a flood.

From the Delta, the 23-mile trip from Pittsburg to Vallejo across Suisun Bay, through the Carquinez Strait, and up the Mare Island Strait is a good day's run. A non-stop passage from the Delta to the Central Bay, with 25-knot winds blowing across Suisun and San Pablo bays, doesn't make good sense. That explains why so many boaters stop in Vallejo.

Plan your departure with a tide guide in hand. From the Bay, pass under the Richmond-San Rafael Bridge just before maximum flood and let the current speed you along. From the Delta, depart just before maximum ebb and ride the current across Suisun Bay.

Whether coming from San Francisco Bay or the Delta, the trip requires only that boaters follow the ship channel.

Because of the private ship repair and dismantling facilities on Mare Island, boaters should be cautious when navigating waters around the island.

ATTRACTIONS

One great attraction of Vallejo, in addition to the exhilarating run across San Pablo Bay or Suisun Bay, is the waterfront along the Vallejo shore of Mare Island Strait. The spiffy new Municipal Marina, with spacious concrete docks and some of the best shower and laundry facilities in the entire Bay Area, is a draw in itself. Combine that with the enhancement the city has added to the waterfront: a wide paved walking/biking path that courses along the water's edge for miles. Vallejo's temperate weather is ideal for outdoor activities.

To make the transition from the waterfront to downtown Vallejo, stop at the Vallejo Naval and His-

Vallejo Yacht Club and Marina and the Napa River

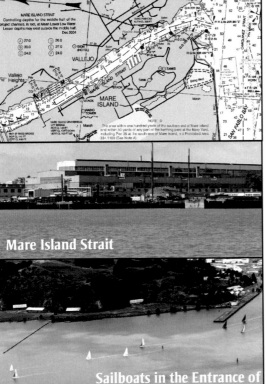

Mare Island Strait

Sailboats in the Entrance of Mare Island Strait

torical Museum on Marin Street in Old Town. Here you can view the city and Mare Island through a working submarine periscope extended through the roof of the museum.

In the city's beautifully restored Old Town is a Heritage Homes District, one of only four nationally recognized districts west of the Mississippi. This District has over thirty architecturally noteworthy Victorian residences, in a range and mixture of styles, this mix sometimes called the "Working Man's Victorian." Although these homes are all occupied and not open to the public, a walking tour through the neighborhood will arouse your appreciation for the skills and imagination of the architects and the craftsmen.

Old Town has a practical attraction: You can lay in a fresh store of produce with a visit to the Farmers Market on Georgia Street every Saturday, 900-1300.

If you've come to the Bay Area with the idea of doing most of your sightseeing from your boat, the Vallejo Transit provides bus service to Discovery Kingdom, a wildlife park especially stimulating to sailors of all ages.

BERTHING

VALLEJO MUNICIPAL MARINA
Contact: 707-648-4370   VHF 16

Having more than 670 slips, with lengths from 20-110 feet, Vallejo Marina is certainly one of the largest marinas in the San Francisco area. This marina is ideally situated between the Sacramento-San Joaquin Delta and San Francisco Bay. For visiting boaters, it is conveniently located at the edge of Old Town Vallejo, at the N end of the Downtown Marina Waterfront.

The newly remodeled portion of the marina has concrete docks and excellent facilities.

FACILITIES AT OR NEAR THE MARINA:

ATM
Boat Maintenance and Repair
City Bus
Ferry Service to Angel Island and San Francisco
    (Ferry Bldg., Fisherman's Wharf, and Pier 39)
Fuel Dock (gasoline and diesel)
Grocery Store
Haul Out
Launch Ramp
Laundry
Pump Out
Restaurants

APPROACH

To get to the Vallejo Marina, enter the Mare Island Strait 1 mile W of the Carquinez Bridge on the N side of the Carquinez Strait. Mare Island Strait is a well-marked ship channel. A dike extends from both shores to control waves and swell inside the Strait. The dike on the E side extends 700 yards into the channel, and the W dike extends 500 yards out from Mare Island. The outer 110 yards of the W dike is submerged. Lights mark the ends of the dikes.

Vallejo Marina is on the starboard side of the channel, 2.6 miles from the entrance to Mare Island Strait. The blue-roofed white buildings of the marina office are easily visible from the channel.

No anchorage exists in the area. Even though Mare Island is no longer a U.S. Naval shipyard, private boaters may not anchor off its shores nor land on the island.

Vallejo Yacht Club

VALLEJO YACHT CLUB
Entrance 38°06.25N, 122°16.10W
Contact: 707-643-1254

Immediately S of the Vallejo Marina is the Vallejo Yacht Club, the fourth oldest yacht club in Northern California. This club offers privileges to members of other yacht clubs.

FACILITIES NEAR THE YACHT CLUB:

Bank
Grocery Store
City Bus Service
Ferry Service to Angel Island and San Francisco
    (Ferry Bldg., Fisherman's Wharf, and Pier 39)
Restaurants

Two Bridges in Mare Island Strait

Much of the pleasure of the trips up the rivers and estuaries that flow in and out of San Francisco Bay comes from the passage itself. On a summer's day you leave the cool, sometimes overcast and windy Bay to pass through another one or more climate zones, each successively warmer than the last.

By the way, if you're averse to the heat, these are trips you might choose to make in the spring or fall; however, if you want a change from the cool fog of a San Francisco Bay summer, a trip up one of the rivers of the North Bay could be just your ticket.

NAPA

Chart #18652 or #18654
Mare Island Strait Entrance 38°04.21N, 122°14.76W
Mare Island Bridge 38°06.64N, 122°16.50W
Highway 37 Bridge 38°07.23N, 122°16.80W

Going up the Napa River, you soon enter a world of flat sloughs lined with dark green pickleweed and punctuated now and then by a Snowy Egret or a flock of Willets. Shortly after, grassy rolling fields appear, golden brown from the dry summer heat, some of them populated with grazing dairy cattle.

Farther along, orderly rows of grapevines march up the undulating slopes of the vineyards that have made Napa prosperous. And then come the bridges, some of them fixed with clearance for sailboats and other ocean-going vessels, others, swing bridges or drawbridges that must be moved before vessels can continue up the river.

Such a trip is also an exploration of history as you pass dilapidated docks, half-sunken barges, and hulls of fishing boats and abandoned cargo ships, reminding you the Napa River was once an important route of commerce between San Francisco and the farms and towns of the Sacramento and Napa valleys and the gold mines of the Mother Lode. Scow schooners and barges carried grain, lumber, furs, and fish down the Napa to San Francisco and returned with manufactured products. Some commercial traffic still travels this river, but the majority of the boats seen today are private fishing boats and pleasure crafts.

ATTRACTIONS

For boaters anchoring out along the River's edge, the attractions are the peaceful nights and the days of watching the waterfowl and the boats going up and down the river. You can take your cruising boat or tender up the river for a look at the river side of the town of Napa. Tie up at the Main Street Boat Dock during summer months and go ashore to explore the city. South of the Highway 29 Bridge you can take a trail along the levee for a couple of miles, with a good view of the fields and hills to the W and the river to the E.

Just N of the bridge is Horseshoe Slough, an ideal vantage point for viewing egrets and herons roosting in the trees. Or you can go into the Napa Valley Marina fuel dock and go ashore for supplies or tie up at one of the docks at the public park just N of the marina, where nearby is the one accessible restaurant in this immediate area.

The John F. Kennedy Memorial Park, N of the marina on the E side of the river, also has a dock. Here, you can go ashore for picnics and hikes both N and S along the levee.

This destination has such a quiet, restful atmosphere you'll regret when your allotted time to spend here has passed.

APPROACH

Boaters cruising to Napa will depart from Vallejo. (See the section on Vallejo for directions to Vallejo Marina.) Immediately N of the Vallejo Marina is the Mare Island Causeway Bridge. Bridge tenders answer on **VHF 13 or 707-648-4313**, and they will also open the bridge if you give them one long and one short blast on your horn.

Plan to arrive at the bridge at some time other than peak highway traffic hours to avoid an excessively long wait. Bridge tenders open the bridge between the hours of 0900 and 1900. Of all the bridge tenders we've encountered in this area on our cruises, the Vallejo tender is unquestionably the friendliest and most willing to help boaters traveling up the river.

After you clear the Mare Island Causeway Bridge, travel 0.6 mile to the Highway 37 Bridge, a fixed bridge with a 100-foot vertical clearance. Past the highway bridge, the scenery changes dramatically, with few signs of civilization for the 12 miles from the bridge to Napa Marina.

Napa Valley Marina

As you transit the Napa River, watch your depths closely to keep from drifting out of the channel. If you stay in the middle of the channel, you will find at least 9.0 feet of water for the entire distance between Vallejo and Napa Slough. If you stray from the channel, however, you will likely find instead water no more than 1 or 2 feet deep.

While making this passage, keep your chart in the cockpit and your eyes on the channel markers. Looking at your chart, you'll see that in some instances you'll not be able to go directly from one marker to another but will have to make a curve to stay in the channel. Local boaters warn that in particular you must swing wide at Marker "11" because of shoaling. If the depth does begin to shallow significantly, slow down and find the channel again by moving very slowly to port or to starboard.

BERTHING

NAPA VALLEY MARINA
Entrance: 38°13.22N, 122°18.65W
Contact: 707-252-8011

Most visiting cruisers stop at the Napa Valley Marina, on the port side just above the railroad bridge. This marina has slips for about 200 boats, and the harbormaster can usually accommodate cruising boaters if they call two days ahead.

Guests are normally directed to tie up at the long dock in front of the haul-out facility. An unusual feature about this marina is the large boatyard, where a large hydraulic trailer hauls out the boats and where boaters are permitted to work on their own boats.

No restaurants are in the marina, but if you have a tender along, you can use it to get to a restaurant less than a mile away. The store by the marina office carries some provisions but also carries a good selection of marine equipment and supplies. This marina is well run, and the people are friendly, making this a pleasant cruising destination.

APPROACH

You will pass through the Brazzo Train Bridge 6.5 miles N of the Highway 37 bridge. It remains open except when a train is approaching. Edgerly Island is on the left for the last 1.5 miles before you arrive at the marina; this island has numerous homes on the port side of the river. The Napa Valley Marina is to port, 0.75 mile above the Train Bridge.

FACILITIES AT THE
NAPA VALLEY MARINA

Chandlery (in the marina store)
Fuel Dock (gas and diesel)
Groceries (limited)
Haul Out
Launch Ramp
Pump Out
Restaurant

NAPA VALLEY YACHT CLUB
Entrance 38°17.13N, 122°17.14W
Contact: 707-252-3342

Visitors from other yacht clubs can tie up at the 185-foot guest dock at the Napa Valley Yacht Club. From this dock, they can take a pleasant half-mile walk into the town of Napa, as well as enjoy the camaraderie and activities at the yacht club.

FACILITIES

Bocce Ball Court
Launch Ramp
WiFi

APPROACH

The Highway 29 Bridge, with a vertical clearance of 60 feet, is another 4.5 miles N of the Brazzo Train Bridge. Immediately above the Highway 29 Bridge, 0.75 mile on the port side, is the Napa Valley Yacht Club, with its guest dock in front of the clubhouse.

A few docks are farther up the river, one being the Sea Scouts dock with its large ex-Coast Guard craft. The end of the navigable Napa River is immediately before the Third Street Bridge in downtown Napa.

Don't confuse the Napa Valley Yacht Club with the Napa Yacht Club. The Napa Yacht Club is an up-scale, on-the-water housing development on the W side of the river, 0.25 mile *below* the Highway 29 Bridge. The Napa Yacht Club has a private marina reserved for tenants only and does not accommodate visiting boaters.

ANCHORAGES

South Slough 38°08.73N, 122°17.30W
Napa Slough 38°11.10N, 122°18.90W
North of Railroad Bridge 38°12.74N, 122°18.45W

Boaters who like to anchor out can find many good spots in the Napa area. Local sailors recommend a site 1.75 miles N of the Napa Valley Marina, on the W side of the river near the eucalyptus trees. Be sure not to anchor in the center of the river because tugs occasionally bring barges up the river. (You should show an anchor light at night because of river traffic.)

Observe the signs warning of cable and gas pipelines crossing the river in the area; anchor between those signs. The current can be strong here, so anchor securely. To avoid being swept into shallow water or into the middle of the channel as the tide changes, boaters use two anchors or tie to a tree on shore and put out a stern anchor.

The Napa River offers many other possible anchorages. Boaters have anchored just N of the Highway 37 Bridge on the outskirts of Vallejo for years. The preferred spot is just S of Marker "2." If you choose to anchor here, anchor out of the channel to avoid the tugs in the river but not so far that you end up aground at low tide.

Local boaters also anchor at the entrance of either South Slough or Napa Slough. In both cases you can anchor just out of the Napa River channel or a short distance up inside the sloughs. Notice that the Napa Slough has markers indicating the center of the slough.

These sloughs can be wonderful anchorages in the fall when the winds are non-existent, but the winds blow strongly during the spring and summer, making them uncomfortable even though the vegetation along the banks of the sloughs keeps the water relatively calm.

We have also seen boats anchored in a wide spot just N of the railroad bridge at Edgerly Island on the E side of the river. This should be a good anchorage because the wind doesn't blow so strongly as in the South and Napa sloughs. In addition, the marina, where you can purchase supplies, is a short run from here.

Boaters anchor, as well, at other places along the W side of the Napa River N of the Napa Valley Marina, taking advantage of the shelter afforded by the eucalyptus trees that line the bank.

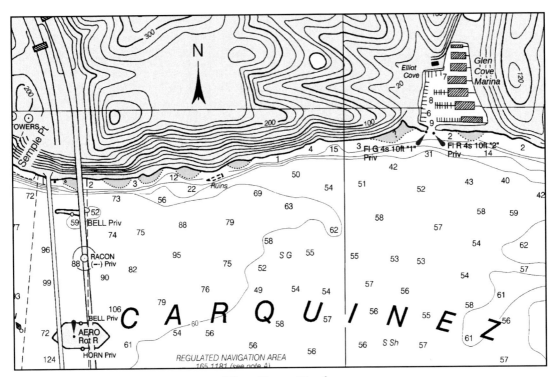

Glen Cove Marina

Glen Cove Marina Entrance

GLEN COVE MARINA

Chart #18652 or #18657
Marina Entrance 38°03.94N, 122°12.81W
Contact: 707-552-3236   glencovemarina@gmail.com

For the Bay Area boater who wants to get way away—and have the twin stimulants of traversing San Pablo Bay and trying to avoid going aground on the shoals once at the destination—Glen Cove Marina is the answer. Until the late 1980s, this was an isolated cove linked to nearby highways by a dirt road to the old Glen farm. Now, houses cover the hills, but Glen Cove Marina still seems far removed from civilization. Adding to the sense of isolation is the tranquil atmosphere of the small marina of 209 slips.

The harbormaster's office is in a building built in 1910 as a lighthouse and lifesaving station. It was brought by barge from the breakwater at Vallejo to Glen Cove in 1957. Except for the removal of the lighthouse tower, it is in its original configuration. To see how it looked as a working lighthouse, observe the refurbished lighthouse, now a bed and breakfast, on East Brother.

The two lighthouses share a common design. Rather than housing a bed and breakfast facility, however, the first floor of the historic structure at Glen Cove houses the harbormaster's office and a separate banquet facility. On the second floor are vacation rental apartments.

Boaters who knew Glen Cove Marina in the past will hardly recognize the current marina. The old docks have been either repaired or replaced, the old lighthouse building has been repaired and repainted, and the grounds are tastefully landscaped.

On the hills around the marina attractive homes line the curving streets. A hiking trail along the cliffs above the water overlooks the busy waters of Carquinez Strait, the Carquinez Bridge, and the rolling hills to the south. Though portions of this trail, a part of the San Francisco Bay Trail, are somewhat steep, the surrounding views will reward the effort.

The pilings W of Glen Cove are remnants of a grain dock, one of the many that once lined the banks of Carquinez Strait to load ships with wheat and barley bound for ports around the world.

At Glen Cove Marina is a fine new 100-foot concrete dock, just E of the old lighthouse building, that can accommodate a number of guest boats, and the harbormaster will gladly put guests in any empty slips.

ATTRACTIONS

Glen Cove has only itself to attract boaters. Steep hills carpeted with wildflowers in the spring cradle this diminutive cove. Across the Strait the lights of the sugar refinery at Crockett gleam at night, but you hear only the sounds of the water lapping at high tide or of the geese and ducks honking and quacking overhead.

APPROACH

Plan for the trip to Glen Cove to offer a little of everything. Coming from the Bay, don't choose your departure time casually. First, choose a time that will allow you to arrive at the marina at or near high tide.

Second, depart on a flood or slack tide to avoid battling a 4- or 5-knot ebb tide. And finally, choose a departure time to take advantage of the kind of winds that are best for your boat. During the morning hours, you will generally encounter light winds and calm seas. Afternoon winds from the NW often blow at 20 knots or more, creating lumpy seas.

The distance between the Richmond-San Rafael Bridge and the Carquinez Bridge is only 14.4 miles, so that part of the trip can be relatively short if you take advantage of tide and wind.

Glen Cove is easy to recognize from the Carquinez Strait. After you pass under the Carquinez Bridge (134-foot clearance), proceed 0.6 mile E. The entrance to the marina appears suddenly off to your port. Identify the metal roofing of the many covered powerboat slips and the large 25-room white lighthouse and lifesaving station tucked back inside the cove. A sign on the E side of the entrance identifies the marina, but, because Glen Cove is the first marina on the port side after the Carquinez Bridge, you'll not likely miss it.

If you are approaching from the Delta, pass under the Benicia-Martinez Bridge and proceed W through the Carquinez Strait for 5.1 miles.

Entering Glen Cove Marina offers as much excitement as most boaters need. Like all other marinas in the Carquinez Strait, Glen Cove Marina personnel struggle to keep ahead of the shoaling. At high water, most boats will have sufficient water depths to go in without going aground, but enter only after checking with the harbormaster.

Be especially observant of the currents when entering the marina. With a strong ebb or flood, you will encounter a number of changes in the direction of the current as you enter. This erratic current can turn around a slow-moving light boat.

FACILITIES AT GLEN COVE MARINA

Many of you probably won't be tempted to walk to town from Glen Cove Marina since the nearest town is Vallejo, about a 3-mile trek up a steep hill.

Laundry
Public transportation
Pump Out
WiFi (free)

Curlew in San Francisco Marsh

View from Boat at Dillon

Dillon Point Anchorage

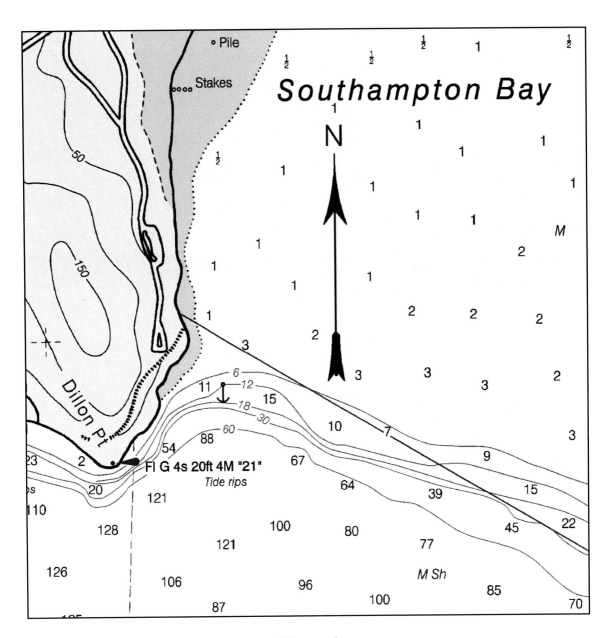

Dillon Point

DILLON POINT
(PREVIOUSLY CALLED ROCKY POINT OR QUARRY POINT)
Chart #18652 or #18656
Anchorage 38°03.66N, 122°11.41W

The anchorage at Dillon Point in Southampton Bay is important because it is the only one for miles in any direction. It is a beautiful and secure anchorage for those who want to spend a few hours or a few days on the anchor.

It is also, however, a convenient stopover for those sailing from the Central Bay to destinations beyond the Carquinez Bridge in the North Bay or in the Delta, where the tides determine when boats may transit the channels, rivers, and marina entrances.

The lands around Southampton Bay were home to the Patwins, approximately 3,300 of whom were living around the bay when the Spanish padres were here between 1800 and 1820, attempting to convert them to Catholicism.

Though Southampton Bay is a good-sized body of water, the anchorage area is small because of significant shoaling, with room for only one or two boats to swing comfortably. The best anchorage is approximately 100 yards N of the "21" light at Dillon Point in 20 feet of water. Use caution as you approach the anchorage: the water shallows quickly, and much of Southampton Bay is marsh.

Drop anchor here in 20 feet on a mud bottom and back down into deeper water, letting out anchor chain as you go. We anchored at Dillon recently, where we let out 100 feet of chain; the current carried us N toward the shallow water in the Bay. When our boat came to rest, we were in 15 feet of water, pointed directly toward the car parking lot on the side hill N of Dillon Point.

Though winds from the W typically funnel through Carquinez Strait and N winds may come over the hills, boats at anchor behind Dillon Point still ride comfortably. The winds in both cases are greatly diminished, and the water's surface in Southampton Bay is protected. In other words, boats anchored behind Dillon have reasonably good protection from the strong winds and uncomfortable waves. We have enjoyed a comfortable stay even though the W winds were blowing 15-20 knots only a few hundred feet away in Carquinez Strait.

In S or E winds, Dillon Point would provide neither a secure nor a comfortable anchorage.

ATTRACTIONS

Though the anchorage at Dillon Point, part of the Benicia State Recreation Area, is close to the Carquinez Bridge and to Benicia and Martinez, it feels remote. Despite houses and business establishments in Benicia visible to the N and E, nothing and no one is close to this anchorage, unless you count the occasional hikers on the Dillon Point trail around the Bay. The head of the Bay is a marshland, where several varieties of endangered plants and wildlife thrive.

The shoreline near the anchorage is rocky, but boaters can land a dinghy or a kayak a short distance to the N of the anchorage area. The trail along the edge of the Bay provides not only excellent hiking but birding opportunities as well.

APPROACH

Boaters arriving from San Francisco Bay will pass under the Carquinez Bridge and proceed 1.6 miles E, passing Glen Cove Marina, on the N shore immediately past the bridge, but before reaching Dillon's Point on the same side of Carquinez Strait. The Green Navigation Light "21" marks the Point. To the N and E of Dillon Point is the Benicia State Recreation Area, easily accessible through Southampton Bay.

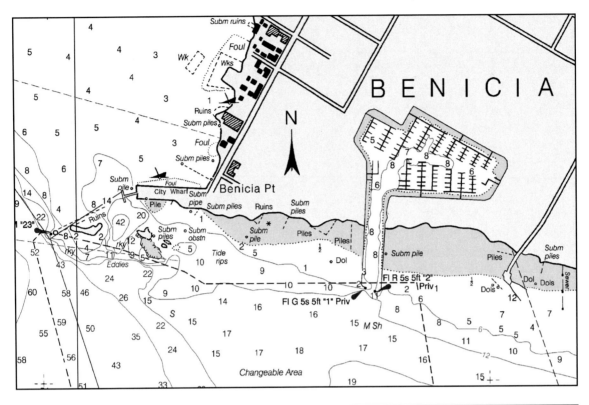

Benicia Marina

BENICIA

Chart #18652 or #18657
Entrance 38°02.49N, 122°09.47W
Contact: 707-745-2628   VHF 16

A weekend cruise to Benicia is popular with Bay Area boaters looking for a relaxing two- or three-day cruise. The run N through San Francisco Bay, across San Pablo Bay, and then down Carquinez Strait can be boating at its best, and Benicia gives one a sense of being in another world and time. It has wonderful spring, summer, and fall weather, with sunny days cooled by the breeze off the strait. In some ways, Benicia will remind you of a town in the Mother Lode: small, quiet, and clean, and on every corner a building or a site that figured in the town's lively past.

Founded in 1847 on land deeded to Dr. Robert Semple by General Mariano Vallejo, Benicia was named after Vallejo's wife. The town soon became one of the most important towns in the Bay Area as a point of departure for gold prospectors traveling from the San Francisco Peninsula to the Mother Lode.

In 1849 the U. S. Army established Benicia Barracks (later renamed *Benicia Arsenal*), one of the strategic forts for the defense of San Francisco Bay. In 1850 Benicia and Monterey were the first two California cities to incorporate.

Benicia's enduring claim to a place in California history is its short tenure as the state's capital. For thirteen months in 1853-54 the legislature met here in what had been the city hall. However, Sacramento's larger size and proximity to the gold fields attracted the legislators, and the governor had a home there. So the capital was moved.

Greater promise for Benicia's economic future came in 1879 when it was designated as the site of a transcontinental railroad depot. Trains were loaded onto the then world's largest ferry and taken across Carquinez Strait to Port Costa, where they continued on by rail to San Francisco. During this same period, Benicia was the principal hide-tanning center of the Pacific Coast and the site of numerous canneries to process both fish and produce.

Then in 1882 one of San Francisco's most successful shipbuilders, Matthew Turner, moved his shipyard to Benicia, where he turned out more than 115 ships in the next twenty years. Turner designed the famous *Nautilus* and the *Galilee*. (The stern of the *Galilee* is on display in the San Francisco Maritime Museum.) Benicia's boom days had come indeed!

Historic State Capitol

ATTRACTIONS

The pleasures of a small town are easy to experience in Benicia. Many sites of historic interest are centrally located and near the marina. The historic California State Capitol, the Fischer-Hanlon House and Gardens, and the Tannery are but three sites meriting a visit.

Walk out to the waterfront and marvel at the skill of the windsurfers in the strait. Or, better still, get out and join them. The strait here is one of the best windsurfing spots on the West Coast.

Benicia Marina Office and Fuel Dock

Benicia Yacht Club

The trip to Benicia can be quick and exhilarating, depending on your time of departure and the tide state. From the Richmond-San Rafael Bridge to the Carquinez Bridge is 14.4 miles, and Benicia is only another 3.6 miles beyond.

Use your tide book to plan your trip. If a 4.6-knot flood tide is running when you make the passage, you can easily cut two hours off the usual time. Conversely, if a 4.6-knot ebb is running, you can add two hours or more. Pass under the Richmond-San Rafael Bridge just before maximum flood to ride the flood into Benicia.

Boaters looking for a calm passage should cross San Pablo Bay before early afternoon, while the winds are light and the seas flat. Sailors looking for more action can enjoy a boisterous broad reach by crossing later in the day. Occasionally, though, the winds blow directly out of the S, providing a beam reach in nearly flat seas.

After passing under the Carquinez Bridge, continue E along Carquinez Strait. At 3.0 miles, Marker "23," on the port side, designates the remains of the old Benicia wharf. The entrance to the marina is 0.5 mile beyond Marker "23."

Though harbor policy is to keep the entrance and marina dredged to a depth of 7 feet at low water, personnel often cannot keep up with the shoaling. While you're not likely to go aground at high water, don't count on more than 3-4 feet at low.

If you are approaching from the E, pass under the Benicia-Martinez Bridge and continue 2.0 miles W to the Benicia Marina.

Recognize the marina entrance by identifying the breakwaters that extend 500 feet into Carquinez Strait. Enter the marina through the 60-foot-wide entrance between the two breakwaters. Traditional navigation lights are at the end of each breakwater.

Note! Begin the trip back to San Francisco Bay early, and take advantage of an ebb. Winds normally blow at 20 knots or more on the nose across San Pablo Bay in the afternoon. By mid-afternoon the waves are steep and choppy. If you depart after midday on a flood, you will find yourself weathering quite a thrash to windward.

BERTHING

BENICIA MARINA

With 350 slips, Benicia Marina can normally provide guest slips for most visitors. Since this is a popular destination, you should call ahead. Tie up at the fuel dock, taking care not to block the pumps, while you sign in with the harbormaster. The Benicia harbormaster's office closes at 1700h, so plan to arrive before that time, or call ahead to make arrangements.

The *Benicia Yacht Club* clubhouse is an elegant structure up the street from the marina. **Contact: 707-746-0739.**

FACILITIES

Benicia Marina is only a block E of First Street, the heart of town, where restaurants, shops, and other businesses abound.

Fuel Dock (gasoline and diesel)
Small Store with drinks and snacks
Launch Ramp
Laundry
Pump Out

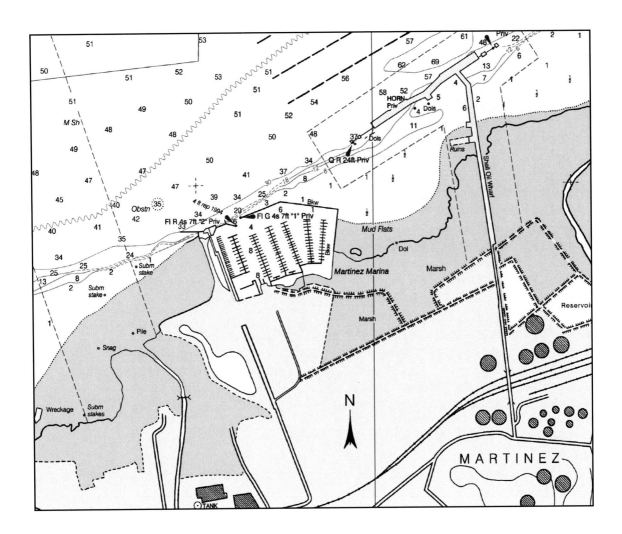

Martinez Marina

MARTINEZ

Chart #18652 and #18657
Entrance 38°01.63N, 122°08.29W
Contact: 925-313-0942   VHF 16

The only skyline of the modest town of Martinez, strategically located at the upper reaches of Carquinez Strait, is the array of monolithic petroleum storage tanks erected for Shell Oil's Martinez Manufacturing Complex. Don't let the dominance of this skyline mislead you, however. Martinez really is much more than a company town, though the petroleum industry contributes significantly to its economic well-being. As a cruising destination, Martinez has much to entice you, even if you're not interested in admiring tanks on hillsides.

Martinez arose on this spot because California's only state-owned ferry began its run from this spot across Carquinez Strait to Benicia in 1847, with the use of true horse power. This ferry, pulled by horses from shore to opposite shore on cables, was the primary access to the Gold Country for gold seekers coming through San Francisco.

Some of the visitors to this stopover on the Argonaut Trail stayed on and founded a town. The sandy beaches (now long since silted over), the mild climate, and the cooling breezes blowing off the Strait were apparently beguiling. On September 14, 1962, the *Carquinez,* the last passenger ferry, then also carrying cars to Benicia, made its final run, ending 115 years of ferry service across Carquinez Strait between Martinez and Benicia.

The Central Pacific Railroad completed its connection to Martinez in 1879. Ocean-going vessels docked in Martinez to load grain brought by rail, scow schooners, and barges. At this time Central California was the largest grain-producing area in the nation. By 1884, grain wharves were continuous along 4 or 5 miles of the strait, but by the early 20th century these wharves were no longer profitable and fell into disuse and disrepair.

Sicilian fishermen stayed on where they docked their *feluccas* used to tend their salmon, shad, and bass nets. One might assume some member of this Italian community was responsible for inventing the "martini," which is reported to have originated in Martinez.

However the local account of the name is that it was a shortened version of "Martinez," this latter name too much to pronounce after two or three martinis. Julio Richelieu is credited with being the first to pour this combination of gin and vermouth to a thirsty returning miner in a Martinez bar in 1874.

Don Ygnacio Martinez, commander of the San Francisco Presidio between 1822 and 1831, held a Spanish grant to this area of rolling hills, the Rancho El Pinole. The town named after him arose on the shores of what was then a much wider and deeper strait.

The site of the present Martinez harbor had just under 50 feet of water before the 20th Century. The silt from the Sacramento and San Joaquin rivers flowing into Suisun Bay continues to create a perpetual challenge to all the marinas in the North Bay-Delta waters.

ATTRACTIONS

Excellent walking and biking trails are close by, many along the shoreline. The East Bay Regional Shoreline Park schedules bird walks regularly. If you miss one, take some bird seed to the small lake SE of the marina, and surround yourself with as many geese and ducks as can fit on the grassy knoll.

In keeping with the Italian influence in Martinez, Waterfront Park has 15 bocce ball courts. If bocce is not your sport of choice, one of the fourteen parks, several within walking distance

Harbor Office at Martinez

Bocce Ball Courts at Martinez

of the marina, will surely have facilities to interest you.

On display in the marina is the inboard runabout of baseball legend Joe DiMaggio. The marina also has one of the better fishing piers around, where striped bass, sturgeon, and flounder are commonly caught. Check with the local bait and tackle shop regarding current fishing regulations.

With a short walk into town, you'll find the largest number of shops selling antiques and collectibles in Contra Costa County. You'll also find one of the cleanest, prettiest towns around. Wide brick sidewalks take you past well-preserved stores and houses from the 1800s and classic structures from the first half of the 20th Century.

On Fridays and Sundays, between May and September, two popular farmers' markets occupy much of Main Street. Martinez has the sort of downtown for a leisurely afternoon of strolling and browsing before returning to the quiet marina to watch sea and shore birds feeding at sunset.

APPROACH

Boaters coming from San Francisco Bay will go under the Richmond-San Rafael Bridge, across San Pablo Bay, under the Carquinez Bridge, and then 4.7 miles through Carquinez Strait. The Martinez Marina is on the S shore of the strait 1.0 mile W of the Benicia-Martinez Bridge and 0.2 mile SW of the Shell Oil pier, where ocean-going tankers tie up. The remnants of the old ferry dock may be the best identifying feature for boaters approaching Martinez Marina, although the sailboat masts behind the breakwater also make the marina location obvious.

Enter Martinez Marina only at high water unless you check with the harbormaster. Like most Carquinez Strait and Delta marinas, Martinez has serious difficulties keeping up with the shoaling. Constant shoaling frequently reduces depths to 5 feet or less at mean low water.

BERTHING

Martinez Marina offers guest berthing at reasonable rates. Tie up at the long 160-foot dock and go to the harbormaster's office to check in.

The **Martinez Yacht Club** has a clubhouse across the street from the marina and will arrange for cruise-ins from other yacht clubs. **Contact: 925-228-5520**

FACILITIES AT OR NEAR THE MARINA:

The marina is only a few blocks from Martinez, where you can find all the facilities of a small town.

Amtrak
Bait and Tackle Shop
Banks
Boat Maintenance and Repair
Car Shows (year round)
Farmers Market (seasonal)
Haul Out
Launch Ramp
Laundry
Pump Out
Restaurants
Shops
WiFi (free and fee)

*There is something about a Martini
Ere the dining and dancing begin
And to tell you the truth
It's not the vermouth—
I think that perhaps it's the gin.*
        —Ogden Nash, "The Primrose Path"

*Why don't you slip out of those wet clothes
and into a dry Martini?*
        —Robert Benchley

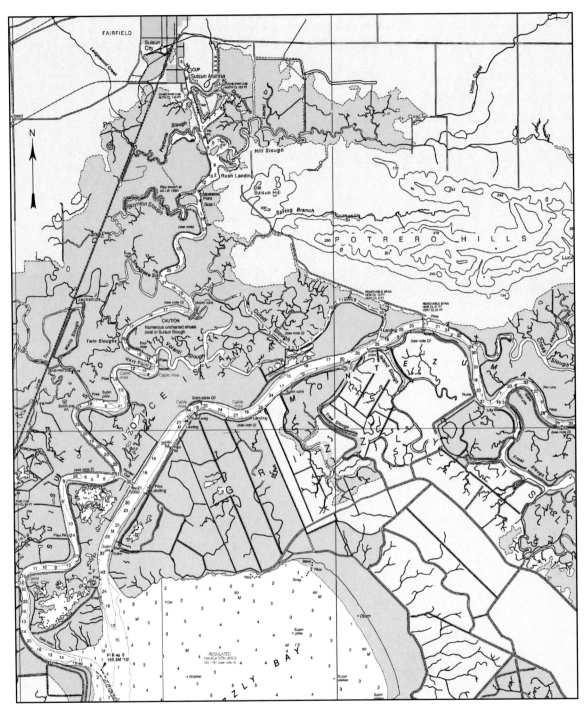

Suisun Slough and Marina

SUISUN CITY

Chart #18656 or #18652
Montezuma Slough Entrance   38°08.55N, 122°03.70W
Hunter Cut Entrance   38°09.35N, 122°03.17W
City Marina Entrance   38°14.31N, 122°02.34W
Contact: VHF 16   707-429-0284   FAX 707-425-7699

As part of its redevelopment project, Suisun City began in 1990 to dredge and widen the badly silted Suisun Slough, a 12-mile waterway emptying into the north end of Suisun Bay. Also part of the city's redevelopment project was the building of Suisun City Marina in 1994. This marina sits in the heart of Old Suisun City, a place with plenty of history and a world of charm.

The native Patwins who inhabited these shores before the arrival of the Europeans harvested the many species of fish, fowl and game abundant in and around the slough.

The Gold Rush was instrumental in the settlement that became Suisun City. Beginning in 1851, miners came up the slough by boat as far as this site and then made their way by land to the gold fields. In 1851, too, steamers began using the slough to transport commercial goods to and from San Francisco. By 1854 the town had streets and a name: *Suisun*, meaning *west wind*, which does indeed blow through these hills.

Suisun City continued to prosper as a port and, later, as the agricultural hub of Solano County. In 1869 Suisun City became a link to the East Coast via the transcontinental railroad. The town's prosperity waned when trucks replaced rail as the primary mode for the transport of commercial goods.

The redevelopment project begun in 1990 restored vitality to the Old Town and its adjacent waterfront. Main Street, one block from the marina, bustles with small-town activity and atmosphere. Ideal for visiting boaters, Main Street invites walking. You'll feel right at home as you stroll along the side streets of turn-of-the century houses and churches and wander into the shops and restaurants along Main.

ATTRACTIONS

In Suisun City you can discover, as did the native Patwins, the bounty of wildlife in these prime wetlands. Fishing is excellent, either from shore or from your tender. Catfish, striped bass, sturgeon, and salmon are among the tasty catches in the sloughs, and local boaters even report catching these behind their boats in the marina.

If viewing is more to your taste, pick up a copy of the Solano History Center publication *Downtown Suisun City Self-Guided History Walking Tour* from the harbormaster or at the Solano History Exploration Center. This excellent guide will enable you to walk the city streets, looking at the historic structures and learning their history.

If natural history is one of your interests, you can walk along the slough to view the abundant waterfowl here and visit the modest but interesting Wildlife Center of the Suisun Marsh Natural History Association on Kellogg Street.

From there, stroll over to Main Street past the attractive Town Plaza, a grass semicircle adorned with a granite and bronze stage and a segmented glass-domed gazebo. At the north end of Main and one block west is Rail Station Plaza, where Amtrak makes an impressive 23 stops each day at its only Solano County stop between San Francisco and Sacramento.

APPROACH

The trip to Suisun City offers challenge, adventure, and diversity. Plan carefully to make certain you use the weather and tide to advantage. To begin, consider the distance. Once at Vallejo, you are still about 18 miles from Suisun City, so plan accord-

Ships of the Mothball Fleet

ingly. Study your charts carefully before making this passage. Observe that two separate channels begin fairly immediately NE of the Benicia-Martinez Highway Bridge. The channel to starboard leads up into the Delta. The one to port leads to Suisun and Montezuma sloughs and on into Grizzly Bay.

After you pass under the Benicia-Martinez Bridge, follow the channel to your port. Identify Buoy R "2," slightly more than 0.5 mile NE of the Bridge, being careful to keep it as well as R "4" and R "6" to starboard. Do not stray outside the channel to starboard, or you'll be aground in short order.

The Mothball Fleet (decommissioned Navy ships) will be on your port side as you proceed up the channel. These ships are currently being removed, however, so, when you make this passage, you can expect to see fewer than the fifteen ships moored there as this book went to press.

After passing Buoy "6," continue on to Buoy G "9" on your port, but do not turn into Suisun Slough at R "10" because of areas of shallow water between this entrance and Hunter Cut.

Instead follow the lead of local boaters, who go from Buoy G "9" to the entrance into Montezuma Slough and take Montezuma to Hunter Cut to take them into Suisun Slough above the shallow water. You may have trouble identifying the entrance into Montezuma Slough because the tule grass blends together and makes the slough hard to see. On a course of about 345° mag., you'll go 2.1 miles to the entrance into Montezuma Slough, approximately at 38°08.55N, 122°03.70W. (**Note:** Because of the possibility of seasonal changes in the stands of tule grass, this waypoint must be considered approximate.)

To reach Hunter Cut, continue NE through Montezuma Slough for 0.8 mile, to approximately 38°09.35N, 122°03.15W, where you'll turn to port into the Cut, which will terminate in Suisun Slough, where you'll wind your way NE to Suisun City Marina.

The trip from Hunter Cut up to Suisun City is picturesque, of course, since you travel through almost totally uninhabited marshlands. Powerboats have the advantage on this trip because those on the bridge can see over the levees, and, of course, because the powerboats generally have shallower draft.

Local boaters warn visitors to be aware of the shoaling on the inside of the turn at Navy Point. Swing this turn wide, or you'll be hard aground, even at high tide. The harbormaster at Suisun Marina advises boaters to stay in the center of the channel up to Suisun City, where they'll find a consistent minimum of 10 feet of water.

Winds are another factor to consider. In the spring and summer, the prevailing westerlies normally blow across Suisun Bay at 20-30 knots during the afternoons. Once inside the sloughs, however, the winds are not a problem.

The passage to Suisun City is challenging, but no more so than the trip to Napa or Petaluma, and it certainly isn't as challenging as the trip to Alviso. Sailboats drawing 6 feet regularly make the trip, so plan the trip with confidence.

BERTHING

Guest Dock Downtown

Metal Art at Suisun Marina

SUISUN CITY MARINA

Guest berthing is generally available at the *Suisun City Marina* (150 berths). On the guest dock, visiting boats may tie up for a maximum of 72 hours with no charge. This dock has neither power nor water. Otherwise, the harbor master will assign guests to vacant berths in the marina for a minimal fee.

The *Solano Yacht Club,* 707-425-7699, VHF 16 or 68, can provide guest berthing for visiting members of yacht clubs who call ahead.

FACILITIES AT OR NEAR THE MARINA:

The marina is on one of the streets of the revitalized historic old town of Suisun City, this convenient location giving boaters easy access to a wide array of shops and restaurants.

At the marina:
Fuel (gasoline and diesel)
Launch Ramp
Pump Out (free)

ANCHORAGE

As you might expect, you can find several spots to anchor in both Montezuma and Suisun sloughs if you just want to get away from civilization and enjoy a quiet evening or weekend. However, don't succumb to the temptation to pull off into one of the many small sloughs that branch off Suisun Slough, or you'll almost certainly find yourself aground. In fact, even if you decide to anchor in Suisun Slough, make sure you have enough water to remain afloat when the tide goes out. As when anchoring in any navigable slough, avoid anchoring in the middle of the slough because of boat traffic. And, because boaters do transit the sloughs after dark, be sure to set your anchor light.

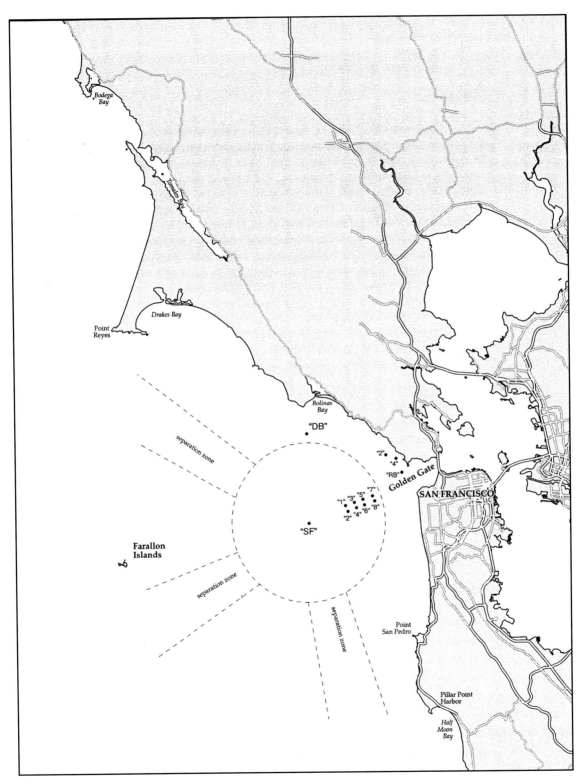

Destinations Outside the Bay

OUTSIDE THE BAY

David Dawson

Schooner Sailing out the Golden Gate

Not farre without this harborough did lye certain Islands . . . having on
them plentifull & great stores of Seals & birds.

—Sir Francis Drake

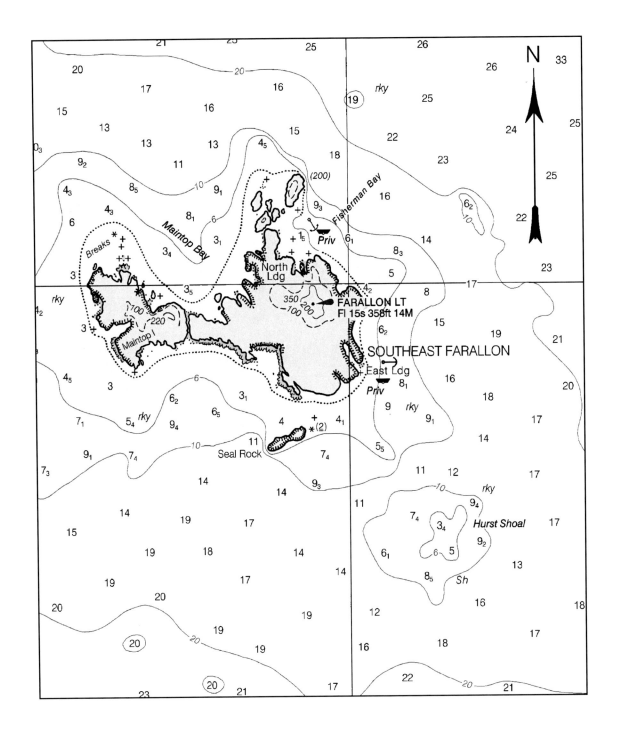

The Farallon Islands

THE FARALLON ISLANDS

Chart #18645

The Farallones (Spanish for "rocks jutting out of the sea") lie 27 miles offshore of the Golden Gate Bridge. These rocky Islands support only meager plant life, notably the Farallon Weed, whose dark green color occasionally relieves the tans and grays of the rock-covered landscape.

The name "Farallones" derives from the Portuguese explorer Juan Rodrigues Cabrillo, who, in 1539, was the first European to land on these islands and record them as "rocks jutting out of the sea." A few years later, in 1579, Sir Francis Drake landed on Southeast Farallon to collect sea bird eggs and seal meat for provisions. He named the group of seven rocky islands the Islands of St. James.

In the early 19th century, Boston fur sealers and Aleut otter hunters from Fort Ross used the Farallones as a base. The last Russian hunters left the Farallones, and California, in 1841. Fourteen years later, the Coast Guard built a lighthouse on the 365-foot peak of Southeast Farallon. From the late 1870s until 1972, when the light was automated, lighthouse keepers and their families lived in the two wooden houses still standing in the lee of this peak.

During the second half of the 19th century, the Farallon Egg Company collected sea bird eggs on the islands to sell in the cities and mining camps of Northern California. The advent of chicken farming near Petaluma in the 1880s ended this enterprise but not before the decimation of the Common Murre and Brandt's Cormorant populations. By 1900, the number of Common Murres nesting on the islands had dropped from 500,000 to a mere 15,000.

Today these islands are a part of a carefully monitored National Wildlife Refuge and Marine Sanctuary, overseen by the staff and volunteers of the Point Blue Conservation Science and the U. S. Fish and Wildlife. Once again the islands are alive with birds.

Breeding here are the largest number of sea birds south of Alaska, including 13 species, among them 50 percent of the world's endangered Ashy Storm Petrels and the largest populations of Brandt's Cormorants and Western Gulls found anywhere. Another 350 species of migratory birds stop off to feed here in the waters of one of California's richest fisheries.

The Farallones are alive, as well, with California Sea Lions, Elephant Seals, Harbor Seals, and, having recently returned to breed after an absence of more than 100 years, Northern Fur Seals. Great White Sharks patrol these waters, preying on the pinnipeds. If you sail near the islands, a school of porpoises may appear to gambol in your bow wave. Farther out you may spot migrating whales, most commonly Grays but occasionally Blues, Humpbacks, and Minkes.

The only anchorages open to the public, Fisherman Bay and East Landing, both on Southeast Farallon, are at best marginal. Landing anywhere on the islands is forbidden by U. S. Fish and Wildlife Service regulations. Nevertheless, the Farallones make for a fascinating day sail when the days are long enough to permit a comfortable round-trip passage in daylight. The outward passage hard on the wind can be uncomfortable, but the abundant wildlife and the prospect of a fast broad reach home in the afternoon more than compensate for the discomfort. Another possibility, of course, is to combine a pass by the Farallones with a trip to Drakes Bay

We have made the trip to the Farallones on our boat at least a dozen times and have found each trip different and exciting, whether we did the trip out and back in one day or combined it with a passage to Drakes Bay.

Golden Gate Bridge and Angel Island

Boat at Southeast Farallon on a Typical Foggy Day

Sara Acosta

PASSAGE-MAKING STRATEGIES

GENERAL COMMENTS

Winter weather is often poor off the Northern California coast. Late spring and early summer with their longer days are ideal seasons for a passage to the Farallon Islands, when the 20-knot winds will give you a thrilling reach home. Late summer and fall often offer lighter winds and calmer seas, but you can encounter boisterous weather here year round. Swells and wind waves regularly reach 7 feet or more, so be prepared for rough seas.

Whatever the season, plan your departure for early in the day, when the prevailing northwesterlies are lighter and the seas are calmer. If tidal conditions permit, pass under the Golden Gate Bridge just before sunrise so that you can be at or near the islands before the wind fills in strongly at midday.

TIDE STATE

Exit the Golden Gate at slack water or during a moderate ebb tidal current. The Potato Patch becomes dangerously turbulent during both heavy ebb and flood tides. *Tides and Currents* shows, however, that heavy currents are running only a few days each month. Simply by moving your departure time an hour earlier or later, you can exit the Gate with a current of less than 4 knots on 20 days of a typical month.

COURSES

Once outside the Golden Gate and well clear of off-lying rocks at Point Bonita, with the lighthouse approximately 100 yards off your starboard beam, set a course of 238° mag. for Southeast Farallon if no wind is blowing to push your boat

Point Bonita Lighthouse

S of the desired course. More ordinarily, though, you'll need to set your course 5-10 degrees more NW to assure landfall N of the island. Don't allow the wind to set you S of Southeast Farallon Island, or you will have a miserable time trying to lay the island against the large ocean swells and heavy winds that are normal in the area. If you depart at dawn, you'll probably motorsail most of the way, the passage taking the average small yacht about 6-7 hours.

The direct course to and from the Farallones passes through heavily traveled shipping lanes and congested fishing grounds. Maintain a sharp look out, and do not attempt this passage in thick, low fog. Most of the time the high fog will allow 1 to 2 miles visibility. For comfort on the outward passage, reschedule your trip if winds are anticipated to be over 20 knots.

DESCRIPTION

The low-lying Farallon Islands are rarely visible from more than 5 miles away. Maintain an accurate DR plot, allow for current and tidal flow, and use radar or GPS if you have it. In typical hazy conditions, your first sight of the islands will be a shadowy protrusion on the horizon, but the main features will not stand out until you are about a mile off. Then you will see the gray and tan rocks of the 365-foot peak of Southeast Farallon, with the white lighthouse atop it.

Visible, too, will be the splashes of white water breaking on the sheer cliffs to the NW of Fisherman's Bay. Then the crane used by the PRBO personnel to hoist themselves and their equipment and supplies up the 70 feet from the water onto the island will come into view. Only then, you may begin to see the few green splotches of the Farallon Weed. The two weathered white houses are not visible from this approach.

A 5-mile speed limit for boats within 1,000 feet of all the shores of the Farallones is in force.

ANCHORAGES

Farallon Islands is a National Marine Sanctuary, with no boats permitted within 300 feet of any portion of the islands except for Fisherman Bay and East Landing, where boats may be anchored.

FISHERMAN BAY
Anchorage 37°42.15N, 123°00.15W

Once you have visually spotted the lighthouse on Southeast Farallon Island, you can locate the anchorage at Fisherman's Bay; it is on the N shore of the island, only 400 yards N of the lighthouse. The anchorage is protected to the NW by several rocky islets upon which the waves crash. An old crane and a small brown building are on the SW shore of the anchorage. This crane, made of timber, in contrast to the modern steel one on the SE corner of the island, is no longer used.

Anchor about 750 feet from shore in a minimum of 50 or more feet of water, or pick up the Coast Guard buoy if it's not in use. However, this buoy, about 1,000 feet from the shore, offers even less protection from the surge and waves than an anchor spot closer in. If you anchor, lay plenty of scope, even on calm days.

Consider Fisherman Bay a temporary stopping place; the surge and refracting waves from nearby rocks make for an uncomfortable stay, even in calm weather.

EAST LANDING
Anchorage 37°41.80N, 122°96.00W

You may also anchor at East Landing, making sure not to block access to the buoys there. You can tie temporarily to one of the buoys at East Landing, but you must move off the buoy if a Farallon Patrol or Coast Guard boat arrives. Although your stay at East Landing should be slightly less uncomfortable than one at Fisherman's, you'll still not likely describe it as comfortable.

Fisherman Bay Anchorage

Annie Schmidt

LANDING AND FACILITIES

Landing on any of the islands is forbidden: They and the waters around them are protected as a wildlife refuge and marine sanctuary. If you want to anchor out overnight, a more appealing plan could be to end your passage with the 18-mile run N to Drake's Bay. The course is to weather, but the anchorage is far more comfortable than that at Southeast Farallon.

No facilities are available on any of the Farallon Islands.

Western Gull at Rest

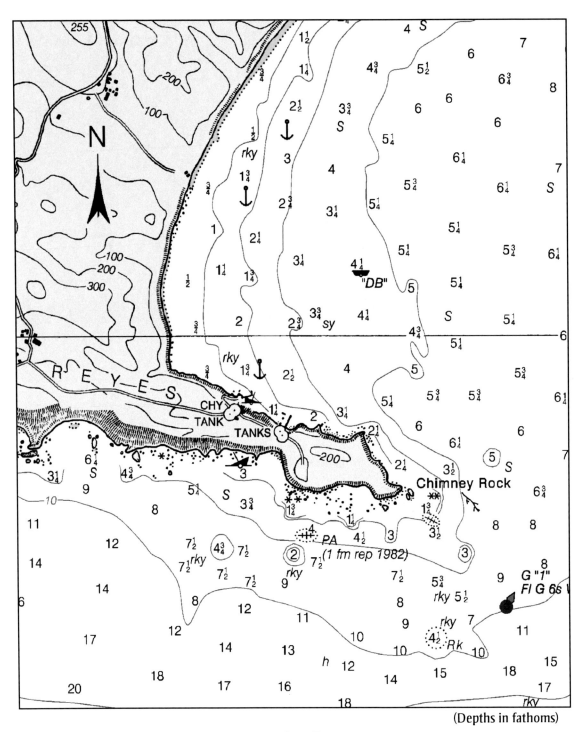

(Depths in fathoms)

Drakes Bay

DRAKES BAY

Chart #18645, #18647, or #18680
Point Reyes Light   37°59.78N, 123°01.40W
Drakes Bay Buoy G "1"   37°59.00N, 122°57.42W
Anchorage   37°59.86N, 122°58.35W

In their journal entries for the year 1579, Sir Francis Drake and members of his crew described a well-protected bay along the Northern California coast, where they careened the *Golden Hind* for five weeks while they made repairs on the ship's keel. In recent years some historians have questioned whether that bay was indeed the one we now call *Drakes* or whether the one Drake found, and used, lay farther north, perhaps in Campbell Cove, at the entrance of Bodega Harbor.

Later explorers, though, clearly found this bay. In 1595 the sailing ship *San Agustin* went aground here in a storm, stranding the captain, Sebastian Rodriguez Cermeño, and his crew. Another Spanish captain exploring the California coast in 1603, Don Sebastian Vizcaino, anchored in Drakes Bay on January 6, the day of the Feast of the Three Kings and thus named the rocky headlands *Punta de Los Tres Reyes*, which subsequently became in English simply *Point Reyes.*

Deer Graze above Drakes Bay

ATTRACTIONS

Drakes Bay as a getaway site has more to offer than escape. For the nature lover, few spots in or around San Francisco Bay rival it.

You might begin with a sportboat ride along the beach from the anchorage to the Kenneth C. Patrick Visitor Center to see the exhibits describing the exploits of Sir Francis Drake in the region. (Be cautious about where you land your dinghy. The opportunities for a wet landing increase at this end of the beach.)

For beach strolling, the golden sands and rocky shores of Drakes Beach curve for 4 miles, from the Historic Point Reyes Lifeboat Station to Drakes Estero. On this beach, you may have to walk around the Elephant Seals hauled out far up the beach or California Sea Lions with pups. Be sure to give them a wide berth so you don't disturb them.

For hiking rather than strolling, a trail leads up into the Headlands to Sea Lion Overlook and Point Reyes Lighthouse, the lighthouse in operation since 1879. A short climb up atop the Headlands will reward you with a view of thousands of Common Murres on the ledges below and Harbor Seals and Sea Lions drying out on the rocky shores or gliding and diving in the near-shore ocean. Between November and April, the migrating Gray Whales pass near to shore on their annual round trip from the Gulf of Alaska to the warm bays of Baja California, where they calve and mate before returning to Alaska in the spring to feed.

Birders from around the country come to the Point Reyes National Seashore that surrounds Drakes Bay to observe the hundreds of thousands of birds that frequent this flyway in their annual migrations, roughly between June and December. From the North come Ospreys, Arctic Terns, Sabine's Gulls, plus phalaropes, fulmars, jaegers, and fifteen species of hawks as well as many species of songbirds.

Best Anchorage is NE of Building on Pier

Anchor 100 Yards off This Pier

Reef, about 8 miles NW of Bonita Light. When you pass the buoy at Duxbury, you can change course slightly for the G"1" buoy off Drakes Bay and travel another 15 miles. Approaching Drakes from the N, go approximately 3 miles E after rounding Point Reyes before arriving at the buoy off Drakes Bay.

We recommend you make a trip to Drakes Bay only when the weather forecast calls for prevailing N or NW winds of no more than 15 knots. (Never anchor in Drakes Bay in either S or E winds.) If possible, depart for Drakes early in the day, before the winds and seas have built up, and on slack water to avoid unpleasant conditions in the waters around Point Bonita and in the Potato Patch.

ANCHORAGE

The best anchorage in Drakes Bay is off the westernmost of the two piers in the SW corner of the bay. You'll recognize this anchorage area by the other boats—primarily commercial fishing boats—

Depending on the month, bird watchers may also see Storm-petrels, Sooty Shearwaters, and Xantus's Murrelets as well as skuas, loons, grebes, and diving ducks. It's a birder's feast for the eyes and the ears.

APPROACH

Drakes Bay is some 25 miles NW of the Golden Gate. After clearing Point Bonita buoy and the Potato Patch, set a course for the buoy at Duxbury

anchored or moored here. In fact, in some seasons you must choose an anchoring spot carefully because of the number of other boats in Drakes. On occasion, we've seen as many as 40 boats anchored in this bay on summer nights. During the winter months, however, you might be completely alone when you anchor here.

As you enter the bay, you'll see the Coast Guard buoy NE of the pier. The water near the CG buoy is about 20 feet deep, but the depth near the old pier, where private and fishing boaters like to anchor, is closer to 15 feet. When the anchorage area is particularly crowded, both private and commercial boaters also anchor off the cliffs to the N of the pier in about 30 feet or less of water.

At Drakes Bay, dig your anchor in carefully. The bottom near the old pier has some grass and kelp that your anchor will have to penetrate. Farther away from the pier, the bottom is sand, especially near the cliffs to the north. For this reason, some boaters anchor near the cliffs even when the more popular area is not overcrowded.

Not only will the conditions on the bottom require you to anchor carefully, but the wind strength can also challenge your anchor. We have spent many nights anchored here when the wind blew in excess of 30 knots, and, yes, we learned about the grassy bottom the hard way, resetting our anchor numerous times until we were finally confident that it would hold. But the good news is that the water in Drakes Bay is calm even in heavy winds.

FACILITIES
At the Kenneth C. Patrick Visitor Center (on the beach, approx. 2 mi. NE of the pier)

Restrooms
Shower (outdoor)
Telephone

Marina at Tomales Resort (see Inverness, page 212)

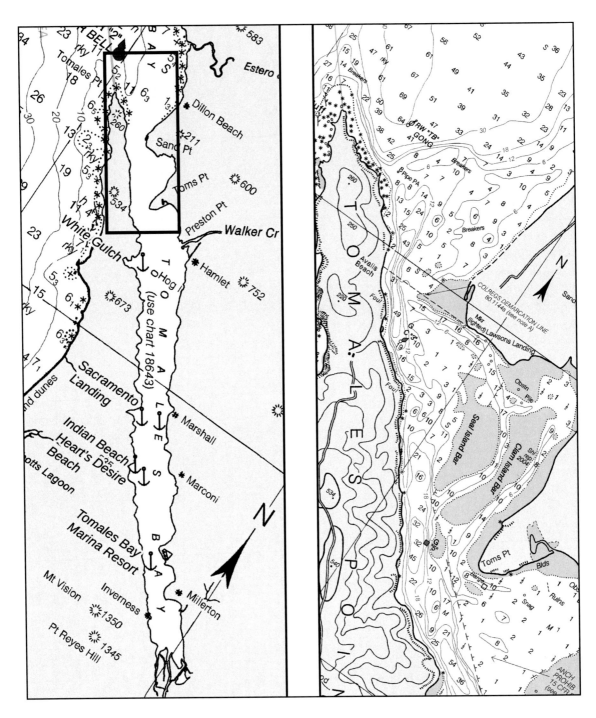

Tomales Bay   **Tomales Bay Entrance**

TOMALES BAY

Chart #18640 or #18643
Tomales Point Buoy #2   38°15.12N, 123°00.21W
Buoy "TB"   38°14.58N, 122°59.28W

The slender, pencil-like bay that opens up through a narrow gap in the southern reach of Bodega Bay is an anomaly of geology. The San Andreas Fault Zone, well-known for the destruction it periodically causes all along this portion of the Northern California coastline, separates the Bolinas Ridge to the E from the Inverness Ridge on the Point Reyes Peninsula. This fault zone runs along the length of Tomales Bay, from its mouth in Bodega Bay to its head, and continues in a more or less straight line to Bolinas Bay. The peninsula is on the Pacific Ocean Plate, and the continual NW shifting of this plate, a generally gradual shift estimated to have begun about 30 million years ago, has created Tomales Bay. The peninsula took a giant leap NW of approximately 20 feet during the 1906 quake.

Spanish explorer Lt. Juan Francisco de Bodega y Cuadra, on the ship *Sonora*, was the first European of certain record to find the well-disguised entrance into Tomales Bay. He called this body of water *de la Bodega* ("wine shop" or "a hold"), though his sailing master described it as *a considerable river*.

After the *Sonora* anchored at the mouth of the bay in 1775, the sailing master, Antonio Mourelle, noted in his journal the hazards of this entrance:

> . . . in de la Bodega [Tomales Bay] on the first flow of the tide, in a contrary direction to that of the currents, the sea ran so high that our whole ship was engulfed while the boat along side was shattered to pieces.
>
> There is not sufficient depth of anchorage at the mouth of this port for a vessel to resist this violent surge. . . .

In 1852, a group claiming title to a Mexican land grant called the five square leagues on the NE side of the bay *Rancho Bolsa de Tamallos,* with *Bolsa* probably signifying a pocket and *Tamallos* being the name of the group of Coast Miwoks that had historically occupied the tract. *Tomales Bay* is the name that has survived.

In the first half of the 19th century, the Aleuts that the Russians at Fort Ross had brought down to hunt fur-bearing animals almost decimated the seal and otter populations of Tomales and other Northern California bays.

The next thriving industry of the Tomales region that remains in evidence today is the dairy industry. While the farming of some crops, notably potatoes and grain, has taken place alongside the bay, these hillsides have proven most nurturing for dairy cattle. With the coming of the Swiss immigrants in the 1870s, dairy farming became the mainstay of the region. Several dairies remain, though many have closed down, and much of the former dairy land has become part of the Point Reyes National Seashore.

ATTRACTIONS

Once you've entered the wonderfully protected waters of Tomales Bay, you'll know all the careful planning to get here has been amply rewarded. This bay, a part of the Gulf of the Farallones National Marine Sanctuary, is a haven for not only boaters but for wilder life of many varieties. Migratory sea and song birds using the flyway along this coast between June and December feed in or around the waters of the bay. Harbor Seals haul out and calve on the mud flats. You may free dive for abalone here, dig clams, go crabbing, or fish for Monkey Face, Wolf Eels, Sea

Entrance into Tomales Bay

Trout, Cabazone, Blue Cod, Striped Bass, perch, and halibut. Or you may simply go to one of the five oyster farms on the E shore and purchase your dinner.

Tomales Bay is replete with hiking possibilities accessible from any of the anchorages. The *Point Reyes* pamphlet available from the National Park Service shows the many trails from the beaches in Tomales.

From White Gulch, a trail heads up the hill, past a herd of tule elk, to the Pierce Point Ranch, a former dairy now a National Park Service display. You can wander through the ranch, learning about the dairy industry that continues to be of economic importance to the Tomales Bay area. After this tour, you can walk down the ocean side of the peninsula for 0.5 mile to McClures Beach or hike the 3+ miles along the Tomales Point Trail and look at all the sea birds on Bird Rock.

Of particular interest, the 0.5-mile Indian Nature Trail, heading NW from the beach at Hearts Desire, has numerous markers identifying native plants, such as the California Huckleberry, Toyon, Poison Oak, California Bay Laurel, California Hazelnut, and Coast Live Oak, and explaining how the Ta-

mallos used these plants for foods, medicines, and ornamentation. The trail continues on another mile beyond the markers.

For a slightly more urban experience, explore the two diminutive towns accessible from the anchorages on foot or by sport boat. Inverness, originally a resort town and then the site of a fish hatchery, is by far the larger of the two. The several restaurants and shops lining its main street attest to its appeal to tourists.

Marshall, on the E shore of Tomales Bay, was a busy railroad stop in the early years of the 20th century. It was also the site of the West Coast's first wireless communications system, run by Guglielmo Marconi, the inventor of the wireless telegraph. Marshall is today in the heart of a thriving oyster farming industry. In each town, you'll have a short but thoroughly delightful walk, especially if you stop to visit with the friendly local people!

Besides Indian and Hearts Desire beaches, other good swimming beaches clustered along the SW shore include Pebble, Shallow, and Shell. On the other side of the bay is Tomales Bay State Park, for swimming, hiking, and picnicking.

Tomales Bay Bar at Low Water—Note Sand Bar Inside

APPROACH

While the name of Tomales Bay may have changed a bit over the years, one characteristic of this bay has remained constant: the hazards at the entrance. We can think of no other destination where the timing of your approach is as critical as at Tomales Bay.

Traveling to Tomales from San Francisco Bay, we like to anchor overnight at Drakes Bay so we can round Point Reyes early the next morning before the winds and large swells make conditions uncomfortable. By leaving at or shortly after dawn and setting a course to round Reyes about a mile off the point, we may still encounter slightly uncomfortable swells, but they are not likely to be dangerous.

One local boater who has spent his entire 80-plus years in and around Tomales Bay told us he crosses the bar only between 0800 and 1000 because the seas are most predictable during those

hours. Although we've crossed the bar far fewer times than he, we too have noticed how much lighter the winds and how much calmer the waters off Tomales Point and Sand Point are before 1000 hours.

The entrance into Tomales Bay lies approximately 16 miles N from Point Reyes. Since the desired time to cross the bar into Tomales is early morning on high slack water on a day when no large seas are running, you may have to spend a day or two at either Drakes or Bodega Harbor to wait for the optimum conditions.

We once departed Drakes Bay just before dawn and arrived at the Tomales Bay entrance at the perfect time, but the odds of repeating that feat are low. The last time we visited, we spent three days happily exploring Bodega Harbor while we waited for desirable conditions at the entrance to Tomales.

Approaching Tomales from the N, you'll probably be approaching from Bodega Harbor. From the entrance into Bodega Harbor, the run to the en-

The Marina in Tomales Bay

trance buoy "TB," some 600 yards from the bar, is a short 5 miles. Examine Chart #18643 before crossing the bar at Tomales.

Although as much as 7 or 8 feet of water covers the bar at the entrance to Tomales Bay at low tide, you must nevertheless cross this bar at high tide. Waves coming directly from the open ocean and into the NW-facing entrance of Tomales can often be 6 feet or higher, with force enough to drive a boat onto the bar.

However, if you carefully time your arrival and departure at the Tomales bar, you can cross it safely. First, do not try to enter Tomales Bay when swells of more than 5 feet are running. Second, enter only at high slack water or just before slack when the flood tide is still running to avoid the dangerous waves that build when ebbing water meets the waves coming in from the open ocean.

Whether approaching from the N or S, you'll be able to assess the conditions at the bar from the "TB" buoy. When you've confirmed that conditions are right, set a course to pass over the bar about 200 feet from the shore. After you're beyond the bar, lay a course for Marker "3," located off Sand Point, watching your chart carefully as you go. (Chart #18643 should be close at hand as you enter.)

Local boaters warn that the bar at Sand Point often extends out into the channel, especially after a winter of heavy rains and shoaling, so favor the shore of Tomales Point as you pass by the marker.

Observe the shallow water some 1,000 yards beyond Marker "3" and proceed cautiously. Providing you're indeed entering on high slack water, you should have no trouble.

Past Marker "3," pay strict attention to the channel markers, for water depths outside the channel are shallow for the first 4 miles. Beyond Marker "10," you need not worry about staying in a channel until you are almost as far S as Inverness.

One member of the Coast Guard who is stationed at Bodega Bay has crossed the bar more than 100 times without incident, and he recommends that visiting boaters faithfully follow these guidelines:

1. Never enter at night; the buoys are not lighted.
2. Never enter on an ebb unless in flat calm conditions.

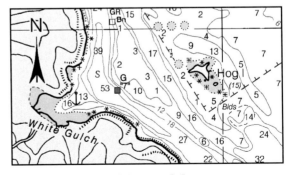

White Gulch

3. Hug the Tomales Point side of the entrance as you pass Sand Point.

4. Call the Coast Guard on VHF 16 or Lawson's Landing (707-878-2443 and VHF 22) if you're doubtful about conditions at the bar.

The foregoing comments underline how treacherous the entrance into Tomales Bay can be. But, with careful planning and attention to the sea conditions, you can safely navigate past Sand Point and revel in the placid waters, generally warm weather (particularly on the eastern side), and slow-paced life of the several excellent anchorages along the shores of this treasure of a destination.

ANCHORAGES

Tomales Bay currently has no marina for cruising boats. Consequently, you will anchor out when you visit this beautiful bay. Anchorage sites are plentiful along the shores of Tomales Bay. We'll simply point out a few favorites.

WHITE GULCH
38°11.71N, 122°56.82W

Slightly more than 3 miles into the Bay past the bar, on the starboard side of the channel W of Marker "7," White Gulch is the first recommended anchorage. Drop your anchor in about 15 feet of water.

White Gulch, a Comfortable Anchorage

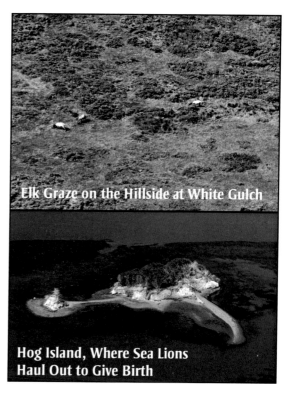

Elk Graze on the Hillside at White Gulch

Hog Island, Where Sea Lions
Haul Out to Give Birth

The mud bottom provides excellent holding (and a messy anchor when you hoist).

On the hillsides above the anchorage, tule elks that have been re-introduced to this peninsula graze as they did for centuries before they were hunted to near extinction after 1860. Friends of ours anchored here recently and watched a mountain lion stalking the elks, although the elks evaded the predator.

In addition to elk-watching, hiking ashore here is excellent, although you can expect to get your shoes muddy as you get from your tender to the land.

Occasionally, winds race down the canyon at White Gulch, but for the most part the days and nights in this anchorage are calm and quiet.

HOG ISLAND
38°11.75N, 122°55.93W

Though we haven't anchored overnight at *Hog Island,* other boaters have told us they like to anchor in 15 feet of water about 100 yards S of the island.

Sacramento Landing Anchorage

Inverness Yacht Club and Dock

This anchorage, protected by the island and within easy sportboat range of many spots worthy of exploration, offers you another option for consideration.

SACRAMENTO LANDING
38°09.18N, 122°54.48W

A second good anchorage on the W shore is in the cove just N of Sacramento Landing and about 3 miles S of White Gulch. The shoreline here provides excellent protection from both N and W winds. Anchor in some 12 feet of water in a mud bottom with good holding.

INDIAN BEACH
38°08.22N, 122°53.73W

A mile farther into the Bay are two adjacent anchorages, the first one at Indian Beach. You can anchor in about 10 feet on a sand and mud bottom. We prefer this anchorage because it is usually quieter than its near neighbor.

You may take your tender ashore on this beach.

HEARTS DESIRE
38°08.04N, 122°53.60W

In the summer months, swimmers, kayakers, and hikers often crowd the beach and the water at Hearts Desire; park personnel put out perimeter buoys in the summer to keep boats out of the swimming area.

You may take your tender ashore on this beach.

FACILITIES AT HEARTS DESIRE

Showers (outdoor)
Restrooms

INVERNESS
38°06.88N, 122°51.39W

Though other small beaches may entice you to stop between Hearts Desire and Inverness, about 6 miles deeper into Tomales Bay, we usually go on to the Inverness anchorage, about 500 yards N of the Tomales Bay Resort, near where a few boats are on moorings. We anchor in an area shown on the chart as having 6 feet of water at low water, recognizing that we might be sitting in the mud in an extremely low tide. Beyond this anchorage, the bay hasn't enough water for boats other than those with unusually shallow drafts.

Put out adequate scope, and set your anchor well when you anchor N of the Tomales Bay Resort, for afternoon winds regularly pick up to 20 knots or so, generating 3-4 foot wind waves that will almost certainly pull out a carelessly set anchor.

From this anchorage, you can go ashore in your dinghy. Obtain permission at the **Tomales Bay Resort (415-669-1389).** if you wish to leave your dinghy while you walk into the town of Inverness, about 1 mile farther S, or have dinner at the Tomales Bay Resort. Take care not to block access for boaters who keep their boats in the marina.

Marshall Boatyard and Houses

FACILITIES AT INVERNESS

Grocery Store, with ATM (1 mi.)
Launch Ramp
Marina (36 slips for small boats
      under 16 feet)
Post Office (1 mi.)
Restaurants (one at the anchorage;
      several others 1 mile away)
Yacht Club Dock (0.5 mi.)

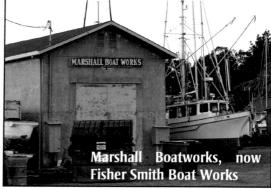

Marshall Boatworks, now Fisher Smith Boat Works

MARSHALL
38°09.70N, 122°53.38W

Along the E shore, approximately across from Sacramento Landing, an anchorage off the small town of Marshall is easy to recognize because of the boatyard on the shore, the boats docked and moored here, and the small community of houses and businesses. Anchor in 15 feet of water, with a mud bottom, just outside the moored boats.

Or you may have the option of renting a vacant buoy from the boatyard at Marshall, *Fisher Smith Boat Works, 415-663-8336.* When space is available at the docks, the owner of the boatyard will also give you permission to tie up to go ashore to have a meal at the deli or the restaurant. Oysters are the specialty on the menus in Marshall.

FACILITIES AT MARSHALL

Boat Maintenance and Repair
Grocery Store and Deli
Haul Out
Restaurant

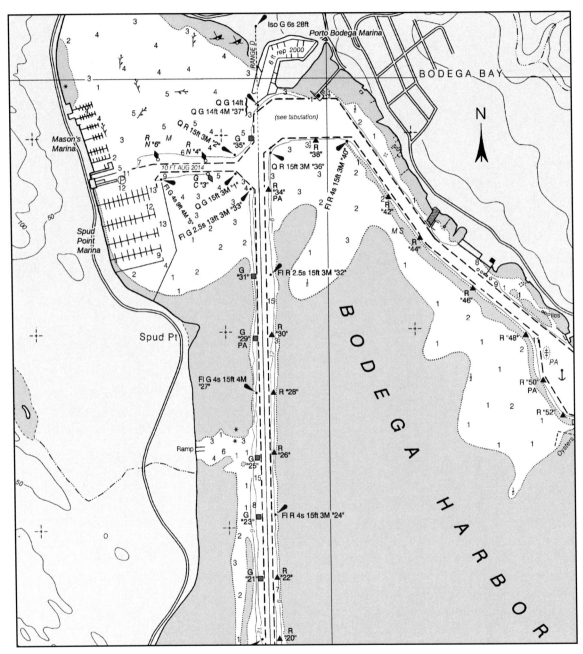

Marinas at Bodega Harbor

BODEGA HARBOR

Chart #18640 or #18643
Buoy "BA" 38°17.21N, 123°02.38W
Harbor Channel Entrance   38°18.33N, 123°02.95W
Bodega Coast Guard   707-875-3596   VHF 16

Historians and archeologists are still debating the location of the one event that may eventually be the greatest claim Bodega Bay can make to lasting fame. In 1579, Sir Francis Drake, frustrated in his attempt to find the fabled Northwest Passage linking the Pacific and Atlantic oceans, turned southward. He found a secure bay lying beneath a headland, where he and his crew sheltered themselves on the beach for five weeks while they repaired the keel of the *Golden Hind.*

Although Drakes Bay, 20 miles to the south of Bodega Harbor, has traditionally gotten the nod as the site of this first landing of a European in Northern California, the discovery in 1963 of a stone wall at Campbell Cove, tucked in behind Bodega Head, has convinced some that this and not Drakes Bay was the site of that momentous landing.

However, none can dispute that some 200 years later Russians used this harbor they called "Port Rumiantsev" for their fur trade out of Fort Ross. The stone wall in Campbell Cove may prove to have been erected not by the English in 1579 but by the Russians in the early 1800s.

Whether the Russians or the English were the builders of this historic wall, both groups were late-comers in the human history of Bodega Bay. The Coast Miwoks harvested food from this bay for an estimated 4,000 years before any Europeans landed here.

In 1841 General Vallejo and the Spanish crown contested the Russians' claim to this port, and in 1843 a Mexican land grant ceded the 35,000-acre Rancho Bodego to an American, Captain Stephen Smith, who three years later became the first private citizen in California to raise the Bear Flag.

With the encouragement of Smith and others, farmers began to migrate here, with potatoes a particularly successful crop. Two prosperous potato farmers, John Keys and Warren Dutton, started a shipping company at Bodega Harbor to transport to market the much prized Bodega Red potatoes, as well as dairy products, grain, fish, and other produce of the region. The busy harbor was also the anchorage for pioneer ships of many nations. Unfortunately, the creeks and bay began to silt badly, and a narrow gauge railway transiting this coastline between 1875 and 1933 became the primary mode of transporting both goods and passengers in and out of Bodega Bay.

Today, fishing is once again the primary export from this bay. At Spud Point Marina, completed in 1985, 80 per cent of the 244 berths are allocated to commercial fishing vessels, and the slips in the adjacent Mason's Marina are almost exclusively taken up by the commercial fishing fleet.

Bodega Harbor, Home to a Large Fishing Fleet

ATTRACTIONS

Besides the opportunity to experience a coastal cruise and good facilities at their destination, visiting boaters can find plenty of other reasons to stop off at Bodega Harbor for a few days, or even weeks. Many of the attractions are, of course, in and around the water.

You might start your day with a hike along Westshore Road and up to Bodega Head. Along the way you'll pass a "pond" where ducks splash down. This pond is, in fact, Hole in the Head, a 12-storey-

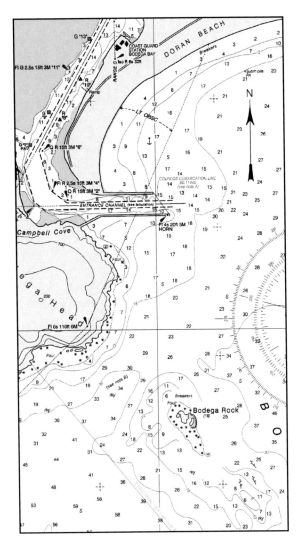

Bodega Rock and Harbor Entrance

deep excavation planned to house a nuclear reactor, a project abandoned in 1964. Atop Bodega Head, you'll take in a coastal scene of rugged brown cliffs and boulders assaulted by crescendos of foaming white water. Between November and April the spouting of the migrating Gray Whales gives away their locations. Orca, Humpback, Fin, and Blue whales, though in much smaller numbers than the Grays, also appear along this coast.

Instead of returning the way you came, you can continue N along trails to Bodega Dunes State Park, its varied habitats offering up a multitude of treasures for birders.

After this vigorous walk, you may be ready to relax on one of the beaches of Bodega. When the sun breaks through the fog (more common in the fall than in the summer), inspiring you to take to the water, Campbell Cove Beach, at the mouth of the harbor on the port side, has a well-protected sandy beach, where even young children can play safely at the water's edge.

Much more impressive is Doran Beach, the long peninsula of sand separating the S end of the harbor from the bay. On the bay side are the beach, hiking trails, clam flats, and a salt marsh. Across the road, on the harbor side, are the mud flats of the southern portion of the harbor, where thousands of Marbled Godwits, Great Egrets, Great Blue Herons, Snowy Plovers, and Killdeer may be feeding at low tide.

You may have guessed that you're sure to see more birds than people around this harbor. In fact, the town of Bodega Bay is well known for its birds, as depicted by the director Alfred Hitchcock in his suspense masterpiece *The Birds*. The only building left in town that is recognizable in Hitchcock's film is the old school house; fire has destroyed the others.

Launch ramps are available to the public at Doran Beach and Westside Park.

APPROACH

Approaching from the S, go approximately 20 miles N from Point Reyes to get to Bodega Bay. Identify the three buoys located in Bodega Bay: R "2" off Tomales Bluff, "BA" (*Jingle Bells* to local boaters) off the S end of Bodega Rock, and R "30" SW of Bodega Head. These three buoys can be difficult to sight if heavy seas are running or low fog has settled in. You will want to use a GPS or radar in case of fog, of course.

Regardless of conditions, do not enter Bodega Harbor until you have a visual sighting of "BA." Bodega Rock will be easily visible from "BA" in all except the foggiest weather, but other rocks NW of the buoy are below the water. Set a course for the entrance from "BA" that will take you E of Bodega Rock.

When the prevailing NW wind is blowing, the surf may break SW of the rocks off Bodega Head as

RW "BA" Buoy, Bodega Rock, and Headland

Channel and Mud Flats at Low Tide

well as to the E of the entrance channel. Although this breaking water appears dangerous, you can readily see the clear water of the channel.

You might be tempted to use the shortcut between Bodega Rock and Bodega Head if you see local boaters doing so, but we can't recommend it unless you can follow someone with local knowledge through the pass. Coast Guard personnel are adamant that this is not a viable channel except in the calmest of weather.

The entrance channel into Bodega Harbor runs from E to W for the first 0.5 mile before making a N run into the harbor between Bodega Head and the peninsula that extends W from the mainland. On this peninsula, called Doran Beach, you'll see many parked RV units as you enter the channel. In the channel, you'll be in protected water, a blessed relief after the rough water typical outside the channel.

The channel changes course three times, but it is well marked. Stay in the channel, which has 12 feet of water, for the water just outside the markers is shallow enough to guarantee going aground. On gusty days, winds blow down the channel briskly.

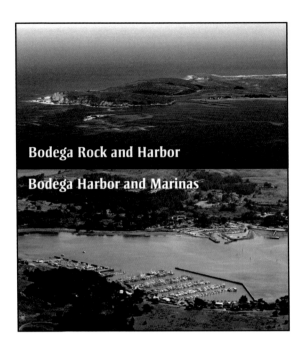

Bodega Rock and Harbor

Bodega Harbor and Marinas

BERTHING

SPUD POINT MARINA
Spud Point Marina Entrance
38°19.84N, 123°03.15W
Contact: 707-875-3535
VHF 16 (weekdays only)

The first marina along the channel, approximately 1.5 miles from the entrance into Bodega Harbor, Spud Point Marina is a modern facility designed and run to serve pleasure and commercial fishing boats, both resident and transient, in this 244-berth marina. "A" dock accommodates boats from 50-80 feet; "B" and "C" docks handle shorter boats.

The harbormaster monitors VHF 16 and 68, but, if you don't have a radio, you may leave your boat in any of the empty transient slips, identified by a 5-inch red anchor on the dock box, while you check in at the harbor office.

APPROACH

To enter this marina, turn to port after passing Buoy G "33," and follow the pairs of buoys past a breakwater on the port side. Depths in the channel and inside the marina are about 12 feet.

FACILITIES

Bait and Tackle Shop
Deli/Mini-market
Dry Storage
Fuel (gasoline and diesel)
Laundry
NOAA Weather Display Station
Public Transportation
Pump Out
WiFi

MASON'S MARINA
Entrance 38°19.84N, 123°03.15W
Contact: 707-875-3811
Mason's Marina, the second marina after you enter Bodega Harbor, is immediately N of Spud Point Marina. The staff at Mason's also welcomes visiting boaters; however, working fishing boats gener-

ally fill all the slips here. Mason's can accommodate boats up to 40 feet, and depths inside the harbor are at least 7 feet at low water.

If you'd like to experience the ambiance of a small working marina, you might be able to get a slip assignment by calling ahead. Spud Point Marina currently handles reservations for Mason's Marina; however, you can call the Mason's Marina number to inquire about space availability.

FACILITIES

Fuel (gasoline and diesel)
Propane

PORTO BODEGA
Entrance 38°19.96N, 123°03.17W
Contact: 707-875-2354
VHF 16 and 71 and CB 35

The third marina, Porto Bodega, is at the N end of the main channel in Bodega Harbor. Marina staff welcomes visiting boaters here, too. Like Mason's, this marina can handle boats to a maximum of 40 feet, and depths here are also about 7 feet at low water. If you arrive looking for a slip, you can call on VHF 16 or 71; however, the marina staff recommends you call before you depart from your home harbor to check for slip availability. Of the three marinas at Bodega, Porto Bodega is the closest to the restaurants, markets, and other businesses of the town, but the docks and facilities are not quite as modern as those at Spud Point.

FACILITIES AT OR NEAR THE MARINA:

Bait and Tackle
Grocery Store
Post Office
Propane
Restaurants

ANCHORAGES

DORAN BEACH
38°18.47N, 123°03.10W

The first anchorage, near the W end of Doran Beach, is excellent in calm conditions or in prevailing NW winds. This anchorage is immediately outside the entrance, N of the north jetty. This jetty, almost 1,000 feet long, provides protection from S swells; and Doran Beach, to the N, provides protection from NW winds. In fact, you're likely to find a few fishing boats or a cruising sailboat already anchored here when you arrive at the entrance into Bodega Harbor. Anchor in 10-20 feet of water.

If a S wind or a W swell is running, you'll not want to anchor here.

Most cruising boaters anchored here take their dinghies ashore on the beach behind the N jetty, but another possibility is to go inside the channel and tie your dinghy to the side of the small dock at the launch ramp S of the Coast Guard station, making sure you don't block access to the ramp.

UPPER TURNING BASIN (NEAR LUCAS WHARF)
38°19.50N, 123°02.50W

The other anchorage area in Bodega Bay is at the end of the channel that branches off the main channel at the N end of the harbor. This channel begins in front of Porto Bodega Marina and ends behind the Bodega Bay Boat Club. Though small, accommodating only two or three boats, the anchorage is secure.

This anchorage provides easy access to the **Tides Restaurant (Contact: 707-875-3652)**, to the post office, and to other businesses in the town. If you want to have a meal at the Tides, call and ask if space is available at the restaurant dock. If not enough space for your sailboat or powerboat is available, you might leave your boat in the anchorage and find enough space to park your dinghy on the dock.

The mud bottom in the Upper Turning Basin provides good holding in water about 12 feet deep. However, a local boater who has anchored here numerous times says he anchors both bow and stern in this basin to prevent the tide from turning his boat beam-on to the W wind that frequently blows through the anchorage during the summer months.

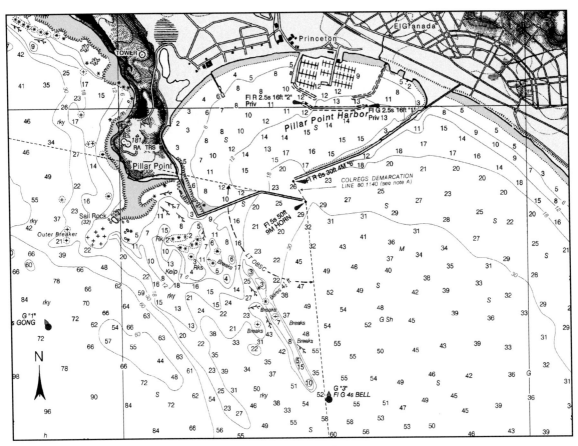

Pillar Point Harbor

Pillar Point Marina

PILLAR POINT HARBOR (HALF MOON BAY)

Chart #18645, or #18682
Buoy G "1" 37°29.19'N, 122°30.37'W
Buoy G "3" 37°28.89'N, 122°28.98'W
Buoy G "1 S" 37°27.53'N, 122°28.10' W
Buoy R "2" 37°28.23' N, 122°29.02'
Harbor Entrance 37°29.68N, 122°29.07W
Anchorage 37°30.00N, 122°29.43W
Contact: 650-515-7792 or 650-726-5727   VHF 16 or 74   sgrindy@smharbor.com

San Francisco Bay sailors planning a trip to Pillar Point Harbor, in the San Mateo County Harbor District, generally call this destination **Half Moon Bay** for good reason: it is tucked into the N corner of Half Moon Bay. However, the town of Half Moon Bay is some 5 miles farther S on Highway 1. Pillar Point Harbor is, in fact, in the tiny town of Princeton-by-the-Sea.

By any name, though, this destination calls sweetly to San Francisco Bay sailors. It is clearly the favored destination for many sailors who want to venture outside San Francisco for a few days.

Despite its proximity to the city, Pillar Point Harbor—protected by outer and inner breakwaters and thus one of the safest harbors in the United States—promises Bay Area sailors a dramatic change of atmosphere. You couldn't call it "sleepy," for this harbor is home to one of the largest and busiest fishing fleets in Northern California, with an annual haul of far in excess of 10 million pounds of fish. (And, by the way, you, too, can easily get in on the act: You may fish off the pier without a license.)

The dozens of fishing vessels daily leaving to go out to sea and returning with their catches of squid, Dungeness Crab, salmon and rockfish keep the waters and docks at Pillar Point alive with the hum of an old-fashioned commercial fishing harbor.

Costanoans lived and fished along these shores for centuries before the Spanish explorer Gaspar de Portolá founded Mission Dolores in 1776. Soon after, the coastal region became the grazing land for the horses, cattle, and oxen from the mission. In

the 1840s Spanish dons with land grants established large ranches here. Today, grazing livestock dot much of the land beyond the neighborhoods and towns around Half Moon Bay.

In the late 1800s Half Moon Bay, the oldest town in San Mateo County, dating back to 1840, grew more and more prosperous. The two wharves N of town, Amesport Landing at Miramar and Pillar Point, handled the large volume of shipping for this otherwise isolated region. Portuguese sailors from the Azores ran a whaling station at Pillar Point between 1860 and the 1890s.

In 1908, the Ocean Shore Railway established a coastal route between San Francisco and Tunitas Glen to carry passengers from the city to the wide sandy beaches of Half Moon Bay. That same year, the railway laid out the resort towns of Princeton-by-the-Sea and El Granada (across Highway 1 from Pillar Point Harbor). The Ocean Shore Railway line lasted only until 1920, after which date these beaches and hills regained their former isolation.

This isolation led to the next spurt of activity, during Prohibition when the rumrunners from Canada hid in this quiet harbor where they could anchor undetected in the hidden coves and thick fog.

Now, Highway 1 has made the area accessible so that houses cluster on the hillsides above Half Moon Bay, and tourists come from the north and the south to sample both the natural and man-made creations. But whether anchored or docked at Pillar Point Harbor, you'll find yourself much more a part of the natural than of the civilized world.

Customers buy fresh fish on boats at Pillar Point.

Busy Fish Restaurant at Pillar Point

ATTRACTIONS

One of the primary attractions of Pillar Point Harbor for pleasure boaters is the vastness and security of its anchorage, making it ideal for rafting up a sizable number of boats for a weekend of merriment.

Whether you are anchored or in a berth, you'll find plenty of entertainment even if you never venture beyond Pillar Point Harbor. Western Gulls, Double-crested Cormorants, Brown Pelicans, and Forster's Terns busily feed in the waters of the anchorage or rest on the rocks. California Sea Lions add their distinctive barking to the commotion on the breakwaters. Great Blue Herons and Snowy Egrets wade in the marsh on the NW side of the anchorage, and Black-crowned Night Herons swoop in overhead for their evening meals.

If you prefer to purchase rather than catch your own fish, a fish market right at the harbor can accommodate your tastes. Fish and crab are available off the boats in the harbor on weekends.

The Half Moon Bay Coastside Trail, traversing the ocean bluffs in both directions from Pillar Point Harbor for about 3.5 miles, promises additional natural wonders. The ocean itself, and the life dependent on it, is, of course, ceaselessly fascinating. Particularly fascinating to many is the overhead view of Mavericks Wave, one of the world's most challenging surfing spots, NW of Pillar Point. Along this trail you'll also see the seasonal wonders of the land—California Poppies, Blue Lupine, and Beach Primroses; song birds and raptors; brush rabbits and jack rabbits.

From this trail, paths lead down to the sandy beaches of Half Moon Bay: El Granada, Vallejo, Miramar, Naples, Dunes, Venice, or Francis.

A much shorter walk is the one through Pillar Point Marsh and Shoreline, on the W side of the harbor. Both fresh water and salt water feed this unique marsh. If you walk on around the point, you'll find tide pools and basking California Sea Lions and a sea-level view of Mavericks Wave.

APPROACH

San Francisco boaters undertaking a cruise to Pillar Point Harbor experience the joys and challenges of coastal passagemaking. To begin, this cruise requires careful timing of the departure from San Francisco Bay. We strongly recommend exiting the bay on slack water or on a *slight* ebb or flood.

Although some boaters choose to depart when a strong ebb is flowing to make the trip from the Golden Gate to the open ocean more quickly, by doing so they increase the risk of encountering dangerous seas as they cross the area between Mile Rock and the ship channel. For, as the strong ebb meets the winds and currents of the ocean, huge seas often form, seas large enough to capsize a boat transiting the area.

Another consideration for boaters making the trip from San Francisco Bay to Pillar Point is the

Pillar Point Harbor Has a Unique Breakwater System

Pillar Point Breakwaters, Anchorage, and Marina

time of day. The winds are generally stronger during the afternoon hours, and, when strong winds blow out of the NW, as they commonly do, these prevailing winds can create a boisterous ocean. To avoid these seas, and the resulting uncomfortable boat motion, time your exit from the Bay early enough to pass under the Golden Gate Bridge well before noon. Then you can have the anchor down inside Pillar Point Harbor by mid afternoon.

After passing under the Golden Gate Bridge, set a course along the S edge of the ship channel. Stay at least 100 yards off Mile Rock and Seal Rocks as you make your way seaward. Large seas build up in these areas, rendering a closer route uncomfortable, even dangerous. Resist the temptation to turn to port for a run down the coastline immediately after clearing Seal Rocks, for shallow water and huge waves make this shortcut dangerous. Instead, con-

Pillar Point Harbor has space for dozens of boats.

tinue along the S side of the ship channel for at least 1.0 mile before turning.

If large seas are running, wait until you are close to the R"8" buoy of the ship channel, some 3.5 miles seaward of Seal Rocks, before turning. If you turn earlier, the almost inevitable erratic seas will not be kind to you and your boat. After the turn, the run to the G"1" buoy off Pillar Point is typically a 19-mile broad reach.

The Pillar Point Harbormaster strongly recommends that boaters making the passage from San Francisco to Pillar Point keep 3 miles offshore as they sail S along the coast. Boaters who stray closer to shore can find themselves in shallow water and rocks off Point Montara.

The G"1" buoy, approximately 1.0 mile SW of Pillar Point, is easily identified by the radar towers and white buildings on the bluffs above the water. Do not attempt to go directly from G"1" to the harbor entrance, however, for shallow water and rocks abound in the area. Rather, go 1.5 miles on a course of 090° mag. to the G"3" buoy.

The harbormaster recommends that, after passing the G"3" buoy, you not turn directly toward the entrance, just under 1.0 mile away, but instead make a wide looping turn to port to avoid the breaking water on the rocks and reef near the direct line to the entrance.

Approaching Pillar Point Harbor from the S, you must navigate around the reef 2.0 miles S of the entrance. A G"1S" buoy marks the S edge of the reef, and an R"2" buoy marks its N edge. You can pass safely on either side of the reef once you've identified it, but be certain to pass well to the E of the G"3" buoy to avoid the breaking water on the rocks and reef to port.

If you're approaching Pillar Point Harbor in thick fog, be especially careful to identify each of the buoys. If you cannot find the buoys, do not attempt to enter the harbor.

Whether you want to anchor inside the outer breakwater or to request a slip, the harbormaster strongly advises all who enter the Pillar Point Harbor to call the harbor office. If you call on your cell phone, use option #4 to reach the Harbor Patrol.

BERTHING

PILLAR POINT HARBOR

Pillar Point marina is behind the inner breakwater. The harbor office attempts to provide guest berths to visiting boaters. Yet, even with 369 slips in the marina, the demand occasionally outstrips availability in the summer months. The harbor is also especially busy in April during salmon season and in November during crab season.

The *Half Moon Bay Yacht Club* has a facility near the marina and has an active sailing program for both children and adults. **Contact: 650-728-2120 and office@hmbyc.org**

FACILITIES

ATM
Chandlery (limited options)
Fuel (gasoline and diesel)
Grocery Store
Launch Ramp
Laundry
Life-saving Vessel
Medical Services (2 miles)
Post Office (0.5 mile)
Public Transportation
Pump Out
Restaurants
RV Park (for boaters only, one night)
Search and Rescue (24-hour service)
Water Taxi Service provided by Half Moon Bay
     Yacht Club on big holiday weekends

ANCHORAGE

Immediately inside the outer breakwater is a large anchorage area with 36 mooring buoys owned by the harbor positioned randomly throughout. These are typically rented to full-time occupants.

Boaters who prefer to anchor out, away from the bustle of this busy commercial harbor, can find ample space around the mooring buoys spread out between the outer and inner breakwaters. The mud bottom here provides good holding for anchoring in approximately 15 feet of water. Be careful to leave enough space between your boat and the mooring buoys so you won't find a large fishing boat sitting a few feet off your gunnel when you awaken the next morning. Inside the inner breakwater directly in front of the harbor office is a convenient dinghy dock for going ashore.

APPENDIX A: GPS WAYPOINTS

Alameda Marina Entrance	37° 46.62 N, 122° 14.84 W
Alameda, Aeolian Yacht Club Entrance	37° 44.98 N, 122° 14.06 W
Alameda, Ballena Bay Entrance Buoy #1	37° 45.81 N, 122° 16.94 W
Alameda, Encinal Yacht Club Entrance	37° 47.00 N, 122° 15.72 W
Alameda, Fortman Marina Entrance	37° 46.83 N, 122° 15.26 W
Alameda, Grand Marina Entrance	37° 46.73 N, 122° 15.13 W
Alameda, Marina Village Yacht Harbor Entrance	37° 47.22 N, 122° 16.19 W
Alameda, Mariner Square Marina Entrance	37° 47.50 N, 122° 16.62 W
Alameda, Pacific Marina (Oakland YC)	37° 47.08 N, 122° 15.89 W
Alviso Slough (exit from Coyote Creek)	37° 27.20 N, 122° 01.36 W
Angel Island, Ayala Cove Entrance	37° 52.10 N, 122° 26.20 W
Angel Island, East Garrison Anchorage	37° 51.86 N, 122° 25.26 W
Angel Island, Point Stuart Anchorage	37° 51.83 N, 122° 26.30 W
Angel Island, Quarry Beach Anchorage	37° 51.57 N, 122° 25.13 W
Angel Island, Sand Springs Anchorage	37° 51.28 N, 122° 25.72 W
Angel Island, West Garrison Anchorage	37° 51.49 N, 122° 26.59 W
Angel Island, Winslow Cove Anchorage	37° 52.25 N, 122° 25.55 W
Aquatic Park Entrance	37° 48.65 N, 122° 25.42 W
Ballena Isle Marina Entrance	37° 45.81 N, 122° 16.94 W
Belvedere Anchorage	37° 52.03 N, 122° 27.56 W
Benicia Marina Entrance	38° 02.49 N, 122° 09.47 W
Benicia-Martinez Bridge, Suisun Point Reach	38° 02.28 N, 122° 07.73 W
Berkeley Harbor Entrance	37° 51.88 N, 122° 19.11 W
Bodega Bay Anchorage, Doran Beach	38° 18.47 N, 123° 03.10 W
Bodega Bay Buoy "BA"	38° 17.21 N, 123° 02.38 W
Bodega Bay, Mason's Marina Entrance	38° 19.84 N, 123° 03.15 W
Bodega Bay, Porto Bodega Entrance	38° 19.96 N, 123° 03.17 W
Bodega Bay, Spud Point Marina Entrance	38° 19.84 N, 123° 03.15 W
Bodega Harbor Channel Entrance	38° 18.33 N, 123° 02.95 W
Brisbane Channel Buoy #2	37° 40.33 N, 122° 22.17 W
Brisbane Marina, Channel Buoy #6	37° 40.20 N, 122° 22.65 W
Candlestick Point, West Anchorage	37° 42.43 N, 122° 23.10 W
Candlestick Point, East Anchorage	37° 42.58 N, 122° 22.39 W
Carquinez Bridge	38° 03.66 N, 122° 13.57 W
Carquinez Strait Anchorage, East	38° 02.47 N, 122° 09.28 W
Carquinez Strait Anchorage, East of Ozol Pier	38° 01.60 N, 122° 09.60 W
Carquinez Strait Anchorage, West	38° 02.70 N, 122° 04.97 W
Central Basin Anchorage	37° 45.96 N, 122° 23.12 W
China Basin Anchorage	37° 46.37 N, 122° 23.13 W
China Camp Anchorage	38° 00.10 N, 122° 27.38 W
Corinthian Yacht Club Entrance	37° 52.30 N, 122° 27.32 W
Coyote Point Marina, Channel Buoy #1	37° 35.62 N, 122° 18.75 W
Dillon Point Anchorage	38° 03.663N, 122° 11.418W

Drakes Bay Anchorage	37° 59.86 N, 122° 58.35 W
Drakes Bay Buoy G "1"	37° 59.00 N, 122° 57.42 W
Embarcadero Cove Marina	37° 46.52 N, 122° 14.68 W
Emeryville, Emery Cove Marina Entrance	37° 50.36 N, 122° 18.72 W
Emeryville City Marina Entrance	37° 50.45 N, 122° 18.69 W
Emeryville City Marina, Channel Buoy #1	37° 50.61 N, 122° 19.33 W
Emeryville City Marina, Channel Buoy #7	37° 50.54 N, 122° 18.64 W
Farallon Islands, East Landing	37° 41.80 N, 122° 96.00 W
Farallon Islands, Fisherman Bay	37° 42.15 N, 123° 00.15 W
Fifth Avenue Marina	37° 47.25 N, 122° 15.86 W
Glen Cove Marina Entrance	38° 03.94 N, 122° 12.81 W
Golden Gate Entrance	37° 49.19 N, 122° 28.71 W
Highway 37 Bridge	38° 07.23 N, 122° 16.80 W
Horseshoe Bay Anchorage	37° 49.95 N, 122° 28.53 W
Horseshoe Bay Entrance	37° 49.90 N, 122° 28.57 W
Mare Island Bridge	38° 06.64 N, 122° 16.50 W
Mare Island Strait Entrance	38° 04.21 N, 122° 14.76 W
Martinez Marina Entrance	38° 01.63 N, 122° 08.29 W
McCovey Cove	37° 46.64 N, 122° 23.24 W
McNears Beach Anchorage	37° 59.64 N, 122° 27.09 W
Napa River Anchorage, north of Railroad Bridge	38° 12.74 N, 122° 18.45 W
Napa River, Napa Slough Anchorage	38° 11.10 N, 122° 18.90 W
Napa River, South Slough Anchorage	38° 08.73 N, 122° 17.30 W
Napa Valley Marina Entrance	38° 13.22 N, 122° 18.65 W
Napa Valley Yacht Club Entrance	38° 17.13 N, 122° 17.14 W
Newark Slough Anchorage, Buoy #16	37° 29.44 N, 122° 05.12 W
Oakland Estuary Entrance, Buoy R "2"	37° 48.15 N, 122° 21.34 W
Oakland, Central Basin Entrance	37° 46.98 N, 122° 14.68 W
Oakland, North Basin Entrance	37° 47.23 N, 122° 15.09 W
Oakland, Jack London Square Marina Entrance	37° 47.58 N, 122° 16.57 W
Oakland, Union Point Marina Entrance	37° 46.63 N, 122° 14.57 W
Oyster Cove Marina, Channel Buoy #2	37° 40.33 N, 122° 22.16 W
Oyster Point Marina, Channel Buoy #2	37° 39.85 N, 122° 22.13 W
Paradise Cove Anchorage	37° 53.72 N, 122° 27.37 W
Petaluma Channel Entrance Marker #5	38° 00.28 N, 122° 24.09 W
Petaluma Marina Entrance	38° 13.66 N, 122° 36.91 W
Petaluma Turning Basin	38° 14.08 N, 122° 38.12 W
Pier 39 Entrance	37° 48.52 N, 122° 24.45 W
Pillar Point Anchorage	37° 30.00 N, 122° 29.43 W
Pillar Point Harbor Buoy G "1"	37° 29.19 N, 122° 30.37 W
Pillar Point Harbor Buoy G "3"	37° 28.89 N, 122° 28.98 W
Pillar Point Harbor Entrance	37° 29.68 N, 122° 29.07 W
Point Reyes Light	37° 59.78 N, 123° 01.40 W
Point Rincon Anchorage	37° 47.47 N, 122° 23.30 W

Portobello Marina	37° 47.36 N, 122° 16.25 W
Redwood City, Channel Buoy #2	37° 33.00 N, 122° 11.67 W
Redwood City Yacht Harbor Entrance	37° 30.15 N, 122° 12.83 W
Redwood City, Bair Island Marina Entrance	37° 30.04 N, 122° 13.23 W
Redwood City, Smith Slough Anchorage	37° 30.11 N, 122° 13.65 W
Redwood City, Westpoint Harbor Entrance	37° 30.87 N, 122° 11.65 W
Redwood City, Westpoint Slough Anchorage	37° 30.68 N, 122° 11.33 W
Redwood City, Westpoint Slough Entrance, Buoy #13	37° 52.08 N, 122° 20.50 W
Richmond Yacht Club Entrance	37° 54.42 N, 122° 22.96 W
Richmond, Brickyard Cove Marina Entrance	37° 54.42 N, 122° 22.96 W
Richmond, Marina Bay Entrance	37° 54.53 N, 122° 21.20 W
Richmond, Point San Pablo Yacht Club	37° 55.38 N, 122° 22.35 W
Sam's Anchor Cafe	37° 52.17 N, 122° 27.20 W
San Francisco Bay Entrance (Golden Gate)	37° 49.19 N, 122° 28.71 W
San Francisco Marina, East Harbor Entrance	37° 48.48 N, 122° 25.96 W
San Francisco Marina, West Harbor Entrance	37° 48.48 N, 122° 26.37 W
San Francisco, Aquatic Park Entrance	37° 48.65 N, 122° 25.42 W
San Francisco, Central Basin Anchorage	37° 45.96 N, 122° 23.12 W
San Francisco, China Basin Anchorage	37° 46.37 N, 122° 23.13 W
San Francisco, Pier 39 Entrance	37° 48.52 N, 122° 24.45 W
San Francisco, Point Rincon Anchorage	37° 47.47 N, 122° 23.30 W
San Francisco, South Beach Harbor North Entrance	37° 46.91 N, 122° 23.10 W
San Francisco, South Beach Harbor South Entrance	37° 46.68 N, 122° 23.14 W
San Francisco Yacht Club Entrance	37° 52.32 N, 122° 27.66 W
San Leandro Channel, Marker #1	37° 40.16 N, 122° 11.21 W
San Rafael Channel Entrance, Buoy #17	37° 57.44 N, 122° 27.41 W
San Rafael Harbor Marina Entrance	37° 58.08 N, 122° 30.78 W
San Rafael Yacht Club Entrance	37° 58.15 N, 122° 31.07 W
San Rafael, Loch Lomand Channel Entrance	37° 58.02 N, 122° 28.96 W
San Rafael, Loch Lomand Marina Entrance	37° 58.28 N, 122° 29.00 W
San Rafael, Lowrie's Yacht Harbor Entrance	37° 57.98 N, 122° 30.45 W
San Rafael, Marin Yacht Club Entrance	37° 58.18 N, 122° 30.00 W
Sausalito (Richardson Bay) Anchorage	37° 51.67 N, 122° 28.55 W
Sausalito Cruising Club Entrance	37° 51.69 N, 122° 29.15 W
Sausalito (Richardson Bay) Entrance, Light #2	37° 51.30 N, 122° 28.28 W
Sausalito Yacht Club Entrance	37° 51.41 N, 122° 28.68 W
Sausalito, Clipper Yacht Harbor	37° 52.29 N, 122° 29.77 W
Sausalito, Schoonmaker Marina	37° 51.89 N, 122° 29.38 W
South Beach Harbor, North Entrance	37° 46.91 N, 122° 23.10 W
South Beach Harbor, South Entrance	37° 46.68 N, 122° 23.14 W
Suisun Bay, Hunter Cut Entrance	38° 09.35 N, 122° 03.17 W
Suisun City Marina Entrance	38° 14.31 N, 122° 02.34 W
Tiburon, Belvedere Anchorage	37° 52.03 N, 122° 27.56 W
Tiburon, Corinthian Yacht Club Entrance	37° 52.17 N, 122° 27.20 W
Tiburon, San Francisco Yacht Club Entrance	37° 52.36 N, 122° 27.78 W

Tomales Bay Buoy "TB"	38° 14.58 N, 122° 59.28 W
Tomales Bay, Hearts Desire Anchorage	38° 08.04 N, 122° 53.60 W
Tomales Bay, Hog Island Anchorage	38° 11.75 N, 122° 55.93 W
Tomales Bay, Indian Beach Anchorage	38° 08.22 N, 122° 53.73 W
Tomales Bay, Inverness Anchorage	38° 06.88 N, 122° 51.39 W
Tomales Bay, Marshall	38° 09.70 N, 122° 53.73 W
Tomales Bay, Sacramento Landing Anchorage	38° 09.18 N, 122° 54.48 W
Tomales Bay, White Gulch Anchorage	38° 11.71 N, 122° 56.82 W
Tomales Point Buoy #2	38° 15.12 N, 123° 00.21 W
Treasure Isle Marina	37° 48.94 N, 122° 22.18 W
Treasure Island, Clipper Cove Anchorage	37° 48.89 N, 122° 22.10 W
Treasure Island, Clipper Cove Entrance	37° 49.08 N, 122° 21.62 W
Vallejo Municipal Marina	38° 06.64 N, 122° 16.33 W
Vallejo Yacht Club Entrance	38° 06.25 N, 122° 16.10 W

APPENDIX B: SAN FRANCISCO BAY AREA YACHT CLUBS

Aeolian Yacht Club
980 Fernside Blvd.
Alameda, CA 94501
510-523-2586

Alameda Yacht Club
1535 Buena Vista Ave.
Alameda, CA 94501
510-865-5668

Ballena Bay Yacht Club
1150 Ballena Blvd.
Alameda, CA 94501
510-523-2292

Bay View Boat Club
489 China Basin St., Pier 54
San Francisco, CA 94107
415-495-9500

Bel Marin Keys Yacht Club
4 Montego Key
Novato, CA 94949
415-883-4222

Benicia Yacht Club
400 East 2nd St.
Benicia, CA 94510
707-746-0739

Berkeley Yacht Club
1 Seawall Drive
Berkeley, CA 94710
510-843-9292

Corinthian Yacht Club
43 Main St.
Tiburon, CA 94920
415-535-4771

Coyote Point Yacht Club
1820 Coyote Point Dr.
San Mateo, CA 94401
650-347-6730

Encinal Yacht Club
1251 Pacific Marina
Alameda, CA 94501
510-522-3272

Golden Gate Yacht Club
1 Yacht Road
San Francisco, CA 94123
415-346-BOAT

Half Moon Bay Yacht Club
214 Princeton Ave.
P. O. Box 52
El Granada, CA 94018
650-728-2120

Inverness Yacht Club
12850 Sir Francis Drake Blvd.
Inverness, CA 94937
(415) 669-7184

Island Yacht Club
1853 Clement Ave.
Alameda, CA 94501
510-521-2980

Loch Lomand Yacht Club
95 Loch Lomand Drive
San Rafael, CA 94901
415-459-9811

Marin Yacht Club
24 Summitt Ave.
San Rafael, CA 94901
415-453-9366

Marina Bay Yacht Club
P. O. Box 281, Station A
Richmond, CA 94808
510-232-6292

Mariposa Hunters Point Yacht Club
405 China Basin St.
San Francisco, CA 94107
415-495-9344

Martinez Yacht Club
        111 Tarantino Rd.
        Martinez, CA 94553
        (925) 228-5450

Napa Valley Yacht Club
        100 Riverside Dr.
        Napa, CA 94559
        707-252-3342

North Bay Yacht Club
        40 Point San Pedro Rd.
        San Rafael, CA 94901
        415-479-3146

North Star Yacht Club
        3300 Powell St.
        Emeryville, CA 94608
        510-428-0505

Oakland Yacht Club
        1101 Pacific Marina
        Alameda, CA 94501
        510-522-6868

Oyster Point Yacht Club
        911 Marina Blvd.
        South San Francisco, CA 94080
        650-873-5166

Peninsula Yacht Club
        1536 Maple St.
        Redwood City, CA 94063
        650-369-4410

Petaluma Yacht Club
        P. O. Box 925
        Petaluma, CA 94953
        707-765-9725

Point San Pablo Yacht Club
        700 West Cutting Blvd.
        Pt. Richmond Station
        Richmond, CA 94807
        510-620-9690

Presidio Yacht Club
        Travis Marina
        679 Sommerville Rd.
        Sausalito, CA 94965

Richmond Yacht Club
        351 Brickyard Cove Rd.
        Pt. Richmond, CA 94807
        510-237-2821

San Francisco Yacht Club
        98 Beach Road
        Belvedere, CA 94920
        415-435-9133

San Leandro Yacht Club
        20 San Leandro Marina
        San Leandro, CA 94577
        510-351-9666

San Rafael Yacht Club
        200 Yacht Club Drive
        San Rafael, CA 94901
        415-454-4661

Sausalito Cruising Club
        P. O. Box 155
        Sausalito, CA 94966
        415-332-9922

Sausalito Yacht Club
        P. O. Box 267
        Sausalito, CA 94966
        415-332-7400

Sequoia Yacht Club
        455 Seaport Ct.
        P. O. Box 5548
        Redwood City, CA 94063
        650-361-9472

Sierra Point Yacht Club
        P. O. Box 899
        Brisbane, CA 94005
        650-952-0651

Solano Yacht Club
        703 Civic Center Blvd.
        Suisun City, CA 94585
        707-429-0284

South Bay Yacht Club
        P. O. Box 100
        Alviso, CA 95002
        408-263-0100

South Beach Yacht Club
        Pier 40, Embarcadero
        San Francisco, CA 94107
        415-495-2295

Spinnaker Yacht Club
        South Dike Road
        San Leandro, CA 94577
        510-351-9930

St. Francis Yacht Club
        On the Marina
        San Francisco, CA 94123
        415-563-6363

Tiburon Yacht Club
        400 Trinidad Drive
        Tiburon, CA 94920
        415-789-9294

Treasure Island Yacht Club
        312 Juanita Ave.
        Millbrae, CA 94030
        650-588-4351

Vallejo Yacht Club
        485 Mare Island Way
        Vallejo, CA 94590
        707-643-1254

Westpoint Yacht Club
        Westpoint Harbor
        1529 Seaport Blvd.
        Redwood City, CA 94063

APPENDIX C: SAN FRANCISCO BAY AREA MARINAS

Alameda Marina
1815 Clement Avenue
Alameda 94501
(510) 521-1133

Bair Island Marina
702 Bair Island Road
Redwood City 94063
650) 701-0382

Ballena Isle Marina
1150 Ballena Blvd, Suite 111
Alameda 94501
(510) 523-5528

Benicia Marina
266 East B Street
Benicia 94510
(707) 745-2628

Berkeley Marina
201 University Ave.
Berkeley 94710
(510) 981-6741

Brickyard Cove Marina
1120 Brickyard Cove Road
Richmond 94801
(510) 236-1933

Brisbane Marina
400 Sierra Point Pkwy.
Brisbane 94005
(650) 583-6975

Central Basin (Oakland Marinas)
1855 Embarcadero
Oakland 94606
(510) 834-4591

Clipper Yacht Harbor
310 Harbor Drive
Sausalito 94965
(415) 332-3500

Coyote Point Marina
1900 Coyote Point Drive
San Mateo 94401
(650) 573-2594

Embarcadero Cove Marina
1 Embarcadero Cove
Oakland 94606
(510) 532-6683

Emery Cove Yacht Harbor
3300 Powell Street
Emeryville 94608
(510) 428-0505

Emeryville City Marina
3310 Powell Street
Emeryville 94608
(510) 654-3716

Fifth Avenue Marina
499 Embarcadero & 1 Fifth Ave.
Oakland 94606
(510) 834-9810

Fortman Marina
1535 Buena Vista Ave.
Alameda 94501
(510) 522-9080

Glen Cove Marina
2000 Glen Cove Road
Vallejo 94591
(707) 552-3236

Grand Marina
2099 Grand Street
Alameda 94501
(510) 865-1200

Jack London Square Marina (Oakland Marinas)
2 Webster Street
Oakland 94607
(510) 834-4591

Loch Lomond Marina
110 Loch Lomond Drive
San Rafael 94901
(415) 454-7228

Lowrie Yacht Harbor
40 Point San Pedro Road
San Rafael 94901
(415) 454-7595

Marina Bay Yacht Harbor
1340 Marina Way South
Richmond 94804
(510) 236-1013

Marina Village Yacht Harbor
1030 Marina Village Pkwy.
Alameda 94501
(510) 521-0905

Mariner Square Marina & Dry Stack
2415 Mariner Square Drive
Alameda 94501
(510) 521-2727

Martinez Marina
7 North Court Street
Martinez 94553
(925) 313-0942

Mason's Marina
1820 Westshore Road
Bodega Bay 94923
(707) 875-3811

Napa Valley Marina
1200 Milton Road
Napa 94559
(707) 252-8011

North Basin I (Oakland Marinas)
1000 Embarcadero
Oakland 94606
(510) 834-4591

North Basin II (Oakland Marinas)
1295 Embarcadero
Oakland 94606
(510) 834-4591

Oyster Cove Marina
385 Oyster Point Blvd
South San Francisco 94080
(650) 952-5540

Oyster Point Marina
95 Harbor Master Rd, #1
South San Francisco 94080
(650) 952-0808

Pelican Yacht Harbor
200 Johnson Street
Sausalito 94965
(415) 332-0723

Petaluma Marina
781 Baywood Drive
Petaluma 94954
(707) 778-4489

Pier 39 Marina
Beach Street & Embarcadero
San Francisco 94133
(415) 705-5500

Pillar Point Harbor
1 Johnson Pier
Half Moon Bay 94019
(650) 726-5727

Porto Bodega Marina
1500 Bay Flat Road
Bodega Bay 94923
(707) 875-2354

Portobello Marina
11 Embarcadero West, Suite 100
Oakland 94607
(510) 451-7000

Redwood City Marina
    451 Seaport Court
    Redwood City 94063
    (650) 306-4150

San Rafael Yacht Harbor
    557 Francisco Boulevard East
    San Rafael 94901
    (415) 456-1600

Schoonmaker Point Marina
    85 Liberty Ship Way #205
    Sausalito 94965
    (415) 331-5550

San Francisco Marina
    West Harbor & Gashouse Cove
    3950 Scott Street
    San Francisco 94123
    (415) 831-6322

San Leandro Marina
    40 Mulford Point Drive
    San Leandro 94577
    (510) 577-3488

South Beach Harbor
    Pier 40, the Embarcadero
    San Francisco 94107
    (415) 495-4911

Spud Point Marina
    1818 Westshore Road
    Bodega Bay 94923
    (707) 875-3535

Suisun City Marina
    703 Civic Center Blvd.
    Suisun City 94585
    (707) 429-0284

Travis Marina (Horseshoe Bay)
    679 Sommerville Road
    Sausalito 94965
    (415) 332-2319

Treasure Isle Marina
    1 Clipper Cove Way
    San Francisco 94130
    (415) 981-2416

Union Point (Oakland Marinas)
    2301 Embarcadero East
    Oakland 94606
    (510) 834-4591

Westpoint Harbor
    1529 Seaport Blvd
    Redwood City 94063
    (650) 701-0545

INDEX